Studies in Australian Federation

ESSAYS IN
AUSTRALIAN FEDERATION

STUDIES IN AUSTRALIAN FEDERATION

Editorial Advisory Board

J. A. La Nauze
A. W. Martin
Geoffrey Serle

This Series was established for the publication of scholarly writing upon Australian Federation. It is open to scholars in all relevant fields, including history, law, political science and sociology. Full-length works may be submitted for consideration, and collections of shorter essays may be issued from time to time. As well as original new works, the Series will include re-publication, in scholarly editions, of important contemporary and documentary material.

ESSAYS IN
AUSTRALIAN FEDERATION

EDITED BY

A. W. Martin

Professor of History
La Trobe University

MELBOURNE UNIVERSITY PRESS

First published 1969
Printed in Australia by
Melbourne University Press, Carlton, Victoria 3053
Registered in Australia for transmission
by post as a book

SBN 522 83915 0
Dewey Decimal Classification Number 994.03
Aus 69-452

Text set in 11 point Fairfield type

PREFACE

Reflecting in 1898, at the close of the last Convention, on the mass of public records which must exist to document Australia's federation debate and its results, Alfred Deakin wrote blandly—and perhaps, as one who has been through the mill, with a touch of irony—of the task that now lay ahead of scholars:

Ample material lies open to the student of the future to comprehend and criticise their work and it asks but patience, together with some acquaintance with the political methods and social and material conditions of the period to enable him to digest and comprehend its significance and the circumstances of its adoption.[1]

But half a century later Manning Clark was still asking for a scholar to tell him 'why the second nibble at federation became a bite, and how the bite developed into the Commonwealth of Australia',[2] while Geoffrey Blainey had justly described the federation movement as 'a subject that has been a no man's land in Australian history for almost a generation'.[3] Today, at the end of the sixties, as men born in the days of the early Commonwealth pass into old age and die, we still lack a comprehensive modern work to answer Clark's question. One can imagine Deakin's shade, on the sidelines, drawing wry amusement from it all.

Ironically enough, Deakin's own contemporaries supplied the closest approach to the kind of History he seems to have had in mind. His palm—'students of the future'—could well be awarded to John Quick and Robert Garran, not on the technical quibble that their *Annotated Constitution* appeared after 1898,[4] but as a way of doing homage to their remarkable achievement. If the most enduring part of that achievement lies in the core of the work—those 700-odd pages of massive 'Commentaries on the Constitution' which display extraordinary historical and legal scholarship—no less impressive is the long 'Historical Introduc-

v

tion' limning the story of how that Constitution came to be. Both men had ardently served the federal cause, and their account of its tortuous history glows with commitment to the belief that federation was the necessary and proper goal for Australia in the late nineteenth century. And yet they also achieved a scholarly balance, a degree of perspective and objectivity which would do justice to skilled historians far removed from the emotion of that time. In a sense, indeed, they did their work too well. That no subsequent scholar has been tempted to write again on the same scale is undoubtedly a reflection as much of the continuing vitality of their account as of the daunting task its replacement would be. But it may also of course be that only now are we on the verge of moving beyond a stage where (as Professor Crisp has put it) our 'Founding Fathers' have been regarded 'as just another generation of run-of-the-mill politicians—a species whose stocks have never stood high in this country which sets no more special store by its leaders than by its historical roots.'[5]

The awakening general interest in Australia's past encourages one to note how scattered fragments of work in Blainey's 'no man's land' hint at the worth of looking towards a new synthesis. Already in Quick and Garran's own day notable contemporaries were reaching out to areas of enquiry beyond an essentially politico-legal narrative. Deakin's *Federal Story*, woven around the delicate interplay of personality and event, moves to a fey conclusion rather at variance with the view, already noted, that for understanding the student chiefly needs a good digestion: the final federal compact was accomplished by a series of miracles.[6] B. R. Wise, though always less discriminating and driven more crudely by grudges against political enemies, nevertheless conveys a similar impression.[7] Men who had taken part in the tense conferences and campaigns of the nineties of course needed no reminding of the force of whim, as much as of conviction, in motivating both political leaders and the frequently apathetic electorate they had to manipulate. But the historian's task is to close as far as he can the gap bridged by chance; in the present context, to replace 'miracle' with explanation. Deakin and Wise offer initial clues to the two great desiderata: satisfactory biographical studies, and a better understanding of the political *milieux*, in the separate colonies, from which the federal compact was wrested.

If the moment is not yet ripe for us to call upon the *Australian Dictionary of Biography* for studies of the men of the later nineteenth century, we are at least assured from the quality already evident in that great project that our hypothetical synthesizer may look to it in the future as his major comforter. Meantime, in the field of full-length biography, J. A. La Nauze offers in his *Alfred Deakin*[8] a study bound to become the main modern stimulus for a revaluing of the events of the nineties, especially in Victoria. Other works include John Reynolds's *Barton*,[9] with its focus on federation intrigues and campaigns in New South Wales, and a range of political biographies which deal at appropriate points with their subjects' attitudes to federation: L. F. Fitzhardinge's *Hughes*,[10] B. E. Mansfield's *O'Sullivan*,[11] G. O'Collins's *Glynn*.[12] Occasional articles offer supplementary insights: light as well as heat has been generated by the McMinn-Fredman exchanges on Reid,[13] and the seemingly obvious explanation of Parkes's federal proclivities has been broadly sketched out.[14]

As these biographical beginnings shade into political history, it becomes obvious that no satisfactory general account of the federation struggle can be written until the federal issue can be properly located in the widely differing political contexts of the separate colonies. Deakin's ignorance of the inwardness of politics in New South Wales might for example excuse his uncharitable view of George Reid, but the historian must consider himself in better case, and seek understanding that transcends a mere balancing of personalities. From another angle, R. L. Reid's brief sketch of South Australian delegates in action at the 1897-8 Convention suggests the crucial importance of assessing local politics if one is to evaluate adequately the role of the smaller colonies in the constitution-making process.[15] A similar point is exemplified, so far as electoral politics is concerned, by J. Bastin's brief treatment of the problem of interpreting the federation referendum of 1900 in Western Australia.[16]

Bastin's work forms part of that small corpus of writing triggered off in 1949 by R. S. Parker's 'Australian Federation: the Influence of Economic Interests and Political Pressures'.[17]

A little earlier, in the introductory chapter to his *Parliamentary Government of the Commonwealth of Australia*, L. F. Crisp had surveyed the federation movement and, like Parker, suggested that scholars might profitably pay some attention to the possibility that identifiable conflicts of sectional and class interests were involved both in the shaping and presentation to the electorate of the Federal Constitution.[18] The entry of political scientists into a field hitherto dominated by lawyers and historians briefly suggested some new beginnings for the study of federation history. While warning against oversimplification, Crisp underlined the usefulness of examining the membership of the federal conventions in the light both of contemporary liberal-conservative divisions and of the operation of socio-economic pressure groups. He also foreshadowed the issue which Parker was to take up more fully: the need to fathom who the voters of 1898 and 1899 were, and what they thought they were voting about. Parker's treatment of these themes opened up what his most severe critic, Geoffrey Blainey, justly called a 'huge, barely tapped field of research'.[19] That investigation of this field rapidly ground to a halt may be attributed largely to the devastating attack Blainey made on Parker's tentative outline of regional voting patterns at the referenda,[20] and to the careful —and therefore depressing—discussion both scholars gave to the technical difficulties of interpreting *any* vote within the framework of the political systems which operated during the late nineteenth century in the Australian colonies. In the early 1950s it seemed that the line of investigation opened up by Parker led into a blind alley. How far this remains true nearly twenty years later remains to be seen: the new interest in regional and local history, our better understanding—in a post-Butlin era[21]—of economic growth in the nineteenth century, and improving techniques of electoral analysis may yet combine to give us a firmer base for fresh investigation of the federation referenda in particular, and the 'grass-roots' of the federation movement in general.

The present volume has to be set against this general background. We deal here with the period 1880-1900, and touch on two distinct, though interlocking, questions: how and why the colonies were led to federate, and, given implicit agreement to do so, why the federal compact took the form it did. These articles are concerned, that is, with aspects of the history of the federation movement on the one hand, and of debate and negotiation about the constitution on the other.

'Federation history' may of course be interpreted more generously than this. As the work of scholars ranging from H. L. Hall to J. M. Ward emphasizes,[22] the federation movement has an important history before 1880. At the other end of the time scale, the political and constitutional history of federation scarcely ends with the establishment of the Commonwealth in 1901.[23] It is hoped that this will be only the first of a number of volumes of essays on Australian federation, and for future collections we shall welcome articles which cover the whole range of federation studies. The aim of this series is to offer a forum for scholars working on all aspects of federation history, in the hope both of rescuing valuable work from the oblivion of thesis-shelves in libraries and of stimulating new monographic work which will help to reawaken a lively interest in Australian federation.

The essays of this first volume deal with important aspects of the federation story not hitherto studied in any depth. In an extended report from his current work on Victorian history, Geoffrey Serle identifies a Victorian ministerial 'campaign' for federation in the 1880s, explains its rationale, and traces the reactions of the other colonies, particularly New South Wales, to it. In elucidating such matters as the colonial response to European imperialism in the Pacific, the history of the Federal Council, the often pathetic rivalry between New South Wales and Victoria and the federal activities of politicians like Service, Gillies and Parkes, this essay offers new insights on the events which formed the immediate background to the constitution-making process of the nineties. J. A. La Nauze and B. K. de Garis both look at particular aspects of this process in detail. 'A Little Bit of Lawyers' Language' discusses the complicated pre-1900 history of that most notorious element of the Constitution, Section 92. This is a type of study hitherto treated speculatively by constitutional lawyers, using only the Convention debates; Professor La Nauze brings to it, instead, the historian's methods and attention to documents, dispelling thereby some long-standing illusions. Dr de Garis examines behind-the-scenes Colonial Office attempts after 1897 to influence the shaping of the Federal Constitution. This also is a subject never before treated by a historian.

The other three essays are concerned with the more public aspects of federation. Janet Pettman analyses the structure of the Australian Natives' Association in South Australia, and examines its role in the federal campaigns of the late nineties. Historians' attention has hitherto been devoted to the Association in Victoria: this study, in emphasizing how the sister organizations in fact differed, demonstrates the impossibility of generalizing, at a time of considerable intercolonial diversity, from Victorian experience alone. R. Norris and Patricia Hewett, stimulated by the Parker-Blainey exchange, look closely at referenda campaigns in South Australia and in south-eastern New South Wales. Both add usefully to the little corpus of published materials originally elicited by Parker's article, and show that it is not necessary to believe in despair that further work on this important theme is impossible.

This collection of essays is addressed to general readers as well as to students; federation is an important—perhaps the most important—political happening in Australia's past. The time may not yet be ripe for the writing of that Federation 'History' that Deakin dreamed of. But if these studies help the ripening process in some measure, we shall feel that our work has been worth while.

A. W. MARTIN

Melbourne,
June 1968

CONTENTS

1

THE VICTORIAN GOVERNMENT'S CAMPAIGN
FOR FEDERATION, 1883–1889

Geoffrey Serle

On 14 June 1883 about one thousand Victorians and New South Welshmen—the Governors, members of Parliament, clergy, judiciary, businessmen and other notables—assembled in the engine-shed at Albury station to celebrate the linking of the two colonies by rail. Electric light dispelled the wintry gloom, flowers covered the pillars and tables, and on high an allegorical painting showed Victoria and New South Wales clasping hands in unity, while behind them an engine was crossing a bridge. Unfortunately the Victorians wore morning dress and the New South Welshmen evening dress. But there was no confrontation: when each discovered his place at the tables, he found he had representatives of the other colony on either side. Lively chaff about the superiority of one colony over the other and the possibility of federation naturally followed until the speechifying began. Old Sir John Robertson was genially uncompromising: Victoria had separated when she was rich and New South Wales poor, but the mother colony bore no ill-will, would gladly receive her daughter back and let bygones be bygones. Alexander Stuart, the Premier, was far more enthusiastic and was heartily cheered when he welcomed the prospect of federation. However James Service, the Victorian Premier, made the speech of the day and the Victorians shook the roof when he said:

We have been long separated, and rivalries and jealousies and ignorance of each other have sprung up in consequence; but now we are looped together with bands of iron . . . Gentlemen, we want federation and we want it now . . . I decline to subscribe to the doctrine that I am to die before the grand federation of the Australian colon-

ies. There is no earthly reason why it should not be achieved . . .
I tell my honorable friend, the Premier of New South Wales, that at
a very early opportunity . . . we intend to test this question. The
Government of Victoria have determined to send a message to New
South Wales asking them what are the obstacles that stand in the
way?

Thus the challenge was made. The fraternal spirit held up well
through the fifteen speeches, invitations to new friends were
freely made to travel on for a couple of days in Melbourne or
Sydney, and Stuart accompanied Service to Melbourne for further talks about the possibility of federation and the current
New Guinea and New Hebrides crises.[1]

When in mid-April the news of Queensland's dramatic annexation of New Guinea had broken, the *Age* exulted:

The timorous policy which fears any further extension of the British
Empire finds no echo here. There is no reason why that large and
fertile island should not be made a new field for immigration, or
why the great colonising race of Englishmen should be debarred
from replenishing this magnificent wildeerness [*sic*]. The enterprising
spirit of the times of
> Raleigh, Frobisher and Drake,
> Adventurous hearts who bartered bold
> Their English steel for Spanish gold
is not yet dead.[2]

Service wired his Agent-General in London to 'promptly and
earnestly support' Queensland's action and urged the other premiers to do likewise; Stuart acquiesced. It seems that neither
Service nor other Australasian premiers had been consulted by
Sir Thomas McIlwraith. Victoria had little direct interest in
New Guinea. Her politicians had until now been far less conscious than those of New South Wales of Australia's possible
destiny in the Pacific. Melbourne's trade with the Islands was
negligible, not one-tenth of Sydney's. There was some business
interest in the potential of New Guinea as a field for investment
but expansion of German trading interests from Samoa to New
Britain and New Ireland and commercial and journalistic pressure on Bismarck to colonize New Guinea were the immediate
causes of concern.[3]

While the colonies anxiously waited for the official reaction

to Queensland's bold action, a further complication arose: the
campaign by the Presbyterian mission to the New Hebrides for
British annexation of all South Sea Islands not under foreign
control was adopted by the Victorian government. On 6 June
Service received a deputation of leading missionaries, prominent
Wesleyans, and Presbyterian and Nonconformist parliamentarians. Having been assured that France was on the point of annexing the New Hebrides, he quickly persuaded the other premiers
to agree to send a deputation of the Agents-General to the
Colonial Office to lobby on both the New Guinea and New
Hebrides questions. Queensland joined Victoria in urging immediate annexation of the New Hebrides.[4]

The New Hebrides had for long been the chief mission-field
of the Victorian Presbyterians and since 1857 the headquarters
of the Reverend John G. Paton. The area was notoriously exploited by 'blackbirders' but the establishment of the Western
Pacific High Commission based on Fiji did not satisfy the missionaries who were becoming more and more concerned about
the threat of French settlers from neighbouring New Caledonia
which had been a convict-dump since 1863. They petitioned
again and again for a British protectorate, but in 1878 the French
and British governments agreed in an exchange of notes not to
annex the islands. In the early 1880s arguments sharpened over
land-ownership, trading rights and French influence on the
natives, and the Presbyterians redoubled their pleas. Service, at
least, was now completely convinced: 'politics, religion, commerce, civilization, humanity', all pointed in the same direction.[5]
Meanwhile, as the Agents-General prepared to see Lord Derby
at the Colonial Office, news of the 'Australian annexation movement' produced uproar in Noumea where the Governor was
urged to annex the New Hebrides immediately. The men on the
spot were beginning to force the hands of the metropolitan
powers.[6]

It was by no means certain that Queensland's annexation of
New Guinea would be ruled out of order. The Colonial Office,
especially the Permanent Under-Secretary, Sir Robert Herbert
who had been the first Premier of Queensland, had recognized
for some time that New Guinea must in the long run be regarded
as vital to Australia. But Gladstone remained implacably opposed

to any annexation, let alone handing over control to a colony with Queensland's record on native labour. The colonies were firmly informed on 11 July that annexation was out of the question for the moment, but might be considered if they federated and arranged to cover all costs; in the meantime it might be possible to extend the protection of the Western Pacific High Commission to New Guinea by strengthening the naval force on the Australian station. Fears about the New Hebrides were brushed aside. The agreement with France was regarded as absolutely binding.[7]

Service and McIlwraith and their governments had expected the worst and were ready to move together, not only to try to produce an agreed Australian policy in the Pacific but to make a deliberate attempt to bring about federation. 'I agree with you', Service wired McIlwraith, 'that Imperial proposal is quite inadequate . . . "Federation and all the islands" should be our watchword.'[8] Service first gained parliamentary support for his annexationist policy. His authority was such that his resolutions passed both houses without dissent in one evening, 11 July. It was agreed that New Guinea and the Pacific Islands lying between New Guinea and Fiji including the New Hebrides should be annexed to the British Crown or that England should establish a protectorate over them; and Parliament consented to carry the costs.[9] A few days later the newspapers carried cables which raised agitation to a new pitch. Vague rumours over the previous months were confirmed: the French lower house had passed a Bill proposing to increase the transportation of criminals, especially to New Caledonia. It was suggested that 20,000 of France's worst criminals, officially described as 'dangerous, steeped in vice, debauchery and crime', should be transported there for life in the next four years. Some speakers had suggested that the New Hebrides be annexed and convicts sent there also.[10]

Few things could have provoked the colonies more. Escaped convicts from New Caledonia had been a growing irritation; since 1874 the colonial governments had made regular complaints to the Colonial Office. The question was central to what little national tradition the colonies had. Migrant colonists were acutely sensitive to Englishmen's doubts about their background, and were subject from time to time to the sneers of the ignorant

and imagined them even when not present; their determination
to cleanse the colonies' reputation had produced major move-
ments of protest.[11] The sustained campaign of the late 1840s,
the Victorian defiance of the imperial veto on legislation to arrest
Tasmanian emancipists and 'bolters', the campaign led by Victoria in the 1860s to abolish transportation to Western Australia
when the threat of cancellation of the subsidy to the mail
steamers finally brought success, were proud features of colonial
history. The worst legacy of the convict system was the lasting
poison in the social relationships of Englishmen and Australians.
So now the reaction was outraged and the annexationist movement was greatly strengthened, especially in the other colonies.

On 24 July Service wired his Agent-General, Robert Murray
Smith: 'England must act promptly and firmly. Latest news
Noumea shows great danger. Intense indignation here if France
is allowed to make New Hebrides cesspool for convicts. Consider
this crisis Australian history.'[12] In Parliament he hoped that England would now be roused to a sense of duty. On the 27th he
pleaded to the Colonial Office for reconsideration of the whole
question of annexation.[13] 'It appears to us incredible', thundered
the *Argus*, 'that British statesmen and British philanthropists
should stand by and allow these virgin territories—christianised
by our martyr missionaries—to be violated by ruffianage from
France.'[14] Scores of public meetings throughout the colony and
resolutions of local councils vehemently assented. Paton stumped
the colony for most of the next six months; the press, the
Chamber of Manufactures, the Congregational and Baptist
Churches and, later, the Intercolonial Trade Union Congress
gave unanimous support. It is difficult to judge how much grass-
roots enthusiasm there was: government supporters were put to
work to produce adulatory local resolutions. But the Governor
confessed he had 'never known any question in Victoria which
has commanded such universal support.'[15]

The Colonial Office regarded the new French policy on transportation as a matter of serious concern and in August the
imperial government made representations to the French government. The immediate consequence, however, was that the agreement that neither power would annex the New Hebrides was
confirmed on 30 August. Despite the flurry of deputations from

and correspondence with the Agents-General, they were not consulted; nor were they or the premiers informed of the new agreement for some time. On 31 August Derby sent a temperate and reasoned reply to the case for wholesale annexation; privately he considered the annexationists to be madmen. By now, however, the Colonial Office at least knew from consular and Admiralty advice that the missionaries' reports about local French activities were fairly accurate. Official policy now was to persuade Service not to be provoking to the French and to use some of the resources of British diplomacy to induce them to abandon or modify their Convict Bill which had been delayed in the upper house.[16]

Meanwhile, with great difficulty, Service had been arranging a 'federal convention'. For tactical reasons, with New South Wales in mind, he had been happy for McIlwraith to approach the other governments in July. But McIlwraith then had to fight an election which he lost to Griffith, so Service had to make the running. At the Victorian election early in 1883 almost every successful candidate had pledged himself to support federation. The government had decided to keep talking federation and to prepare the ground as much as possible. There was wide agreement in Parliament that Victoria's recent protectionist excesses and especially the behaviour of its delegates at the 1880–1 Intercolonial Conference, when they had led the opposition to Parkes's proposal for a Federal Council, had been narrowly provincial and that the time had come to think in national terms.[17] Previous intercolonial conferences were recognized as having been largely futile: Service once remarked that of twenty-three subjects dealt with in ten conferences over twenty years only three had been effectively settled and not one agreement for uniform legislation had been carried out.[18] In May, however, a postal conference in Sydney had been successful; despite immense suspicion Graham Berry had carried the Victorian government's proposals. Crisis in the Pacific now appeared to make a genuine move possible.

The other colonies agreed to confer with varying enthusiasm. Stuart had accepted McIlwraith's invitation, but when Service announced that at McIlwraith's request he was proposing to convene the conference and suggested 25 September in Melbourne, Stuart replied that the time was inconvenient. When Service suggested October or November, he replied that his pending Land Bill (which was, indeed, of crucial importance) made it difficult for him to agree to any date. On 29 August Service replied vigorously to this aloofness which he

greatly deplored; it will cast a damper over the movement throughout the whole colonies, and will be regarded in England as an evidence that we are not all truly in earnest . . . I think the other colonies will scarcely be able to help feeling that, after being led up to the very point of fixing a date for the Convention, the whole thing is knocked on the head by New South Wales backing out of the agreement.

Surely the matter was so important that Parliaments should be adjourned. In reply Stuart remarked that his government did not feel that federation was as urgent as did Victoria and Queensland, but he had no desire to prevent discussion and would be happy to meet in Sydney. It had been quite evident, replied Service, and it was surprising, that New South Wales was lukewarm:

I could understand it so long as we were not threatened with annexation by France of some of the most important of the islands, and with the avowed intention of making them the receptacle for the moral filth of that country; but that any Australian can coolly contemplate an irruption of people into these parts, in comparison with whom the Goths and Vandals were civilised races, is to me quite incomprehensible. But for these two dangers . . . we might have contented ourselves with nudging the old folks at home . . . The people of England are at our back. If we are prompt and resolute, the battle is as good as won; if we are cool, or hesitating, or indifferent, I believe the New Hebrides, and probably some of the other groups, will be lost to us.

Stuart now revealed his position. He was not indifferent to the activities of foreign powers or to the convict threat, but he disagreed basically on methods. He believed that urging annexation of the New Hebrides and violating the existing agreement would only encourage France and give her some justification to annex the New Hebrides herself. The best solution would be a British protectorate over New Guinea and a joint protectorate with France over the New Hebrides. Annexation would be costly and contrary to free trade principles; they would do best to work for a general policy of non-annexation.[19]

Stuart was a Gladstonian with no jingoist feeling, and although a Scot was an Anglican; nor was he subject to local political pressure. 'In New South Wales', he wrote to his Agent-General,

there is marked contrast between the feeling of the masses of the people and that which obtains in Victoria or in Queensland. I don't know whether we are more phlegmatic in our temperament than they are, but assuredly it would be a hard task to get up upon this subject the enthusiasm which is displayed by our neighbours on either side of us.[20]

In effect he stymied the Victorian campaign for annexation of the New Hebrides when on 17 September the New South Wales government formally dissociated themselves, stating that they were unwilling to embarrass the imperial government and were satisfied with the understanding with France not to annex; South Australia had already taken up this position.[21] It was clear, too, that the New South Wales government had no intention of federating at this stage and that there was little point in meeting for that purpose. In October Stuart told Service that the meeting would really be just an intercolonial 'conference' and not a 'Convention': 'the Colonies here have not unanimously expressed an opinion that the time has arrived. We have all more or less expressed our opinion that the time will come; but there has been, so far as I can judge, no general consensus of opinion that the time has arrived.' Service must by now have realized that the 'Convention' could not be one of Founding Fathers. He replied that 'the Colonies have already approved of the principle of Federation, and that the business of the Convention will be to discover how far and on what points Federal action can be carried out at present.' At least they could create an organization, with legislative and executive powers to deal with pressing questions, which could develop into a full union.[22] But Service knew that there was no immediate hope of tariff union and recognized that the question could not even be raised. The Victorian government none the less believed that external dangers justified and were sufficient to bring about confederation or a limited federation. The government of New South Wales did not.

So delegates from all the colonies' governments, including New Zealand and Fiji, met in Sydney on 28 November for the 'anti-convict' or 'annexation' Convention. On arrival, Service and his fellow-delegates, Berry and G. B. Kerferd, and accompanying pressmen were appalled at the lack of interest of the Sydney politicians and press; they and other delegates were not even met at the station. Service tactfully arranged that Stuart, who throughout was to be moderate and conciliatory, should preside over the proceedings. The other New South Wales delegates, W. B. Dalley and George Dibbs, were at first frankly hostile to the purposes of the conference. The Victorians had to be persuaded not to reply to Dibbs's opening speech which seemed to be deliberately provocative. The conference proceeded to discuss rival sets of resolutions by Service and Griffith. The Victorian policy in support of wholesale annexation of the islands by Britain won support only from New Zealand; the other colonies broadly supported Griffith's view that New Guinea was far more important than the New Hebrides and that the agreement with France over the latter must be respected. Nearly all delegates were firmly impressed with the danger of German or French annexations and with the French convict menace, especially the immediate question of escaped convicts reaching the colonies. Hence, while a firm recommendation was made to Britain to annex eastern New Guinea and a crucial guarantee was made to bear 'such share of the cost . . . as Her Majesty's Government . . . may deem fair and reasonable',* Britain was urged only to work for control of the New Hebrides. None the less a resounding declaration was made against any foreign annexations in the Pacific south of the Equator in the confidence that the imperial government would 'promptly adopt the wisest and most effective measures' to ensure this. Moreover a firm protest was made against French convict transportation and agreement reached to pass uniform legislation to forbid escapees or time-expired convicts landing in Australia.

The Victorians were half expecting the New South Welshmen to withdraw when the time came to discuss federation, but cordiality was growing especially between Service and Stuart.

---

* 'Fair and reasonable': mystic words. Is there an earlier instance of their use?

Service's remarks, it was said, were sprinkled with 'apposite quotations from Scripture' and 'occasional Scotticisms . . . unintelligible to all but Mr. Stuart who relished them immensely'.[23] And at a Sunday picnic Service made a happy speech with appropriate praise of the harbour he had seen for the first time and recognition of Port Phillip Bay's inferiority. Service, with Griffith's general support, wanted a real federal government if he could get it, though he said he was asking for no more than a beginning, a 'slight attachment' which would develop into a closer union. No delegate imagined that anything more was possible. Griffith's resolution in favour of a Federal Council similar to that proposed by Parkes three years earlier was agreed to, but when the Bill drafted in committee was discussed the proposals were diluted to the point of futility. The vehement protests of Sir John Robertson and others against the creation of any federal body persuaded the New South Wales delegates to hold out against any but the most sketchy arrangements and even they were hard-won. In the end the Council was to have no executive powers and no revenue. Legislative powers were to cover relations with the Pacific Islands and 'prevention of the influx of criminals', also 'fisheries in Australasian waters outside territorial limits, the service of civil process beyond the limits of a colony, the enforcement of judgments and of criminal process beyond the limits of a colony, the extradition of offenders, and the custody of offenders on Government ships beyond territorial limits.'[24]* The colonies were to have equal representation, Victoria having led the way in abandoning any claim for greater representation on grounds of population. Before the Council could be formed, the imperial government would have to legislate and at least four colonies pass enabling Acts. Service offered to call a special session of the Victorian Parliament to adopt the Bill as quickly as possible, but deferred to Stuart when he argued

---

* Many other matters (defence, etc.) could be dealt with if two colonies referred them. Many of the delegates must have been uncertain about how they expected the Council to operate. Service probably thought the most important probable gain was a regular conference at which informal agreement on common action might be reached. In April 1884 he made the baffling remark: 'We have no intention that the Federal Council should originate one single law or measure of its own accord.' Despite the lack of executive power he said the intention was to make it an executive body for carrying out laws passed by colonial parliaments (*Argus*, 24 Apr. 1884, p. 9).

that it would be preferable for his government to make the first move. Having agreed that Service should act as executive chairman in any necessary consultation, the Convention amicably dispersed.[25]

Sir William Des Voeux, Governor of Fiji and a delegate, was highly impressed with the 'very great ability' of most of the Convention's members; he believed Australasia 'had reason to be proud of its democratic selection'.[26] Yet, while Service's partial success speaks volumes for his enthusiasm and force of character, the proposed Federal Council was, as Herbert commented in the Colonial Office, a 'very rudimentary and lax arrangement'.[27] Victorian allies like C. H. Pearson and John Quick were highly dubious; Deakin in retrospect justly considered it all 'a doubtful gain'.[28] But the Victorian government had now committed its prestige and grimly settled down to fight the issue out.

Graham Berry stayed on in Sydney for a few days and was present at the Speaker's dinner. After hearing the Governor, Lord Loftus, and the visiting Earl of Rosebery speaking warmly of the prospects for federation, he let himself go when asked to speak late in the night. The way in which the Convention had been spoken of in Sydney over the last fortnight was disgraceful. So was the attitude of the local speakers that night, in their lack of recognition that recent events amounted to 'the greatest work done since Captain Cook discovered the land!' Overriding dissent, Berry went on to make a rousing plea for federation and was loudly cheered at the close of his speech.[29] However, at another banquet in Melbourne, Service was being characteristically forthright and tactless: 'We felt really as if we were about to perform a great work, and that all the world was looking on . . . But to our astonishment, when we got to Sydney, we found our friends there fast asleep.' There was 'complete oblivion', 'ignorance' of the fact that a Convention was being held to eliminate the possibility of future generations of Australians having 'an enemy dwelling on their borders'. 'I found what I had often heard of . . . and could not have believed without having experienced it, namely, the most intense jealousy on the part of Sydney in respect to Melbourne . . . We had to do the best we could.' Sir John Robertson was warm, earnest, kind-hearted, but antiquated in his ideas with 'curious delusions' about Victorian motives; Dibbs was 'really the greatest enemy we had at the beginning'; Dalley was 'cold' at first; but eventually the delegates, at least, had become enthusiastic about the Federal Council. As was his habit, he concluded by calling for three cheers for friends in New South Wales.[30] Reactions in Sydney were violent: the speech 'almost drove the Sydney people mad', one journalist reported. One parliamentarian announced that New South Wales was as far above Victoria as heaven was above earth, while another spoke of the agreement as a disaster which would have terrible consequences and condemned the 'high treason' of the New South Wales delegates.[31] Deakin in *The Federal Story* refers to this 'one irreparable blunder' by Service which could not be excused:

a considerable quantity of bitterness was thereafter infused into the always jealous relations of the two colonies. Worst of all, it was made perfectly plain that the Convention . . . had really been Victorian and thus the Federal Council became branded as a Victorian invention. As such it became a point of patriotism with many New South Welshmen to belittle and oppose it.[32]

Deakin was exaggerating, for only those who wanted to be angry were made so; nothing was basically altered.

In view of the evident lack of national feeling, Service's campaign of 1883 was obviously premature and ill prepared. The colonies were still very largely isolated from each other. Certainly there had been much movement of population from one to another; miners and shearers especially were less prone to take colonial loyalties seriously. None the less few politicians or businessmen had ever met their equivalents in other colonies and hardly any knew each other well enough to be friends; Service and Higinbotham set foot in New South Wales for the first time at the Albury celebration in 1883. Few businesses, other than banks, insurance companies and shipping lines, were conducted in more than one colony. The colonial economies were largely insulated from each other; the nationalizing of the Australian economy in the eighties and nineties greatly smoothed the path to federation as the hindrances of colonial barriers to day-to-day business became increasingly irritating. Although New South Wales imported much wheat and flour from Victoria and South

Australia, and Victoria depended on coal from New South
Wales, trading contacts were limited, as the economies were not
complementary to any great extent. The sense of intercolonial
rivalry, however absurd in retrospect, was keenly felt by politicians, businessmen and press proprietors at least; competition
for British capital and migrants left little room for any sense of
interests in common. Many New South Welshmen, clutching
at pretensions to historical dignity, found it difficult to look
calmly on upstart breakaway Victoria whose astonishing progress
had rested on the chance presence of gold deposits. Victorians
were 'people to be mistrusted', Sir Robert Garran remembered
from his childhood.[33] Migrant Victorians knew little and cared
less about the supposedly backward 'mother colony'; the convict
poison operated here too. Anthony Trollope had said the last
just word on Victorians' distressing propensity for 'blowing'.[34]
George Reid recalled in old age that one of the characteristic
attitudes of New South Wales politicians

was the strong suspicion expressed as to the *bona-fides* of Victorian
statesmen . . . The Victorians put our feelings down to jealousy
and petty provincialism. But we thought they pushed a proper regard
to self-interest to extremes. We used to call our ways British, their
style American. As a matter of fact our 'British' needed quite a lot
of their 'American'!

He put the turning-point of rivalry down to the capture by Victoria in 1872 of the P. & O. mail contract which made Melbourne
the terminal; after that 'our people cultivated a livelier interest
in public affairs'.[35] In 1883 Henniker Heaton, a former New
South Wales politician, warned Victorians to beware of

old and narrow-minded politicians who are now whispering to the
young politicians that New South Wales is so outpacing all com-
petitors, and taking the lead, that she will positively lose by federation . . . it was through the power of one of those utterly selfish
and narrow-minded politicians that the joining by railway of New
South Wales and Victoria was for so many years delayed.[36]

Sir John Robertson was Victoria's most frequent detractor with
his contemptuous references to that 'cabbage garden' and his
paranoid fears that the federal movement was really a Victorian
plot to capture part of the territory of New South Wales. Yet

he had some small justification, for David Syme in the *Age* was prone to argue that a pre-condition of federation must be a readjustment of colonial boundaries so that Victoria might regain its lost territory of the Riverina.[37] The *Age* also sometimes asserted that New South Wales was favoured by the Colonial Office because of its free trade policy and more compliant loyalty. Social climbers in both colonies were from time to time aggrieved at the distribution of honours to one colony rather than the other. Governments even sometimes suspected that their loan prospects in London were being sabotaged by their rivals.[38]

The ideological clash over protection was in fact just entering its most intense period. Protection against the other colonies had not originally been envisaged and until Berry's tariffs of the late seventies there was hope for reconciliation. By now in free traders' eyes Victoria had made the Murray 'a barrier as effective as the great wall of China to the elevating influences of civilising commerce'.[39] For Robertson, federation meant 'marrying our living free trade to the dead carcase of the protection of Victoria'.[40] Rabid Victorian protectionists would only consider federation with protection as the agreed national policy. The *Age* occasionally showed its true feelings. In its editorial of 30 November 1883, surprisingly written by Charles Pearson,[41] it found 'a natural division' between Victoria and South Australia on the one hand and New South Wales and Queensland on the other:

A great part of their populations grew up in the days when education was not enforced by the State, and their disadvantage in this respect has placed them at the mercy of the squatters and importers, who together control the legislatures of Sydney and Brisbane. The growth of the sugar plantations in both colonies has promoted the introduction of colored labor, and the lavish expenditure on assisted immigration has introduced a large class of voters who have no knowledge of democratic institutions, and no proper feeling of loyalty to their adopted countries. The proportion of Catholics to Protestants is also larger . . . Our natural ally would seem to be South Australia . . . We can . . . develop our own resources without troubling ourselves about our neighbours. In time of peace we have no great need of them, and in time of war it is they who will need to be supported by our arms, fed by our corn, and clothed by our manufactures.

Such madness and arrogance was, however, hardly typical.

The battle for the Riverina pre-dated the ideological conflict over protection. The Riverina was predominantly settled by Victorians, both squatters and selectors; Victorian governments made every effort to exploit this natural geographic sphere of influence whose boundaries are still defined by the predominance of brand of beer and code of football. Control of Riverina trade meant, it was believed, more business done in Melbourne and greater status and prosperity for the colony. So the first major trunk railway out from Melbourne was extended on from Bendigo to reach Echuca in 1864 and the north-east line was hurried on to reach Wodonga in 1873. Victorian capitalists were even permitted to construct a Victorian-gauge line from Moama to Deniliquin. The New South Wales counter-attack began from the mid 1870s; the main line slowly snaked down to reach Albury in 1881 and the branch to Hay, which tapped the feeders to the Deniliquin line, was opened in 1882. Meanwhile both colonies adopted a policy of differential freight rates; Victoria charged half or less the standard rates on Riverina wool coming down to Melbourne and commodities consigned to north of the Murray.[42] Victoria pressed on with new lines to the Murray. In 1886 New South Wales began running early newspaper-trains to the Riverina at considerable financial loss to combat the insidious influence of the Melbourne papers.[43] So the wasteful competition, which had such serious financial implications, proceeded.[44]

Perhaps the greatest irritant of all was the tax on stock brought into Victoria. The motivation of the tax which Berry imposed in 1877 was devious and largely to be explained in terms of internal politics, but it was also the most conspicuous act of aggression in a series of ruthless retaliatory moves following the lamentable breakdown of the 'free border' agreement between the two colonies which had lasted from 1867 to 1873. When a Victorian minister visited Sydney in 1879 in the hope of patching up a new agreement, Parkes insisted that first the stock tax be repealed; negotiations broke down.[45] Then at the 1880–1 Intercolonial Conference, the Victorians brushed aside Parkes's proposal for a Federal Council.

All in all there was some reason why many in Sydney reacted with surprise and suspicion to the Victorian initiative of 1883. Yet the problem remains, whose explanation can be sought only in the differing historical nature of the two colonies, of why one was now ready for the federal debate and the other was not; and why in particular one was so sensitive and the other so indifferent to European incursions into the Pacific.

At a dinner in honour of the Earl of Rosebery on 9 January 1884, Service claimed that the colonies had no lust for territory as such, but wanted to establish 'a Greater Britain in these southern seas, which will be freed in all time to come from those disastrous wars . . . which have torn Europe to pieces'. The islands must be annexed to prevent them becoming sinks of pollution; Britain's 'providential mission' was to exterminate 'moral and material evils' such as convict transportation and blackbirding; that odious and wicked trade must be policed from the colonies. But Britain must pay attention to the views of the colonies, for in fifty years' time Australia's population would be larger than Britain's and she would be ready to relieve the mother country of the task of governing India. Would the Earl of Rosebery be so kind as to tell Mr Gladstone that he might spare some sympathy for three million of his own flesh and blood and not just for Italians, Greeks and Bulgarians? And would he tell the French ambassador that if the convict policy was continued, Australians would come to hate Frenchmen whom they would know only as convicts and burglars? Berry, in his speech, remarked that Australians were waking to the fact that they had a foreign policy. Victoria was the smallest colony but it had a mission: 'within her territory might spring up a matured public opinion that would govern the whole of the Australian colonies. She might be to Australia what the New England States were to the United States of America . . . great in ideas.'[46]

Such pretty conceits were only exaggerated expressions of a world view which was coming to be overwhelmingly accepted in Victoria, with mounting enthusiasm and almost without dissent. Some indication of the order of priorities may be gained from the report of part of Service's speech. He wished to tell Rosebery that they wanted federation (cheers), prevention of 'further foreign domination in the islands of the Pacific' (loud cheers), and 'annihilation of the introduction of convicts into the Pacific' (continuous cheering). The convict threat was to become the

major agreed and unifying aspect of the Pacific question everywhere in Australia, but nowhere more so than in Victoria. The
strength of the Presbyterian interest helps to explain the peculiar
Victorian emphasis on the New Hebrides, and especially such
aspects as the support for Griffith's Kanaka policy in Queensland
and the strait-laced tone of attacks on the 'immoral' and 'licen-
tious' French. Service was also expressing an element of the
Australian dream when he spoke of the need to keep old-world
imperialistic conflicts out of the Pacific so that Australia might
be free to work out its ideal society; soon this was to become
an assertion of Australia's destiny to rule the Pacific. The emphasis on jingo-imperialism was also central to the argument: the
need to forestall and resist rival empires and to develop the potential contribution of the colonies to imperial unity and strength.
But the 'antiquated autocracy or bureaucracy' which was the
Empire must be reformed. Colonial governments had no representation in the imperial system, were 'outside petitioners to the
Colonial Office with scarcely more influence than a country
member of the House of Commons', needed some tangible means
of asserting their rights. As things stood, colonists were patron-
ized, humiliated, treated like children; they wanted to be received
in England 'as simple citizens, and on a footing of perfect
equality'.[47] Hence federation was the necessary course, so that
the colonies could reach a united view on Pacific and imperial
questions and present them to the imperial government; thus the
Empire would be strengthened and an Australian nation formed.
Any possible economic benefits to Victoria from federation were
insignificant as motives at this stage. As yet, though all expressed
opinion seemed unanimous and there was a 'curious obliteration
of party lines',[48] the movement was largely confined to the government circle, the Presbyterians and the newspapers. There was
a slight air of spuriousness about the public campaign of 1883
with its half-filled halls and whipped-up petitions. But overwhelming support was to come both from the old gold migrants
and, with only the slightest variation of emphasis, from their
children.

1884 was to be a very bad year for the cause: the convict
threat deepened, no progress was made with the Federal Council,
and the Germans occupied north-eastern New Guinea. There

was a curious lull for the first half of the year. The imperial government was unwilling to take seriously the possibility that either Germany or France had annexationist intentions. Derby was appalled at the 'mere raving' of the Sydney Convention in laying down a Monroe Doctrine for the Pacific and Gladstone thought the proposals preposterous.[49] Pressure was, however, kept up quietly on France on the convict question: the Bill was still delayed in the French Senate.[50] Service, fretting at the delay, kept striving as best he could, and wrote to the premiers in April suggesting a meeting. Stuart would not agree but concurred in a unanimous telegram requesting the imperial government to protest emphatically to the French government about the Convict Bill.[51] When Parliament met in June, Service was warmly supported by the great majority; the Convention resolutions were passed without a division and the proposed Federal Council was approved fifty-four votes to five and unanimously in the Legislative Council.[52]

At last in mid-June the colonies received Derby's formal response to the Convention. He unkindly pointed out that none of the parliaments had adopted the Convention proposals, or provided the funds for extension of the activity of the Western Pacific High Commission in the New Guinea area which he had suggested a year before. The colonies must combine and cover the costs before action could be taken. Service, of course, had been only too willing to act, but it had been agreed to wait on New South Wales. He now quickly won the agreement of the Australian premiers to provide the necessary annual £15,000. Victoria and Queensland agreed to provide the sum together in case there was a hitch, and prepared identical legislation.[53]

In June Bismarck clearly signalled a change to an active colonial policy and forced the British government's hand. In response the Colonial Office advised an immediate protectorate over all eastern New Guinea; the cabinet agreed early in August. But after a German declaration of interest the protectorate was confined to the south-eastern shores. The need to conciliate Germany prevailed over colonial interests. The protectorate was declared early in October; but Germany had decided in August to annex the north-east.[54]

Meanwhile Service was very much in the dark. The cabled

news of the intended protectorate, which was assumed to cover
all eastern New Guinea, was welcome, but there was no news
yet of imperial legislation to establish the Federal Council and
the French Convict Bill was still under discussion. Then, early
in August, the New South Wales government, perhaps trying
to conciliate its opponents, asked the imperial government to
delay the Federal Council legislation until the New South Wales
Parliament had expressed an opinion. Service reacted angrily.
'Is Sydney to dominate Australia?', he asked when cabling the
news to Murray Smith. He now unwisely, quite impractically,
decided to campaign again on the wide annexation question. He
wired again: 'Can you get Derby to promise annexation Islands
when the Federal Council constituted? That I think would fetch
Sydney . . . I trust New Guinea may be deemed secure . . . the
position of the other islands is critical in the extreme.'[55] Then in
mid-September Murray Smith reported rumours of an arrangement with Germany to partition New Guinea. Service sprang
into action and cabled the premiers to urge again annexation of
New Guinea and a protectorate over all available islands. This
was too much for Stuart and Dalley who believed it was no time
to embarrass the imperial government over New Guinea and that
the proposals for the other islands went beyond the Convention
agreement.[56] Even Griffith thought it better to confine the issue
to New Guinea, though the other colonies gave Service general
support. Service pleaded with Stuart, to no avail, for help in
resistance to European annexation: 'nothing but continual
knocking at the door will arouse the Imperial Government to
action'. Dalley wrote to Griffith: 'Service is unquestionably mad.
And any doctors of experience would certify to his insanity on
reading his telegrams.' Eventually all the Agents-General but
New South Wales's joined in a strong letter to Derby on New
Guinea. Murray Smith wired that the New South Wales attitude
was doing infinite mischief in weakening the Australian case.
To his dying day, Service never forgave Stuart and, quite erron-
eously, attributed to this 'betrayal' the failure to annex north-
eastern New Guinea before Germany.[57]

When the limitation of the protectorate was revealed, there
were disgusted reactions in Parliament. 'Everybody disappointed
by piddling policy', Service wired Murray Smith.[58] But mean-

while a great campaign, led by the Australian Natives' Association, was developing. The A.N.A.'s first major public demonstration was on 22 September in the Melbourne Town Hall. The colonies were now protecting themselves, claimed Deakin, it was appalling so to confine the New Guinea protectorate because of 'some conjectural fear of offending Germany or Russia', and he quoted:

> We don't want to fight,
> But, by Jingo, if we do;
> We've got the ships, we've got the men,
> And we've got the money too.

Australia's duty was to point out the errors in British colonial policy and to 'revive the colonial policy of the days of Raleigh and Drake, and the traditions of Sir Henry Lawrence in India, and of General Gordon, alone to-day in Khartoum'.[59] Tension grew as a German man-of-war was observed passing Port Phillip Bay and Port Jackson. 'Altogether things look ugly and demand prompt action', Service cabled. The wild man, Hugh McColl, called on the Victorian government to annex north-eastern New Guinea itself.[60]

Then on 30 October, on the last day of the session, the Federal Council proposals were defeated in the New South Wales Assembly by one vote.* Parkes had just won the day, but purely local political factors had influenced the voting. Stuart had been away ill and the Legislative Council had approved. The New South Wales government, however much it disagreed on policy on the Pacific, had kept faith with the Convention and had observed its promise to support the creation of the Federal Council. Dalley defended the leaders of other colonies who 'have acted as men under the influence of a solemn conviction; and while we have, perhaps, had an imperfect sympathy with their enthusiasm, we have had no good cause to suspect their good faith nor to complain of their want of courtesy.'[61] Then the imperial government, preoccupied with its proposed reform of the franchise, was only too glad to drop the enabling legislation for that year.

---

* Bede Nairn has pointed out that several absentees who had been expected to vote for the Bill were already in Melbourne for the Spring Racing Carnival! See *Official Report of the National Australasian Convention Debates* (Sydney, 1891), p. 301.

'At last the end has come', Service cabled Murray Smith on 20 December:

Information received reliable source that Germany has hoisted flag on New Britain, New Ireland, and north coast of New Guinea. The exasperation here is boundless. I protest in the name of the present and future of Australia. If England does not yet save us from the danger and disgrace, as far at least as New Guinea is concerned, the bitterness of the feeling towards her will not die out in this generation.[62]

Service tried and again failed to convene a meeting of premiers; once again New South Wales was unco-operative. Stuart was ill and Dalley, the acting Premier, went so far as to welcome the German annexation and to claim it was impudent and absurd to protest and embarrass the imperial government; but this 'scuttle' speech got him into trouble with the press.[63] There was little Service and his government could do. They had considered sending an embassy of protest to Britain, but only Queensland and New Zealand could be relied on to join. 'The difficulty of the position from the first', he wrote privately,

has been that the colonies have not been perfectly united even in saying what they wanted. N.S. Wales' back-draft ruined the annexation question, and left us at the mercy of Lord Derby—who seems as blind as a mole, and as cold as an icicle. And the more vigorous we are, the more sulky N S W appears to become. Action therefore which seems obviously right on the face of it, is rendered impossible —or if not impossible, almost useless, because what Victoria feels to be of national importance is regarded as the result of provincial arrogance and self assertion.[64]

There was nothing to be done but to protest: under instructions Murray Smith bombarded the Colonial Office with requests that the annexation be not recognized. 'New Guinea must be got back', wired Service,[65] in total ignorance of the diplomatic context which made it essential for the imperial government to submit, despite the humiliation which Bismarck's deception had brought. Ultimately Service could only call on posterity, his conviction that Australians would never recognize any German right of occupation and would one day take the island back.[66] J. A. Froude, the visiting historian, was nearer the mark than in most of his comments when he remarked that it was just as well that Australia was not federated with its own navy or these 'hot-headed men' might have 'sent their ships round to warn the Germans off'. 'Young nations', he concluded, 'are like young men, sensitive and passionate, and even their most experienced statesmen do not escape the contagion.'[67]

The long-drawn-out siege of General Gordon in Khartoum had roused deep emotion. When the news of his heroic death arrived early in February 1885, 'most of the people seemed to run mad . . . and were red hot for revenge';[68] indignation meetings hooted Gladstone's name and called for his removal from office. There was great excitement when it was heard that Dalley had offered a New South Wales contingent for service in the Sudan. Victoria hastened to follow suit, planned to send a naval brigade and mounted infantry, and began recruiting. Service hoped that a joint contingent from the colonies might be arranged in order to boost the federal cause. But the New South Wales offer was accepted by a surprised imperial government and the Victorian (and Canadian) offers declined for the time being, and Dalley suavely rejected the suggestion of a national contingent on the ground that it would mean delay.[69] The Victorian government kept a stiff upper lip, but there was special cause for rancour for only twelve months before Derby had rudely snubbed their offer, for use in the campaign, of two new Victorian gunboats on their way out through the Suez Canal.[70] Service genuinely admired Dalley's coup and believed it had 'precipitated Australia in one short week from a geographical expression to a nation'; 'while we have a man, a ship, or a shilling, England shall never want assistance' in time of peril.[71] He sent warm fraternal greetings to the contingent on its departure. The *Argus*, however, remarked that New South Wales had been favoured as the most subservient colony; acceptance of Dalley's offer was a 'reward for his desertion of the Australian cause' over New Guinea. Dalley was greatly insulted and told his Governor that he had 'quite resolved to take no step with [the Victorians] or have anything whatever to do with them'. The *Argus* meantime pointed out that in fact Victoria had been the first colony to have military or naval assistance accepted by the mother country when in 1860 H.M.S. *Victoria* served in the New Zealand wars![72]

However, just as in New South Wales Parkes was supported

strongly enough to lead a damaging campaign against Dalley's
gesture, in Victoria public opinion cooled rapidly. As early as 19
February Service cabled Murray Smith: 'Public opinion H.M.G.
do not require assistance. Reuter's telegram that offer declined
has been received with satisfaction on the part of many . . . not
desirable to press offer.'[73] The imperial government's indication
that a Victorian force for service in the Sudan might be welcome
later in the year was ignored in the months of crisis between
March and May when it was believed that war with Russia was
inevitable. Victoria's armed forces, which were far more highly
developed than those of any other colony, must stay at home to
ward off likely invasion.

Such threats, real or supposed, from Germany, France and
Russia in turn must surely, thought Service, build up enthusiasm for federation; yet there was little response in New South
Wales. Despite much shilly-shallying, the senior colony would
not join the Federal Council. Early in 1885, after consultation
with the New South Wales government, Derby proposed an
amendment to the Draft Enabling Act which would give any
member colony the right to withdraw from the Council once
established. The Victorian government dickered but eventually
agreed with Queensland, South Australia and Tasmania—the
four governments now described themselves as those 'prepared
to confederate'—to oppose the proposal strongly. They had been
prepared to agree if it would mean that New South Wales (or
New Zealand) would join, but as even this proposal appeared
to be insufficient to satisfy New South Wales the objection was
maintained.[74] None the less Derby introduced the Federal Council of Australasia Bill in April with the offending clause and
other minor amendments still included. Then in July, too late,
Stuart asked for delay as he might have further proposals to
make. After consultation the other premiers, suspicious that this
was an attempt to shelve the Bill, agreed that it must proceed:
'all attempts to meet Sydney seem fruitless', Service remarked.
When the Bill was passed on 14 August, Stuart said that now
there was no chance of New South Wales joining.[75] Service
wrote sadly to him:

In place of sending in an occasional note of encouragement, or
speaking a seasonable word of sympathy, or aiding us with your
counsel, or kindly telling us that on some points of the Bill you had

altered your mind . . . we never heard either from or of you, excepting via London.[76]

The Sydney *Bulletin* had no doubts about what had happened. While it deplored Service's imperialism, it also deplored the 'deep-rooted suspicion of every project emanating from Victoria' which characterized New South Wales politicians: 'From the beginning, their object appeared to be not only to stand aside themselves, but to prevent the other provinces from coming together.' Queensland, Tasmania, Western Australia and Fiji quickly passed adopting Acts, and Victoria in October with a roar of 'aye' and cheering.[77] Then the forlorn cause seemed almost lost, for South Australia would not proceed, and Service almost abandoned the whole enterprise. He consulted Murray Smith: was it worthwhile, if less than half the population of Australasia was to be represented? 'What do you think? You can imagine my chagrin should it fail.' Murray Smith advised perseverance. But although Service 'wined Downer', Adelaide stayed out, and the Federal Council when it first met in January 1886 was a poor puny infant.[78]

Tension was lessening over the New Hebrides. The French Senate modified the terms of the 'Relapsed Criminals Bill' and as promulgated in May 1885 the number of criminals proposed to be transported was greatly reduced; it was understood that no more than 2,000 would be sent to the Pacific. The Victorian government regarded this as at least a negative victory. There was little point now in passing the prepared quarantine legislation against French convicts, especially as New South Wales had shown so little interest.[79] Moreover in May, just before going out of office, Derby made the crucial promise that no French proposal to annex the New Hebrides would be considered without consultation with the colonies and the securing of satisfactory conditions.[80] In fact, however, the annexation movement was growing stronger in France. New Caledonian lobbyists were pressing their case that the colony needed both convict and New Hebridean labour and French newspapers were whipping up resistance to the provocation of the Australian colonies.

Early in 1886 the storm broke. While the Federal Council was meeting at Hobart news arrived that Germany and France had reached an agreement whereby Germany would not object to French annexation of the New Hebrides. Service and Griffith rallied the Council and produced a flurry of resolutions and telegrams. In Melbourne Duncan Gillies, who had just succeeded Service as Premier, set about mobilizing the other colonies. For once all the colonies did act together. On 23 February the Agents-General met Earl Granville, the new Colonial Secretary, to urge the prevention of convict transportation and protection of the *status quo* in the New Hebrides. But Granville now told them that France had proposed that she be allowed to annex the New Hebrides in return for abandonment of transportation. In line with Derby's promise he formally asked the colonies for their opinions, but gave a cautiously favourable response to the French initiative and then cabled the colonial governments urging acceptance. With the Foreign Office, the Colonial Office and several of the Agents-General in agreement, the matter appeared to be all over bar the recriminations.[81]

When the news became public on 12 March the pressure groups swung into action again and Gillies was 'daily besieged' by deputations; the clamour was sustained at high pitch for months. Every manse became a hive of activity again; the A.N.A. organized public meetings all over the colony; a united press and the great majority of politicians drove the government on to a last-ditch stand.[82] Service appealed privately to Rosebery, now Foreign Secretary: 'We are sick and wounded at heart that Home Government does not recognize our interests and protect them. Our hope now rests on you.'[83] Gillies was proving an apt pupil; he cabled Murray Smith:

What would be use speaking of Imperial Federation in face of an act which would proclaim stronger than any language contemptuous indifference for our wishes and future prospects?

Should English Ministers give away or allow to be taken New Hebrides today, Australia will assuredly take them back when able.[84]

Herbert sourly noted that the cable was 'no doubt instigated by Mr Service and prompted by his disgust at finding that the more loyal Colonies are assisting and not impeding Her Majesty's Government in the attempt to carry out the wish of Australia that transportation may be finally ended.'[85] 'The more loyal Colonies' were New South Wales and New Zealand.

Gillies and Griffith were in constant communication. By 12 March they had agreed on a draft protest by members of the Federal Council, who all agreed within a few days, and South Australia too. Support from Sir John Thurston, Governor of Fiji and a respected expert on Pacific affairs, was especially welcome. Gillies released a secret memorandum by Thurston which had a marked impact in England: Herbert angrily noted that the Victorian government was 'absolutely untrustworthy'.[86] Still, despite prompting, no reply to Gillies came from New South Wales. But on the 22nd Sir Patrick Jennings, the new Premier, cabled home that his government favoured the French proposal. When on the 29th the decision was made public, Gillies angrily wired: 'This dissension between the Colonies may, I fear, breed serious disaster in the future. Cannot we act together for once.'[87] Griffith bitingly rebuked New South Wales for always isolating herself. This time, however, Parkes, the *Daily Telegraph* and the Presbyterians provided powerful opposition in which Jennings's Catholicism was featured. The *Bulletin* supported the government, deploring the 'parsonical land grab' of the 'holy howlers' and applauding England's indifference to 'the ravings of Paton and the cocoa-nut-oil party'.[88] On 22 April the Colonial Office sent another firm memorandum urging acceptance. But the tide was beginning to turn. Lieut.-General Sir Andrew Clarke—a staunch Liberal Party candidate, old Victorian colonist and former colonial Governor—was now acting as Victorian Agent-General and threw himself into the fray. On 30 April he addressed an emotional, yet formidably competent statement to the Colonial Office,[89] and then succeeded in seeing Gladstone himself—in the midst of the Home Rule crisis! Berry arrived to take over as Agent-General and proceeded to lobby forcefully as only he could. But the decisive event was that New Zealand finally came down on the Victorian side. Its government had been inclined to accept the French proposal, especially if the coaling-station of Rapa could be ceded as part of the settlement. A ferocious campaign by the Presbyterians, however, had so roused opinion that in mid-May it announced a change of policy.[90] New South Wales was now isolated. Rosebery and Granville accepted the verdict and on 19 May Berry proudly cabled that the French ambassador had been informed that there was no prospect of British assent. Melbourne rejoiced: the right of consultation had been established, colonial advice had been accepted, the Federal Council had got off to a great start.[91]

The triumph was brief. Early in June 400 French marines from New Caledonia occupied the New Hebrides. There is doubt to this day about whether the coup was ordered from Paris or was the initiative of the militant local commandant. Whatever the truth, the French government skilfully exploited the situation, claiming that the troops were sent to protect French settlers from native outrages and that there was no act of annexation. Alarm in Victoria was intense. Gillies suggested to Rear-Admiral Tryon that he strengthen his forces in the area and offer the Victorian gunboats; Tryon did quickly send H.M.S. *Diamond*. The English reaction was reassuring: 'Press, Parliament, Government unanimous defending Australian interests . . . Public opinion excellent', Berry cabled Gillies. Rosebery was indeed very angry, protested strongly several times and finally dismissed the original French offer for a settlement. In Australia Gillies and Griffith continued to use the Federal Council mechanism to make their protests. Despite strong local pressure, Jennings refused to co-operate, did not reply to a letter from Griffith suggesting revival of the proposed legislation against French convicts, but was eventually forced by public opinion to protest at the French occupation. He still continued, however, to support the original French offer and when he made a highly indiscreet speech to a French Club dinner in Sydney, Parkes made a great parliamentary scene.[92]

It was a stalemate and negotiations dragged on and on. France, while denying its intention of annexing the New Hebrides, used the occupation as a bargaining counter in a series of British-French differences in the Pacific and North Africa of which the most important was over Suez.[93] Agonizing reports of the consolidation of French interests continued to spur the government, but Gillies was floundering far out of his depth, as his letters to Berry show.[94] His main recommendation was to send a rival British force to occupy parts of the islands. He later developed a more sophisticated view: that because of the touchiness of French public opinion, Britain should secretly seek French agreement to sending a British force, and that then both would withdraw by agreement, thus preserving each other's dignity. Occasionally he and Berry dropped clumsy hints, which may have had some substance, that Victoria was seriously considering 'going it alone' and sending a force to occupy or rather to take by force, the New Hebrides.[95]

By the close of 1886 the outlines of a probable settlement appeared clear. The Foreign Office, the Colonial Office and the Agents-General all took the view that, after French withdrawal, a system of joint Anglo-French control of the New Hebrides might be devised, if possible with a French guarantee to abandon transportation. Meanwhile the first conference of British colonies, which was chiefly to discuss defence, was preparing to assemble in London. Gillies stayed home, while Deakin was to lead the Victorian delegation whose other members were Berry, Service and James Lorimer. Early indications boded ill for Australian unity. On board ship Deakin found Downer of South Australia and Griffith full of self-will, undecided about what should be attempted at the Conference yet anxious to assert their individuality, and jealous of Victoria and New South Wales. In London Berry was thinking much the same thing: 'Each colony has an axe to grind and all join in bitter jealousy of Victoria. Those subjects which we regard as the most important sink into insignificance before some local *fad*.'[96] However, Gillies had been in touch with Parkes, who had recently become Premier and appeared to be willing to co-operate.[97]

On the opening day of the Conference Deakin, alone of the colonial spokesmen, went beyond polite formalities to state Victoria's view on the proper relationship between colonies and mother country.[98] The confrontation which followed three weeks later had an accidental quality. Salisbury was worried about broad serious problems in dispute with France, was not well informed on the history of the New Hebrides dispute, and became impatient with the discussion as it proceeded. By the most likely account,[99] Wisdom of New South Wales, Service and Downer had all stated their determination that France should not have the New Hebrides, and no doubt Service had pressed again for British annexation. Salisbury apparently scathingly derided the idiocy of quarrelling with France about so trivial a matter and saw no reason why France should not retain possession if she would abandon transportation. The speech was either a poorly calculated piece of bullying or, more likely perhaps, an uncalculated loss of temper. But in effect this was a return to the French proposals of 1885 which had been rejected before the French occupation, and a reversal of the line of British negotiation over the previous ten months. No wonder there was consternation among the delegates! Berry replied immediately—'one of the best and smartest speeches' he ever made, according to Service.[1] Then Griffith made his protest, though more temperately, and Deakin made his famous speech. Then followed Jennings of New South Wales to deny that there was Australian unanimity, as a large party in his colony was still prepared to accept the French offer; but if that was to be rejected New South Wales would act in co-operation with the other colonies. The delegates demanded further discussion on the 28th when Service, who led off, was supported by all the other Australian colonies, but not New Zealand. Service subsequently often referred to the striking unanimity of the Australian delegates over the New Hebrides issue and its effect on the imperial statesmen; he gave credit to Parkes for taking such a firm line in settling the issue and even claimed that Wisdom expressed himself in strong language 'which I hardly think a Victorian representative would have ventured to use'.[2] Certainly Deakin, Berry and Service, no doubt on the basis of private assurances, were all convinced that their defiance had produced a firmer imperial stand against France.[3]

All the delegates seemed to regard the Conference as having been highly successful. But still, although agreement had been reached in principle, the French government stalled while Gillies niggled away at the Colonial Office and the Presbyterians complained about harassing of their missions. Late in August Gillies pressed for an ultimatum and, failing action, the landing of a military force. Herbert actually agreed, probably unfairly, that the Foreign Office was dilatory: 'Proper step tell France if occupation extends beyond certain point, military forces will be landed', he minuted.[4] At last late in October the agreement for an Anglo-French joint naval commission and French evacuation was reached. Berry wrote exultantly to Gillies: 'At length our time has come.'[5] It was of course only a negative victory which left the Presbyterians aggrieved, but still a famous victory. The major question settled at the Colonial Conference had been naval defence. As international tensions grew, proposals to reinforce the navy's Pacific squadron had been discussed. The Intercolonial Conference of 1880–1 had recommended additions paid by Britain while the colonies built up their defences. Carnarvon's royal commission of 1882 had firmly recommended that the colonies contribute to the cost of reinforcing the Pacific Fleet. The Admiralty also became concerned about the growth of colonial navies, outside its control, for local defence. When Rear-Admiral Tryon took charge of the Australian station, he was instructed to attempt to negotiate an agreement whereby the colonies would agree to pay for a British-built and British-manned auxiliary cruiser squadron and allow their 'navies' to be brought under his command. Tryon quickly found there was no chance of agreement to the latter point; moreover the Victorian government, broadly supported by Queensland, wanted a 'fleet built, manned, and owned by Australia itself'.[6] Throughout, however, the government of New South Wales broadly accepted the Admiralty's proposals. The other governments did not press their plan for a national fleet or even insist on opportunities for colonial sailors in the Royal Navy. Another difficulty was the amount of the colonial financial contribution; the discussion provided many opportunities for argument about what was proposed to be protected—British investments and shipping or Australian interests. Late in 1885 the Admiralty ceded the point about local control of colonial navies and guaranteed that the auxiliary squadron would be confined to Australasian waters. Tryon negotiated on, but many details remained at issue; Victoria especially, chiefly because of its greater expenditure on its own navy and some feeling that Australia, rather opportunisitically, was being singled out from the rest of the Empire for discriminatory treatment, was holding out for a smaller contribution to the new squadron.[7]

The details were harmoniously settled by compromise at the Colonial Conference. Late in 1887 the Victorian Parliament, in the presence of the Earl of Carnarvon and the Marquis of Drogheda, made the passing of the Australasian Naval Force Bill an imperial occasion. Gillies reviewed the history of the negotiations,

proudly claimed the agreement was a federal triumph, and significantly remarked that—however desirable—Australian acceptance of full responsibility for naval defence would have cost
twice as much. Only three others spoke and the Bill was carried
nem. con. Gravely, nineteen Councillors spoke in agreement.
Proceedings in the upper house concluded with three cheers and
one cheer more for the Empire and a unanimous vote.[8] In New
South Wales Parkes carried the proposals, after an all-night
sitting, by forty-one votes to nine whereupon three cheers for
Australia were given followed by three for Old England.[9] But
Queensland delayed provision of the five new cruisers, for it
did not ratify the agreement until 1891. Then the brave little
colonial navies, ignored by the Royal Navy, went into decline.[10]

In mid-1885 Robert Harper, a maverick conservative, attacked
the Victorian government: it seemed that 'the men who rule in
Melbourne thought they ought to rule the universe'. Leading
men in New South Wales were asking, 'Has your Premier lost
his head? Are the people in Melbourne mad?'[11] What was, in
fact, the basis of the beliefs which Service, Gillies, Berry, Deakin
and the mass of politicians, press proprietors, the A.N.A., Protestant clergy, leading trade unionists and so many others held
with such fervent unanimity? The government certainly had no
need to create a political diversion, as a few parliamentary critics
and the exasperated men in the Colonial Office sometimes asserted; motives of economic interest were barely more significant.
In the first place there was a rudimentary but widely held
feeling that national interests, the interests of the colonies as a
whole, were threatened by the European powers. The neglect of
these interests by the imperial government and the 'air of icy
superiority' of the Colonial Office[12] which treated the colonial
governments like unruly children, were infuriating. The more
moderate thought chiefly in terms of keeping European powers
out of the Pacific; the more extreme, like Deakin, were genuine
Australian imperialists. 'We intend to be masters of the Pacific
by and by', he could say, and he even used the specious argument of Victoria's confined territory as a justification for colon-
ization in the Pacific.[13] Few as yet actually talked in terms of an
Australian nation, though Service did:

As far as France is concerned, Australia is simply a geographical expression. But we want to make it more than that; we want to make ourselves a nation, a united people . . . who are able to command respect.

Every one of us must feel our hearts beat strong and more strong when we think of ourselves not merely as Victorians, or New South Welshmen . . . but as Australians.[14]

Yet Service was a fervent imperialist. Jingo enthusiasm swept Victoria remarkably early; nowhere else in the colonies was there more consciousness of growing threats to the Empire or stronger demands for a no-nonsense imperial policy. Service agonized over the shameful weakness of Gladstone's policy. England, in the Pacific and elsewhere, was so often giving way 'instead of taking her stand upon the ground that if a thing is right we must *insist* on it'.[15] Again and again he stressed the love and affection of Victorians for the mother country: 'We cling to the idea of the Unity of the Empire. We do not wish to see anything of estrangement between Young Australia and Great Britain. We want our sons and daughters to grow up to love the Old Country.'[16] Berry also from time to time made the easy assumption that not following colonial interests would lead to the dismemberment of the Empire, that the way to achieve real imperial unity was militantly to protect the extremities equally with the heart of the Empire from all injury and insult.[17]

Patiently on the whole, British officials tried to restrain these wild colonial boys. With ineffable tact the Earl of Carnarvon reiterated the facts of life in Melbourne in November 1887:

Whilst we are bound to the best of our power to reduce such a nuisance and to safeguard your interests, on the other hand, let us count upon your patience, your support, your forbearance, very often in difficult matters. In dealing with great nations we cannot always invoke the mere engines of force. Diplomacy is the sole treatment. European diplomacy, as you well know, is a very complex matter . . .[18]

Of course Britain could not partition the Pacific at her pleasure, was trying to delay the partition process in other parts of the world as well, and believed (as Stuart did) that the colonial policy of bold annexation would create more diplomatic difficulties than maintaining the *status quo*. When the process was forced on Britain from 1884 to 1886 she was not in a strong bargaining position. France was hostile to British policy in Egypt and Russia was threatening on the Indian border, so Germany had to be conciliated. There could be no vehement protest at the German annexation in New Guinea or any strong stand when settling the demarcation of the boundary; Gladstone saw it as urgent to wind up 'these small colonial controversies', to get 'out of the way the bar to the Egyptian settlement'.[19] Similarly the New Hebrides was one minor issue in dispute with France among several which were settled together in 1887.

In this situation the Victorians must be seen as elephantine blunderers. It is almost certainly true, as many in the Colonial Office and local critics like Higinbotham[20] believed, that the antagonism they created in Berlin and Paris spurred the Continental powers on towards annexation. On the other hand it is arguable that the German and French governments under pressure themselves would have annexed anyway and that Victoria, by rousing the imperial government barely in time, at least gained compromise solutions instead of total losses. In calmer moments the Victorian leaders recognized their ignorance of the wider diplomatic situation but defended their behaviour on the grounds that the imperial government refused to take them into its confidence and was blind to colonial interests unless forcibly brought to its attention. The 1885 pledge that the colonies would be consulted in future on matters directly affecting their interests, though it was frequently not to be observed in the following half-century, was a significant break-through. The Agents-General were consulted more and more, minor confidential information was revealed to them, and they partly replaced the Governors as channels of communication.[21] Service for one believed by 1888 that there had been a basic change in attitude and that relations between colonies and mother country were highly satisfactory.[22] Rosebery's behaviour over the New Hebrides, Lord Knutsford's conciliatory attitude as Secretary of State and the success of the Colonial Conference were evidence of the change. In 1888 the imperial government treated the colonies most considerately and tactfully, as we shall see, over the Chinese crisis. But no other major external issues, which might have revealed the always possible clash between imperial and colonial interests, were to arise for many years.

Parkes's electoral victory early in 1887 had raised the hopes of the Victorian government. He visited Melbourne in February and met Gillies who wrote to Berry:

he speaks (tall) of all the Colonies being federated—but while this is all very well in its way: to strain after the unattainable and pass by the attainable . . . I hope that he will give practical effect to his general opinion as often expressed and join us: if he does we will be at one on this continent.[23]

Parkes's co-operation over the Colonial Conference in London was highly encouraging and for some time no intercolonial tiffs occurred. Parkes and Gillies conferred again in September. The Victorian government prepared for its intercolonial exhibition of 1888, having carefully ascertained that New South Wales had no objection to a lavish festival in Melbourne after its own centennial celebrations. On the A.N.A.'s suggestion, Gillies won the agreement of the other colonies to observe 26 January as a national holiday from 1888; Anniversary Day had long been celebrated in New South Wales. (It is ironical that the Sydney *Bulletin* was campaigning for commemoration of Eureka instead of 26 January.)[24] The Victorian government had already in 1883 abolished Separation Day as a public service holiday as out of keeping with the spirit of the times; however it still remained a bank holiday.

But the centennial year was to mark the low point in relations between the governments of the two colonies. The issue which led to the widening of the breach was ludicrous: Parkes's attempt to alter the name of New South Wales to Australia. For long there had been discontent and recent press discussion revealed much support for a new name. But few anticipated Parkes's bold approach later in November 1887. He won the support of his cabinet and of Dibbs, the Opposition leader; both pledged with signed statements as many of their supporters as they could gather. When Parkes asked for leave to bring in the Bill, two outraged members, Henry Copeland and J. P. Abbott, took the unusual course of forcing a debate there and then; an angry and highly revealing discussion followed. Copeland thought the proposal monstrous and absurd, it would make New South Wales a laughing-stock; Abbott moved an amendment to alter the name to Wentworth (his own seat). Parkes made his case uncompromisingly: there was wide discontent with the name, New South Welshmen had no easy collective name like Victorians and Queenslanders, it was ridiculous to be saddled in perpetuity with Cook's fancy that the coast of Queensland resembled that of South Wales. For nearly half a century they had represented the whole of Australia to the world, 'we were the original Australian people':

by right of being the founders of Australia, of being the pioneers who did all the hard prolonged work, of being the persons who carried the flag of England into the desert, and maintained it there, who planted homes, towns, industries, and opened the fields of civilisation, we are entitled to this name.

Dibbs supported him:

I have no sympathy with the people of Victoria or Queensland who may object to the change . . . The other colonies left the wing of their parent, but the day is not far distant when they will return. They will then sink the names which they have taken, and join us in forming a great nation, to be known for all time as Australia . . .

Three opponents of the Bill stood out for their common sense: W. J. Lyne who believed that nothing could 'dissever' the the colonies more than this proposal, E. W. O'Sullivan (who, however, suggested 'Arcadia' as an appropriate name), and W. McMillan who regarded 'the attempt to jump the name of Australia' as 'one of the most outrageous and contemptible things I ever heard of.' The three divisions were carried by a majority of about forty, with only eighteen or nineteen in opposition; because of loyalties to Parkes and Dibbs, the votes should not be taken as a close reflection of opinion.[25]

The *Sydney Morning Herald* and *Daily Telegraph* were hostile to the proposal and the *Bulletin* despaired over Parkes's 'narrow parochial policy of intercolonial hatred and distrust' and seriously predicted ultimate civil war.[26] The rest of Australia displayed mingled mirth and anger. In Adelaide it was suggested that South Australia should immediately change its name to Australasia; alternatively it was proposed that every colony change its name to Australia. The *Australasian* unkindly suggested that the appropriate name for New South Wales was

'Convictoria'. Most Victorian parliamentarians at first thought the proposal was meant as a joke, but the government moved quickly and Victoria, Queensland and South Australia jointly protested. In London Berry rushed round to the Colonial Office to see the Secretary of State and publicized the assurances he was given. The Governor of New South Wales was instructed to reserve the Bill if passed and Herbert had no doubt that it would be disallowed.[27] No more was heard of the measure beyond an angry, sarcastic and patronizing public letter from Parkes to Gillies.[28]

What were Parkes's motives? Despite his vehemence, it is doubtful if he was more than half-serious for he must have known that in the long run the proposal was almost certain to fail. He wanted to satisfy some influential citizens who felt strongly on the matter, but if it was a 'popular' move aimed at what was believed to be dominant sentiment and the strengthening of electoral support, it was a bad miscalculation since he was so sadly humiliated. He could not have seriously believed that the other colonies would not bitterly resent the proposal. It is possible that he believed that New South Wales needed, as it had been on the defensive so long, to assert its 'supremacy' before a serious move towards federation could be made. The debate is most useful in demonstrating the reality of New South Wales provincialism, the extent of rankling resentment towards Victoria, and the gulf between the New South Wales patriots (of whom Robertson was the classical example) and those who naturally thought in Australian terms. A strong group in New South Wales (which included a disproportionate number of leading politicians) insisted on regarding federation as a rejoining of the mother colony by her errant children; none the less the strength of existing federal opinion should not be overlooked, as it so often is.

Gillies undiplomatically chose this moment to propose a conference to aim at ending the railways war by eliminating differential rates for goods. The South Australian government was willing, but Parkes replied with a vague letter which probably led Gillies to believe that there was no point in pressing him.[29] In December also, Gillies took up a proposal which, on Victoria's initiative, had been discussed at the London Conference and later with Parkes: that the colonies should jointly request that a general officer of the imperial government inspect the colonial troops and advise on planning for 'united defence in case of an invasion'. It was hoped that Lord Wolseley himself would be made available. Parkes delayed a decision, but after Gillies had pressed him twice in March 1888 rejected the proposal on the 30th: 'we must act for ourselves, and act upon our own resources'. Gillies wrote again at length, but Parkes did not reply.[30] Twelve months later the imperial government took the initiative and offered to make General Edwards available, whereupon Parkes and Gillies agreed to accept the offer. Another Victorian plan was to establish a federal ammunition factory. At the Federal Council early in 1886 they won the broad assent of Queensland and South Australia to the proposal that governments purchase from such a factory and consider sharing any necessary subsidy; negotiations with English manufacturers were begun by the Victorian government. By early 1888 Captain Whitney, the representative of the chosen English firm, had settled on a site at Footscray on the Maribyrnong River. In response to overtures from Gillies, Parkes began a long stalling operation. He remarked that supporting the factory 'would be more correctly described as subsidising a Victorian factory than as assisting to establish a federal one'; the site had been selected without consultation. Gillies assured him that Whitney had spontaneously selected the site, that New South Wales was being asked only to agree to purchase cartridges and not to share in any subsidy, and that he would be willing to have the factory built in New South Wales if Whitney could find a suitable site and New South Wales paid for it. Whitney journeyed to Sydney to inspect possible sites and seemingly was not satisfied. (It is almost too much to believe that Whitney and Gillies were not in agreement that the site must be in Victoria.) Parkes wrote to say that to be truly federal the factory could not be in Melbourne or Sydney but should rather be in a border town like Albury, Echuca or Moama; that New South Wales would share expenses if it were located in a border town; that if built in Victoria New South Wales might establish another factory; but none the less would agree to purchase from it for the time being. By now the border towns were excitedly urging their claims. Whitney demanded an extra bonus of £20,000 if the site had to be in a border town. Gillies asked Parkes if he would be willing to share the extra expense. Parkes agreed to submit the matter to Parliament and suggested joint examination of possible sites, preferably Moama or Echuca. Whitney now refused to agree to a border town, the Victorian government decided to call it a day and Whitney built at Maribyrnong his Colonial Ammunition Factory from which the munitions industry was to grow.[31]

The outstanding case of disharmony was on the most important question of all in the period—Chinese immigration. The crisis came in May 1888 but tension had been mounting for some twelve months. In mid-1887 the visit of the Chinese Commissioners surveying the welfare of their compatriots had aroused suspicion; Chinese were flocking into the Northern Territory and a major agitation led by the trade unions was seething in most of the colonies. On 3 November 1887 Gillies, seeking a united approach, wired the premiers: 'Do you propose to legislate on Chinese question this session? If so can we come to an understanding . . . as to proposals?' Parkes replied next day, agreeing that all should legislate in the same terms. On the 19th Gillies urged a conference before anyone took action. But the next week saw Parkes's fiasco over the change of name. On the 26th he threatened, despite his anxiety 'that we should act in concert', to proceed unilaterally; however he did not do so at this stage. On the 30th Gillies pleaded with him to confine any action for the moment to 'temporary expedients' and made suggestions about how existing legislation might be brought into conformity. In December the imperial government received a note from the Chinese government protesting at existing discriminatory legislation and on 23 January 1888 the colonial governments were asked to comment. Before replying, Gillies again circularized the premiers on 22 March to suggest a joint answer to the effect that while all agreed that further restriction of immigration was necessary it would be preferable to seek a treaty with China through the imperial government rather than to legislate: 'Thus might be accomplished inoffensively—through the means of diplomacy—all that we desire, while legislative measures . . . might engender an international bitterness.' The Victorian government was impressed by the recent negotiation of a treaty between China and the United States (which was never ratified).

The New South Wales government, however, was not prepared to discuss the matter with anyone. On 31 March Parkes
sent a long and strong telegram to Lord Knutsford requesting
the imperial government to open treaty negotiations, and told
the other premiers that separate answers on similar lines from
the colonies would carry more weight than any joint representation. Then late in April the crisis broke when the *Afghan*
arrived at Melbourne and in response to public pressure the
government refused to allow most of the migrants to land. It
did not want to resort to further legislation, was anxious to test
the prerogative power to exclude aliens by executive action, and
was ultimately upheld by the Privy Council against the majority
of the Victorian Supreme Court in *Musgrove* v. *Ah Toy*. The
arrival of the *Afghan* in Sydney, however, coincided with several
other vessels bringing more than 500 Chinese. The mass outcry
was far more vehement than in Melbourne, the government was
faced with a major crisis and resorted not merely to exclusion
by executive action but also drafted harsh legislation which
passed the Assembly in one day. Parkes opportunistically chose
to pick a row with the imperial government, which had actually
begun sounding out Peking but had omitted until prodded to
acknowledge by cable Parkes's telegram of 31 March. Although
the imperial government had to wait on replies from the other
colonies before committing itself, Parkes condemned this 'pro-
crastination, negligence, and unwarranted delay . . . we cannot
patiently stand to be treated with the frozen indifference of
persons who consider some petty quarrel in a petty State of more
importance than the gigantic interests of these magnificent
colonies.' Early in May the South Australian government called
urgently for a conference; the Queensland and South Australian
governments then appealed to Parkes not to pass his Bill before
the conference was held; the Victorians, who were furious at
Parkes's unilateral action, asked that the Bill be vetoed if passed
before the conference was held. The Foreign Office complained
that the proposed New South Wales legislation would make
negotiation of a treaty almost impossible.

The intercolonial conference was held at Sydney from 12 to
14 June and no doubt there was some plain speaking. The Victorians had been doubtful whether it was worth proceeding, but
considerable agreement was reached. The imperial government's

proposal for a general immigration law to put all nations on the
same footing and thus remove apparent discrimination against
the Chinese received short shrift. It was agreed further to encourage the imperial government to negotiate a treaty and, to
aid the objective, to abolish existing poll-taxes. It was further
agreed to pass uniform restrictive legislation based on the formula
of one passenger to 500 tons of a ship's burthen, although Victoria
unwillingly followed majority opinion only for the sake of unity
and New South Wales flatly refused to abandon its Bill (which
was still before the Council), though it did consent to amend
it when two other colonies had passed the agreed Draft Bill. In
the event Victoria passed the Bill late in 1888 after Queensland
(with additional severity) and South Australia had done so; but
the original New South Wales Bill was passed, retaining the
individual poll-tax of £100, and was not subsequently amended.
By August the ambassador in Peking had agreed on moderate
terms of settlement* with the Chinese government and on 14
September the imperial government formally asked the colonial
governments whether the proposed terms were satisfactory. The
Victorians were happy to agree; so ultimately were all the other
colonies—except New South Wales which never replied to the
despatch, despite regular requests until 1892 when the proposed treaty was abandoned. It might be argued that the consequences of neglecting this opportunity were tragic for Australian
history and important in judging Parkes's claims to statesman-
ship. Throughout this issue Victoria had acted as the 'loyal'
colony, reflecting the new harmony in its relations with the
imperial government following the Colonial Conference of
1887.[32]

On the economic front, despite good intentions, the Victorian
government did not succeed in reducing the problem of divergent tariffs. There was little protectionist fanaticism among the
members of the stable Service-Berry and Gillies-Deakin ministries in the years 1883-90; they were a combination of moderate

---

* The terms were: abolition of the poll-tax; restriction of entry of Chinese
labourers to one to 300 tons; free entry for merchants, travellers, officials and
students; most favoured nation treatment for Chinese already in Australia with
full rights to leave and return (Knutsford to Australian Governors, Very Confidential, 14 Sept. 1888).

protectionists and 'free traders' who were compelled to accept
protection as a settled policy. Despite their apparently assured
control of the Assembly, they were continually threatened by
the demands of extreme protectionists, the numerous farming
representatives and the Melbourne *Age*. Much though the government would have liked to eliminate protectionist excesses
which were irritating to other colonies, it was in no position
politically to do so. It was known that smuggling was rife; the
barbarous searching of travellers at Wodonga or Spencer Street
station was bad publicity for the colony.[33] Hostility in the
Riverina because of the stock tax was producing commercial
retaliation; yet even when the protectionist-dominated royal commission on the tariff recommended abolition of the stock tax in
1883 the government took no action for fear of rural interests.
None the less the coalition ministries, despite constant pressure,
refused to adopt any new provocative tariff measures, until forced
to in 1889.

The Chambers of Manufactures and Commerce supported
throughout the government's policy of intercolonial pacification.
Protection was all very well, but those manufacturers well established behind tariff walls were finding that it had its confining
aspects. They were looking now more and more to an Australia-
wide market, especially to New South Wales; but very often
the Victorians could not compete for price with overseas manufactures in that colony. So their natural objective became intercolonial free trade behind a national tariff wall. The free traders
in the Chamber of Commerce naturally supported the principle
of intercolonial free trade for, even if a national protective policy
were adopted, the immediate area of free trade would be
widened. Moreover Victorian protection kept out some products
of other colonies; for example, in so far as Victorian farmers were
protected, Tasmanian and South Australian primary producers
were harmed; their governments were tending to impose retaliatory tariffs which harmed Victorian manufacturers. From about
1879 the Chamber of Manufactures began spasmodically to press
for federation or intercolonial free trade as a step to that end.
As early as 1882 a prominent businessman remarked that 'It is
an undisputed fact . . . that the employers of labour have arrived
at the conclusion that federation, or some system of intercolonial

free trade, is necessary for the proper carrying on of the industries of the colony.'[34] By 1883 the two Chambers were conferring
regularly and, although there was violent disagreement over what
the national tariff policy should be, both came out strongly for
federation and immediate intercolonial free trade with for the
moment separate colonial tariffs against the world. It was noted
that Victoria levied duties on 203 items and New South Wales
on 86; yet 'free trade' New South Wales's customs revenue was
almost as high as Victoria's.[35]

Immediate intercolonial free trade was politically out of the
question. Yet something might be possible. The Victorians had
been alarmed by the no doubt half serious and tactical discussion
by some members of the 1883 Convention of the possibility of
a customs union excluding Victoria.[36] As the largest exporter
Victoria had to placate the other colonies, and go on to capture
wider markets; it would be disastrous if protection against Victoria developed further. Those colonies which joined the Federal
Council would at least consider a customs union. The Tasmanian
government in mid-1883 had suggested a reciprocity treaty. Late
in 1884 the Victorians responded and at a conference in January
1885 both governments agreed harmoniously to a near-complete
customs union for a three-year trial period, subject to parliamentary ratification. The *Age*, the *Argus* and both Chambers
(which continued jointly to lobby the government in favour of
intercolonial free trade) warmly approved. Berry, who had negotiated the agreement, was sharp with protesting delegations of
primary producers; it was ridiculous to regard Tasmanians as
foreigners or to claim the treaty was inconsistent with a standing
policy of protection. Yet the opposition grew, not merely from
sawmillers, hopgrowers, oats and barley producers, orchardists
and berrygrowers, potato-farmers and jam-manufacturers (and
Tasmanian manufacturers), but also from doctrinaire protectionists led by James Mirams, and, even more serious, from the
dogmatic Trades Hall Council which seemed to be guided more
by protectionist theory than the immediate interests of its con-
stituents. Late in 1885, when the government proposed ratification, the Opposition, scenting a useful election issue, was
hostile. The government caved in and dropped the measure.
Although Service in later years was to refer to his own humili-

ation and his ministry's great failure, it is difficult to believe that the government could not have rallied its ranks. Certainly Adye Douglas of Tasmania believed his colony had been sold: once they had agreed to join the Federal Council no more was heard of the reciprocity treaty. But the answer probably is to be found in a remark by Deakin nearly two years later: that the treaty was abandoned because it was considered unfriendly by another colony—was it New South Wales or South Australia?[37] Negotiations for a reciprocity treaty with Queensland in 1886 failed to get far; Queensland and South Australia also failed to reach agreement.[38]

In 1887 the Victorian Chamber of Manufactures became very active under the leadership of Emanuel Steinfeld, a Ballarat furniture manufacturer. It arranged a conference of the three Australian Chambers at Adelaide in October when Steinfeld called for an end to the tariff war. It would be sinful and criminal to delay union, limited markets had caused many manufacturers to fail and had deterred investment, if operations could be enlarged beyond one colony plenty of capital would become available. 'Base insinuations are promulgated that Victoria wants to fatten into prosperity at the expense of the other colonies. This is false. The people of Victoria are animated by a sincere desire to unite the Australian colonies, to prosper with, and through, each other.' Anyway, he continued, Victoria had an unfavourable trade balance with New South Wales and Queensland, and manufacturers in the other colonies would always be protected to some extent from the Victorians by transport costs. Some South Australian delegates, for fear of Victoria, opposed intercolonial free trade but the New South Welshmen, who believed they had more to gain from national protection than to lose from Victorian competition, were enthusiastic. The conference formed an Australian Federal Union—'really the first practical step towards the Federation of the Colonies', said Steinfeld —and broke up with great backslappings and expressions of friendship.[39] A few months later a joint conference with Chambers of Commerce was held at Sydney, but the local Chamber of Commerce boycotted it. The Sydney and Melbourne manufacturers were still working closely together and won unanimous agreement to a resolution in favour of intercolonial free trade and a uniform national tariff on the understanding that the motion did not imply that the tariff was to be protective. It was also agreed that it was desirable to negotiate reciprocal treaties immediately. But the Victorian protectionists ran into some strong criticism. Douglas of Tasmania believed Victoria was only trying to serve its own purposes: 'The greatest enemy Tasmania had had was her child Victoria, for when Victoria grew up she did all she could to cripple Tasmania.' A commercial Victorian delegate remarked that if he were a New South Welshman he would take no part in the conference: 'It was all very well for Victoria . . . to say to her neighbours, "Pull down your fences, and we shall have a fair fight".' Other Victorian delegates, in sorrow rather than anger, denied that they were wolves in sheep's clothing.[40]

More significant still, at the first congress of Chambers of Commerce in Melbourne late in 1888 there were strong demands for uniform legislation on such common interests as the estates of deceased persons and insolvents, the recovery of debts, partnerships, patents, trade-marks, insurance, etc. In introducing the federal question, the President, Robert Reid, a Melbourne merchant, deplored the 'great darkness which still prevails in Victoria' on fiscal matters. Yet E. Pulsford, the able free trade propagandist, had difficulty in carrying a motion in favour of absolutely unrestricted free trade in all aspects. Steinfeld had been invited to join the Melbourne delegation and to read a paper; his motion for a customs union with a uniform tariff was carried against the Sydney delegates who were prepared to support a customs union only if each colony could retain its own tariff against the world outside Australia. Then, after a rip-roaring speech by Service, a resolution in favour of all colonies joining the Federal Council was carried unanimously.[41]

Proceedings at these conferences show to what extent businessmen in all the colonies, with the notable exception of the Sydney merchants, were recognizing the need for federation. In this regard the movement was gathering strength. But from 1887 the Victorian government was faced by a serious internal challenge which came close to wrecking its federal policy. Tens of thousands of farmers organized in the Victorian Farmers' Protection Association and adopted as their policy a large increase in the

stock tax, import duties on dairy produce and most crops, bounties for wheat exports, and lower freight charges.[42] As the government well knew, the stock tax was the standing evidence of
Victorian selfishness and determination to get the better of its
neighbours. It was hurled in their faces again and again by the
Sydneysiders; as late as January 1889 Parkes bluntly said in Melbourne that 'so long as Victoria indulged in the pastime of this
most barbaric tax it was useless to ask the other colonies for
federation'.[43] There was even talk of New South Wales imposing an export duty on wool bound for the port of Melbourne.
With some justice on their side the farmers were now demand-
ing a share in the benefits of protection; their demands were
sharpened by the distress of many of the new wheat-farmers in
the north and north-west. The trouble was, it was not clear that
higher agricultural protection would afford at the most more than
marginal benefit. Nevertheless it became widely believed in rural
areas that higher protection would be of great benefit, especially
a higher stock tax, even though only a few hundred graziers
(and those were larger landowners for the most part) could possibly benefit. The low stock tax became a symbol of the farmers'
wrongs; beside it the lofty case for federation was as nothing.
In June 1888 the Farmers' Protection Association approached
the Trades Hall Council and the Chamber of Manufactures for
support. The T.H.C. resolved to give aid, recognizing the justice
of the case for protection, though it disapproved of a wheat
bonus. The manufacturers were made of sterner stuff: farmers
were already 'the most favoured class in the community', said
Steinfeld, their demands would endanger federation, no support
could be given to a policy which would raise the price of bread
and meat.[44] In August, James Munro, the leader of the Opposition, moved a motion of no-confidence in the government in the
hope of attracting the rural members, but at the last moment
the Protection Association decided not to support a change of
ministry.[45] The government did not waver; Deakin warned that
the New South Wales protectionists had told him that, if they
came to power they would try to shape a tariff which would not
injure Victoria, but if Victoria meanwhile unsheathed the sword
these assurances could not hold.[46] Early in 1889 the election was
largely fought in rural areas on the issue of the stock tax; the

ministry's promises of assistance in other forms largely carried
it through, although the new Assembly was 'the most strongly
protective House that ever came together in Victoria'.[47] In
August 1889 the government survived again when Allan McLean
led most of the country members and the doctrinaire protectionists in an attempt to raise the stock tax.[48] (Eventually in 1892
there was indeed a massive increase.) But the government, faced
with an alliance of country members, protectionists and the
Trades Hall, ashamedly conceded higher duties on oats, barley,
fruit, jam, eggs and timber. The *Argus* deplored the government's abandoning of the federal cause and 'the cannibalistic
prospect of another season of gnawing at our own Australian
vitals.'[49] There was much resentment in Adelaide and Hobart;
the Adelaide Chamber of Commerce refused to co-operate with
the Melbourne Chamber in drafting a national tariff because of
'the present course of Victorian legislation'.[50] The issue provides
a useful illustration of the limitations on national feeling in some
quarters and of the importance of fancied or real economic interests in conditioning attitudes to federation.

The other curb on the Victorian government was the *Age*.
Syme's attitude to federation over the years was invariably suspicious and fluctuated according to immediate tactical estimates
of the prospect for protection under federation and the maintenance of his paper's influence. He retained his obsession about
the colony's limited territory and resources which might in the
long run mean that Victoria would be a comparatively junior
partner in a federation; in 1886 he recommended amalgamation
of Victoria and South Australia as the latter's answer to its current depression. He regularly attacked the official New South
Wales statisticians for allegedly misleading compilations* and
suspected that federation was a plot of the free traders, especially
when Parkes came to power and held private discussions with
Gillies. In the long run he and his parliamentary lieutenants,
Mirams and Munro, feared that the national tariff might be a

---

* An entertaining note might be written on the attempts over many years
of Hayter in Victoria and, from 1886, of Coghlan in New South Wales to
produce statistical series to show their respective colonies in the more favourable light. Much offence was caused in New South Wales by Hayter's series
on the incidence of crime. He also produced comparative figures on suicide
and promiscuity among single women.

free trade one; in the short run moves for higher protection in Victoria were inhibited.[51] By 1888 he was openly sabotaging the government's policy. He was basing his hopes now mainly on the growth of protectionist political parties in the other colonies. Protective policies by one colony against another were to be encouraged; this would assure a national protective policy and was probably the quickest road to federation.[52] He supported the farmers' case for a higher stock tax:

There is not a great deal of force in the federation argument, since it is time enough to ask Victorian producers to make sacrifices for a national object when there is some immediate prospect of that object being attained. Meanwhile, the farmers and graziers of the colony have a clear right to participate in the advantages of the protective policy of the country to its fullest extent.[53]

By May 1889 he was resorting to the argument that Gillies's chief motive for opposing the stock tax was to support the 'Toorak squatters', the clique who owned Riverina stations.[54] Syme's mischief-making went further: he set out deliberately to rouse intercolonial hostility. There was no need to worry about reprisals from New South Wales to protective increases in Victoria, he asserted. To make reprisals they would have to go protectionist and, whether they did or not, they would be forced for many years to buy Victoria's surplus manufactures and agricultural produce.[55]

Mr. Gillies' continual coaxing of Sir Henry Parkes as of a pouting child is not only useless, but is mischievous, by ministering to the morbid vanity of small minds in Sydney who are encouraged in the notion that the other colonies are powerless to do anything without the assistance of New South Wales . . . Up to the present the public affairs of the colony have been dominated by the mercantile class in Sydney, who have used as their tools men of inferior intellectual calibre—such as Sir John Robertson, Sir Patrick Jennings and Sir Henry Parkes. It is quite remarkable that whilst Victoria during the last thirty years has produced a host of able public men, New South Wales has brought to the front few men above the intellectual standard of the parish vestryman. We are justified in assuming that ability has been studiously kept out of the political arena by the dominant ring as being incompatible with subservience . . . To prevent the spread of Victorian ideas and the limitation of free imports, the Sydney importers have set all their creatures in the Press and on the platform to stir up animosity against the people of this colony. [But with the progress of the protectionist cause] it will probably be found that New South Wales can produce statesmen of a higher stamp than Sir Henry Parkes, and that the cultivation of hostile feelings towards Victoria will be denounced as a crime or laughed at as an absurdity.[56]

A couple of months before, old Sir John Robertson, in response to a similar *Age* editorial, had dashed off a furious letter to the Sydney press. The Victorian population included

hundreds of thousands of the very scum and filth of the criminality and rascality of all mankind, including those from the two convict colonies adjoining them . . . [By] the early drain from our lands . . . although we lost great numbers, much intelligence, much unscrupulousness and general floating rascality, we gained in having our atmosphere purified of the effects of their presence. As gold was to be obtained in Victoria very easily, and as their vicious propensities were then unrestrained by either law, order or decency, it was not likely that they would return to the good old-fashioned, sleepy, law-abiding and well governed colonies like New South Wales or Tasmania.

Victoria was 'insolvent, bombastic, unjust and inconsistent' and her 'rotten and thoroughly exploded fraudulent federation scheme' should be treated with contempt.[57] Syme was Victoria's Robertson, the ultra-provincialist, the classic 'Victorian nationalist' even. We may also acknowledge that one of the strengths and justifications of the coalition was that the government was able largely to emancipate itself from control by the *Age*.

Things were not altogether easy for the Victorian government in its policy of intercolonial pacification. Apart from its domestic difficulties, the trouble was that it was morally compromised in that Victoria had been the economic aggressor and remained so despite all good intentions. James Service, honest as always, summed it up in 1888:

from the first to the last the Victorian policy has been a selfish one, and it is a selfish policy now. People say that when it suited Victorians to establish protection the protectionists were supported by a great many of those identical gentlemen who are now crying out for intercolonial free-trade. It is to our political advantage now, they say, that we should have this intercolonial free-trade. The feeling in the other colonies is that this is but another movement in favour of our noble selves. It is very natural that they should have this feeling, and it is no use shutting our eyes to the fact. What we in Victoria have to do is to join with the other colonies rather than endeavour to take the lead. Let the Sydney people lead, and let us follow them.[58]

Gillies agreed that Victoria could not make any new major initiative. He, too, resorted to flattery and cajolery of Parkes, appeals to him to get on with the great work.

We did not desire unnecessarily to press for the lead in this matter. Victoria has offered to assist New South Wales, as it was its place to take the initiative. Victoria has offered, if New South Wales will take the lead, to follow. We have no pride except the pride of duty, and we are willing to follow.[59]

In January 1889 there was a reconciliation, after a year of disharmony, when Parkes came to Melbourne to speak at a medical congress and to see the Exhibition. Nothing is known of the nature of the conversations, beyond the fact that the possibility of federation was discussed.[60]

The Victorians were also bringing tactical pressure to bear through the Federal Council. In 1887 they appear to have been uncertain about whether or not to abandon the enterprise. No meeting was held that year—possibly as the *Age* asserted 'lest its action give umbrage to the free trade and anti-federal faction in New South Wales',[61] more likely because no action was of much use in the absence of South Australia. In 1888, however, the two governments were in close contact and both were delighted when late in the year the Bill to join the Council passed the South Australian Parliament. The Council meeting in January–February 1889 was harmonious. C. C. Kingston went out of his way to praise the Victorians' handling of Council affairs:

Victoria exhibited a spirit of liberality in dealing with the smaller colonies which was worthy of all praise, and was obviously prompted by a desire to promote the federation of Australasia. It could never be said that Victoria had sought any advantage which could be questioned by the other federated colonies.[62]

(Was this really a remark for Parkes's ears?) The Council agreed to enlarge its membership from each colony and then, at its

next meeting, formally to consider the question of federation. As
Deakin subsequently wrote, 'The Federal Council became influential by the excitement it occasioned around Port Jackson.'[63]

There were, of course, other powerful reasons why Parkes
made his move in 1889, especially local political exigencies and
consciousness of how little time he had left to earn the plaudits of
posterity. Before General Edwards had even arrived in the country, on 15 June Parkes boasted to Lord Carrington that he 'could
confederate [sic] these colonies in twelve months'.[64] On the same
day he wrote to his daughter to say that he was 'seriously thinking . . . of offering myself as leader in a great movement to
federate on a solid basis all the colonies'.[65] On that same day (or
night, in all probability) he opened negotiations with Gillies:

> I am writing to you now in consequence of remarks which have
> fallen from you at different times, both in private and public, as to
> my taking some prominent or leading step in the cause of Australian
> Federation. Other persons of importance from other of the Colonies
> have expressed opinions similar to yours.
> I am prepared in all good faith to undertake this great responsibility,
> if you, after mature consideration, and consultation with South Aus-
> tralia or Queensland, still think it wise for me to do so. If thus
> authorised I will convene what may be termed a Parliamentary Con-
> vention of Australasia, that is, a body to be clothed with the authority
> of the Executives of the respective Colonies . . . Should my idea of
> the initial step receive the approval of Victoria and one other Colony,
> I shall be prepared to act and at the proper time to submit a draft
> measure for a Federal Constitution.[66]

Gillies's reply of the 21st has not been preserved, but he probably
queried whether this was the right moment for moving to full
federation, for Parkes replied on the 25th: 'I think I see grounds
for apprehending that difficulties in the way of any comprehensive scheme of federation will be increased by further delay
especially in this colony. It was indeed this apprehension which
induced me to open communication with you on the subject.'[67]*
Deakin was probably reflecting governmental scepticism about
Parkes's move when on 5 July he wrote to Dilke: 'Parkes has

---

* Parkes concluded this letter with the delightful suggestion that 'the seat
of the Federal body should be unitedly in Victoria and New South Wales
. . . at some point on the Murray the Executive offices on one side and the
Legislative chambers on the other.'

recently made *private* overtures but as he wishes it accomplished only in such a manner as will recognise the hegemony of N.S.W. and put all the rest of us in the position of penitents it is not likely to lead to much.'[68] Gillies eventually wrote at length on 12 August to say that he believed there was no chance of achieving full federation at the moment and appealing to Parkes to join the Federal Council. On the 23rd Gillies told the South Australian Premier confidentially of Parkes's proposal. There was no reply from Sydney.

Parkes's next move, which for want of any better explanation than pique or playing to the gallery might be seen as an attempt to bring pressure to bear on the Victorian government, was to make an outcry about the Murray River waters. When the Victorian government began to plan major irrigation works, it sought a treaty in 1886 with New South Wales over use of the Murray waters, but negotiations broke down, largely because of South Australian hostility, and each colony was haphazardly giving water-rights to irrigators.[69] Early in September Parkes came out with a wild statement that Victoria was draining the Murray and jeopardizing future navigation; he threatened to 'assert the right' of New South Wales to control the river by stopping Victorian works and giving the Chaffeys at Mildura notice that they were trespassing in their use of water; he proposed to establish a New South Wales Conservancy Commission. The basis of his claim was the odd fact that the bed of the river was New South Wales territory; but of course either party could, if it came to a conflict, check the other by manipulating the sources within its territory. The obvious answer, recommended by many parliamentarians in New South Wales, was an intercolonial authority. The Victorian government took no notice of the provocation.[70]

Six days after the release of the Edwards report, Parkes telegraphed the premiers on 15 October to suggest a conference to consider the implications; the second instalment began of the long-drawn-out correspondence with Gillies. Parkes made his premeditated move to Brisbane to consult with the Queensland government and on the way back on the 24th made his call to the nation at Tenterfield and thus forced the issue. The story is familiar of how the premiers unitedly forced Parkes to agree, not to the convention he had suggested, but to a meeting of members

of the New South Wales government with the Federal Council
to discuss his proposal, with the face-saving compromise that they
would meet as 'representative public men'.[71] There was, of
course, a great deal of prestige at stake. Despite their calls to
Parkes to take the lead, when it came to the point the Victorians
found it intolerable that the Federal Council should be bypassed.
They had been long suffering, had kept their tempers continually in the face of provocation by the man who, they believed,
had wrecked almost every recent attempt at intercolonial co-
operation. Their dignity could not be outraged to this extent. But
all this understood, it perhaps needs to be pointed out also that
Gillies believed what he said when he argued that the prospects
for federation were hopeless, but that confederation in a reformed Federal Council was attainable; his letter of 12 August
rings true. Ironically, the government was now much more pessi-
mistic than the A.N.A. and the Chamber of Manufactures and,
despite the potential benefits to Victoria of intercolonial free
trade, had come round to the view—Gillies implied it as early as
February 1887—that the recent history of intercolonial relations
and the evident balance of opinion in New South Wales placed
the possibility of agreement on full federation out of the question
for the time being. Moreover, it was now very doubtful whether
they could carry their own Parliament with them in view of the
recent selfish excesses of the farmers and protectionists and the
power of the *Age*. Gillies's case for confederation at this time is not
strong, perhaps, but deserves more attention than it is commonly
given. The entry of New South Wales and an increase in powers
and authority might have made the Federal Council a suitable
body to handle matters of defence and external affairs for an
interim period. It happened that these questions were not nearly
as urgent in the 1890s as in the 1880s. And Gillies's case lost all
force when South Australia failed to legislate to enlarge the
Council in 1889 and then resigned its membership. But Gillies
was at least correct in his assessment of the immediate possibility
of federation.

We may end this story at the familiar point of the assembly of
the Conference at Melbourne in February 1890 which led to the
Convention of 1891. The detailed story of intercolonial relations

has displayed only too well what Josiah Royce, the eminent American philosopher, described as 'absurd neighbourhood squabbles' of 'shameful triviality'.[72] It has also displayed extensive differences in tone and temper between Victoria and New South Wales on national and imperial questions which are much more easily delineated than explained. A score of times, as we have seen, the Victorian government took the initiative in seeking agreed policies on issues of common concern in order to promote the federal cause. It was generally backed by the governments of Queensland and South Australia, but the government of New South Wales, though it occasionally co-operated, generally either disagreed with the particular policy recommended or disagreed merely for the sake of disagreement.

Adequate explanations of the differences in attitudes between the two colonies will only be reached when sufficiently detailed studies have been made of the social composition and intellectual climate of both colonies, and when it is fully realized how isolated the colonies were from each other in the mid to late nineteenth century and how it was possible for such divergent views to develop. Some preliminary suggestions may, however, be made.

The unity of Victorian opinion is to be explained largely by the homogeneity of its ruling class—politicians, businessmen and other opinion-makers—who were nearly all still (with rare exceptions like Deakin) the young migrants of the 1850s. They were more urban middle-class in origin, intellectually more provincially English than the ruling class of any other colony; the society they created was more metropolitan-dominated, more industrially developed, more closely in touch with the currents of English opinion and hence more sensitive to the rise of the new imperialism and threats to imperial security and less isolationist than other colonies. Its mere half century of history did not allow any deep-rooted provincial loyalty based on long tradition to exist. (Apart from Syme, Mirams was a rare example of a man who occasionally expressed something like a Victorian nationalism.)[73] Peculiarities of its short history had produced a protectionist orthodoxy and a discrediting of free trade internationalism (partly because of the reactionary nature of the free trade organ, the *Argus*, which the *Bulletin* not unreasonably once dubbed 'The Squatters' Friend and Vested Interests Guardian').[74] The strength of Scottish Presbyterianism added militant zeal to advocacy of British annexation in the Pacific. Predominant economic interests inclined Victorians to seek federation. A period of political calm, in which governments were not worried by major internal issues apart from developmental works, permitted attention to constructive national questions. A freak period of politics produced governments dominated by honest idealists like Service (and even those supreme professionals, Berry and Gillies, might just come under this head) and idealist intellectuals like Deakin, Pearson and Wrixon. Victorian businessmen had huge investments in New South Wales and Queensland and were more accustomed than businessmen elsewhere to think in intercolonial and national terms. Sectional interests enabled other businessmen to prate in terms of national idealism though they perhaps cared no more for federation in itself than the hard-headed protectionist fanatics and farmers who regarded it as so much pie in the sky. In short, by the accidents of history, the Victorian governments had history on their side, were developing that blend of imperial and Australian loyalty which the young men in the A.N.A. branches were thrashing out in their debates, and were groping towards a conception of equal partnership of ex-colonial nations in the British Commonwealth of the future.

New South Wales was a much more complicated and diverse society. Its ruling class was made up of migrants of various periods, among whom those of an earlier generation than Victoria's were still prominent, and a sizeable minority of native-born. A century's history had produced some sense of 'national' New South Wales identity and a strong provincial loyalty. Free trade orthodoxy was still intellectually dominant and Gladstone remained a power in the land; his anti-annexationist policy inhibited recognition of alleged Australian interests in the Pacific. The conservative imperialists, like Dalley, were horrified by their Victorian equivalents presuming to advise on imperial policy. At the other extreme the isolationist and separatist national party, typified by the *Bulletin*, was fast growing in influence and was barely reflected at all in Victoria. The Irish Catholics were a very important political bloc whom it was necessary to conciliate,

while the Presbyterians had little influence. It happened that
Parkes, who was closer to Victorian views on Pacific questions
and on the desirable future relationship with Britain than any
other leading politician, was overseas for eighteen months in
1883–4 and out of office until 1887. It is possible to explain the
attitudes of New South Wales governments on national-imperial
issues largely in terms of such factors.

Yet the extent of opposition to federation, the lack of desire
to co-operate with other colonies, the strength of New South
Wales provincialism and the weakness there of a sense of Australian identity remain baffling. There is no reason to doubt
Dalley's estimate in 1884:

There is here a considerable party who regard the ultimate federation of the colonies as a doubtful advantage, and an immediate
attempt to accomplish it as dangerously premature. The party which
here regards the prospect with favour is divided as to the means by
which it can be safely and efficiently accomplished. And there is
. . . a large party who, having given the matter little or no consideration at all, is influenced more easily by a cry than by an argument, and which is consequently disposed to regard the eagerness
and activity of other colonies as signs of peril to the interests of
their own.[75]

We shall never know how much or how often Parkes believed
his own propaganda; but we may be sure that his cavalier treatment of other colonial governments reflected his view that there
were no votes to be lost by such behaviour and even possibly
that he saw such assertions of New South Wales hegemony as
a positive vote-catcher. The 'Geebungs' were not negligible in
importance; the evidence of anti-Victorian sentiment, of the most
crass and primitive kind, is abundant. Some of it, however, was
based on coherent ideology, for the dogmatic free trader, who
was increasingly being driven to the wall by the rise of the local
protectionist movement, had every reason to suspect and fear the
motives of the economic wing of the Victorian federation movement. But there is another factor which was crucial and which
distorted the surface appearance of New South Wales opinion:
this was a period of extreme political instability and local
conflict. Great questions were in process of resolution in New
South Wales politics; attention was all turned inwards and con-

sequently the broad matters which the Victorians persistently brought forward must have seemed to governments to be irritating distractions. The Stuart ministry was absorbed in its attempt to achieve land reform; the conflict between free trade and protection had reached a bitter pitch; the 1885–7 Parliament sank to lower depths of turbulence and disorder. In such a situation, federation appeared to be a minor issue and, as we know from the later history of the movement, its achievement required the full concentration of governments and the shaping of political groupings based on it as a major issue.[76]

2

A LITTLE BIT OF LAWYERS' LANGUAGE
THE HISTORY OF 'ABSOLUTELY FREE'
1890–1900*

J. A. La Nauze

Section 92 of the Constitution of the Commonwealth of Australia reads:

On the imposition of uniform duties of customs, trade, commerce and intercourse among the States, whether by means of internal carriage or ocean navigation, shall be absolutely free.

A second paragraph, dealing with transitional arrangements, became exhausted two years after the imposition of uniform duties by the Federal Parliament in 1902.

Sir Robert Garran, who died in 1957, had lived with the Constitution for most of his long life, as secretary to the Drafting Committee during the Federal Convention of 1897–8, as the first Secretary of the Attorney-General's Department after the inauguration of the Commonwealth, as Solicitor-General until 1937, and in old age as a still alert and active commentator on its mysteries. Not long before his death he wrote that from

* Historians and lawyers, to their mutual loss, rarely read each other's professional journals. This enquiry was completed, and the article written in its present form, before (to my shame) I knew of Professor F. R. Beasley's series of articles, 'Commonwealth Constitution: Section 92, its History in the Federal Conventions', *Annual Law Review* (University of Western Australia Law School), vol. 1 (1948-50), pp. 97-111, 273-88, 433-44. Since we both refer frequently to the discussion of Section 92 in the debates of the Federal Conventions there are necessarily coincidences in our quotations, but rather than my drawing attention to these as they occur, it seems sufficient to acknowledge generally the priority of Professor Beasley's articles in this respect. Our main purposes are different, and for my enquiry—the authorship and history of the phrase 'absolutely free'—I have been able to draw on a wider range of sources than the Convention debates. I am not concerned, as he is, to discuss the history of Section 92 in relation to the other Sections referring to trade and commerce and as a layman have absolutely refrained from comment on its interpretation since 1903.

1920, the year of the High Court judgment in McArthur's Case, 'Section 92 occupied the centre of the stage as the most troublesome provision of the Constitution'. He imagined a law student beginning his constitutional studies with an historical survey. After considering the interpretations of Section 92 made by the High Court and the Privy Council over fifty years, 'The student closes his notebook, sells his law books, and resolves to take up some easy study, like nuclear physics or higher mathematics.'[1]

There has been trouble with both 'trade, commerce and intercourse' and 'absolutely free'. The first phrase is peculiarly a matter for lawyers, since its interpretation has been assisted or hindered by awareness of a mass of legal argument in the United States about the 'interstate commerce' clause. This essay concentrates on the phrase 'absolutely free', in a constitutional context a native Australian invention, which has probably been the more troublesome of the two, and certainly has had the larger politico-economic implications. A lay historian, if he has any sense, will refrain from expressing opinions about the meanings given to these words since 1903, the year of the establishment of the High Court; he may have opinions, but the grave duty of interpreting the Constitution is not laid upon him. In looking through some of the celebrated judgments of the High Court and the Privy Council, however, he cannot fail to be intrigued by a curious sort of hypothetical history indulged in by various learned judges, including some of those who had been closely concerned as draftsmen with the framing of Section 92. Moreover, it is slightly nettling that lawyers, who on the whole owe a good deal to the words 'absolutely free', should be inclined to refer with half-affectionate condescension to the opinion of George Reid expressed during the last discussion of the phrase in the Convention of 1897–8:

This clause touches the vital point for which we are federating, and although the words of the clause are certainly not the words that you meet with in Acts of Parliament as a general rule, they have this recommendation, that they strike exactly the notes which we want to strike in this Constitution. And they also have the further recommendation that no legal technicalities can be built up upon them in order to restrict their operation. It is a little bit of laymen's language which comes in here very well.[2]

The words of the Leader of the Convention and Chairman of the Drafting Committee, which immediately follow, are not so generally recalled: 'MR BARTON—It is the language of three lawyers.'

This enquiry began as a polemical exercise, a defence of laymen; for there is no doubt that, of the statements of these two barristers, Barton's more nearly expresses the truth. But as it proceeded it became evident that the history of Section 92 was a good deal more complicated than seems to have been generally realized, and in itself needed some clarification. How far the actual history behind the words of a statute or a constitution is relevant to their formal interpretation is of course a delicate question. Even the layman appreciates that it is dangerous to suppose that a statute has any meanings except that which its words express; and how far those whose duty it is to deduce this meaning may or should take account of its original penumbra is a matter for their discretion. A practising lawyer's business is to know, in the light of judicial decision, what the words mean, or are likely to mean, now; and not what they may have meant perhaps seventy years ago. And whose opinion about their meaning would he take as authoritative anyhow, if he were interested enough to look at the history of the words before they were finally embodied in a legally binding instrument? These points are familiar, and more obscurely behind them, the layman perceives serious issues in the philosophy of legal interpretation.

Yet judges do indulge in a kind of history, part hypothesis, part based on rather obvious public documents like the Debates of the Conventions: when the framers of the Constitution inserted these or those words (it is said) they must have intended this, or could not have intended that. Thus Dixon (then simply J.), a very great and very learned judge, on the phrase 'trade, commerce and intercourse' in Section 92:

Those who introduced s.92 into the Australian Constitution did so in the full light of American experience. In s.51(i) they coupled the word 'trade' with the word 'commerce' which stood alone in the United States Constitution to define the subject matter of the power of Congress to regulate commerce with foreign nations and among the several States. *Not content with the expression 'trade and com-*

merce' for the purposes of s.92 they there added the word 'intercourse' . . . 'Intercourse' *was doubtless added because of the view* . . .
that commerce might not extend to intercourse that was not concerned with business profit or pecuniary gain.[3]

Now, as a matter of historians' history, from the very first
appearance of the present Section 92 as one of the Resolutions
moved at the beginning of the Federal Convention of 1891, to
the very last business day of the Convention of 1897–8, the
relevant words in the many versions of the Section were simply
'trade and intercourse'. It was the word 'commerce' which was
inserted at the last moment as a mere drafting amendment, and
approved by the Convention, with some hundreds of others, *en
bloc* and without discussion.

Suppose, *per impossibile,* that the High Court had attached
to it a research officer trained both in law and in history. Suppose
that, as a mere matter of interest, he were instructed to investi-
gate the origins of the troublesome Section 92, with particular
attention to the contentious words 'absolutely free'. As a lawyer
he would very likely (and rightly) confine himself to the documents and discussions that bear directly on the point, ignoring
the wide and vague assumptions of a society and era in which
free trade versus protection was a serious and familiar issue. As
a historian he would, using these documents, come to something like the conclusions which follow.

There were many versions, and many stages of discussion, of
most Sections (then called Clauses) of the Australian Constitution before it reached the form embodied in an Act of the
imperial Parliament, 63 and 64 Vic. c. 12, assented to on 9 July
1900. A Federal Convention, its members authorized by the
legislatures of the various colonies, met in Sydney in 1891 and
approved a Constitution in the form of a Draft Bill to be enacted
by the imperial Parliament. For some years no action followed
In 1897 a second and quite independent Convention assembled
for its first session in Adelaide, with a membership now directly
elected by popular vote. After two further sessions, in Sydney
and Melbourne, a Draft Constitution Bill was approved in
March 1898. It was twice modified thereafter before it came into
operation on 1 January 1901; first as a result of a premiers' con-

ference in 1899 and secondly by the imperial Parliament in 1900. Section 92, however, remains in the form finally approved in March 1898.

Despite their formal independence, there is strict continuity between the two Conventions as far as the words of the Constitution are concerned. Although it was decided in 1897 to make a fresh start, the Draft Constitution of 1891 was in fact taken as the basic document with the explicit or tacit approval of the great majority of the members, and became the first draft discussed in Adelaide with few except drafting modifications. In both Conventions a long and detailed Constitution, in full legal form, was constructed on the basis of a short set of guiding general Resolutions first discussed and approved. There were many drafts: those presented to select committees, discussed, modified and re-drafted; those then submitted to the same processes in Committee of the whole Convention; finally in 1898, after the fourth re-committal by the Convention, about 400 final drafting amendments approved in one sitting.

The present Section 92 first formally appeared as a Resolution moved by Sir Henry Parkes at the beginning of the Convention of 1891. The wording of its various forms underwent a series of modifications which will be noticed in passing, but only one of these calls for special mention before we concentrate attention on the words 'absolutely free'. The Draft Bill of 1891 referred to 'trade and intercourse throughout the Commonwealth' and this stood through many versions until a late stage in 1898, when it was changed to '. . . among the States' as a matter of deliberate decision rather than of approval of a mere drafting amendment. The second paragraph of Section 92, as it now stands, was 'exhausted' in 1904, and has no further relevance.

Before the Convention of 1891 assembled in Sydney Sir Henry Parkes drew up a set of Resolutions which he proposed to move. These were discussed among the New South Wales delegates at a preliminary meeting in his house. The first of these ran:

That the trade and intercourse between the Federated Colonies, whether by means of land carriage or coastal navigation, shall be free from the payment of Customs duties, and from all restrictions whatsoever, except such regulations as may be necessary for the conduct of business.[4]

At least three other delegates, all formidable lawyers and draftsmen, also came to the Convention with words prepared for the same purpose. Sir Samuel Griffith (Queensland) had set down briefly a 'Draft of suggested instructions to committee', in which the fourth of seven points was 'That customs should be under the sole control of the Federal Parliament &c.'[5] This is not explicit, but what the '&c.' would have included may be gathered from a letter from Inglis Clark to Griffith, to be mentioned presently. Inglis Clark (Tasmania) himself came to the Convention with a complete draft constitution, prepared from his notes by the Tasmanian Parliamentary Draftsman, and printed apparently in the first half of February 1891.[6] The provisions intended to secure internal freedom of trade were taken almost verbatim from the Constitution of the United States: no 'Province', without the consent of the Federal Parliament, to lay any taxes or duties on imports or exports, nor any duty of tonnage; revenue from state inspection laws to be for the use of the 'Federal Dominion'; federal taxes to be uniform.[7] It is not so well known that Kingston (South Australia) also came equipped with a complete draft constitution.[8] Among the powers to be assigned to the Federal Parliament was:

To impose and collect taxes and duties of Customs and Excise, but so that all taxes and duties shall be uniform throughout the Union; and no tax or duty shall be imposed on any article exported from one colony into another

and this was buttressed by the familiar prohibition of the imposition by any colony of tonnage, taxes or duties on imports or exports without the consent of the Federal Parliament.[9]

The Convention formally opened in the Legislative Assembly chamber of the Parliament of New South Wales on the morning of 2 March 1891, and adjourned an hour later. That afternoon there was an informal meeting in Parkes's office, a meeting of considerable importance for the history of Section 92. Writing seven years later, Deakin (Victoria) referred to a meeting of premiers which 'considered and somewhat amended' the Resolutions to be submitted by Parkes.[10] Those present, however, were not only the premiers. The *Sydney Morning Herald's* reporter mentioned 'about a dozen of the Federation Convention delegates', representing all the colonies except Western Australia, whose delegates had not yet arrived, while Parkes alone represented New South Wales.[11] The Premiers were Parkes, Griffith, Munro, Fysh and Playford; others present were certainly Inglis Clark, Gillies and Kingston, so that, with perhaps one or two others and a New Zealand delegate, the reporter's 'dozen' was about right. There is some direct evidence about the proceedings of this meeting. Though he was speaking six years later, Fysh was not likely to be mistaken in his recollection of its tone: 'I well remember what took place in respect to the resolutions of 1891. They were framed in Sir Henry Parkes's office in a spirit of liberality.'[12] In the Griffith papers there is a printed copy of the original draft Resolutions already tried out by Parkes on his fellow-delegates from New South Wales, clearly the copy used by Griffith at this meeting.[13] And it is certain that Griffith expanded verbally his own brief document of 'Suggested Instructions' because Inglis Clark wrote to him next day. He had come away from the meeting in Parkes's office (he said) convinced that if some of them did not draw up a set of satisfactory resolutions they would ultimately be committed to whatever Parkes, with his misty notions, might put upon paper. He had therefore attempted to draw one up. 'I could not recall the exact language of any of your resolutions'; his own were 'simply attempts to express from memory the same proposals that are embodied in yours'. He was sending copies to Gillies and Kingston.[14] His version of what Griffith had proposed presumably as a modification of Parkes's draft on the same theme, ran:

After the establishment of the Federation all Trade and Commercial intercourse between the several Colonies whether by transit on land or by coastal navigation shall be free and exempt from all Customs duties whatever.[15]

Now it is certain that Parkes did consider and partly adopt the Griffith-Clark suggestions for additions or alternatives to his original draft Resolutions, for those he actually moved in the Convention reflected them in one unmistakeable way. They may have been based on notes taken at the meeting on 2 March, or Clark's draft may have been shown to him next day when the Convention itself met for only two hours. Though the wording of Parkes's Resolutions, in a notice of motion endorsed by Griffith as 3 March, generally inclined more to that of his own draft than to Clark's, his first Resolution was entirely new. This affirmed that the powers, privileges and territorial rights of the existing colonies should remain intact, except for agreed surrenders of power to a Federal government. Now Griffith, Clark and Kingston, all three, had included a sentence to this effect in their 'Suggestions' or draft constitutions. It must have been one of the points discussed at the meeting in Parkes's office. Its relevance here is that if he agreed to add a whole new Resolution he could equally agree, in the 'spirit of liberality' that prevailed, to suggested changes in the wording of others. Certainly, when his formal notice of motion went to the printer some time on 3 March, the Resolution concerning intercolonial trade was significantly different from that which he had submitted for discussion on the previous afternoon. It now read:

That the trade and intercourse between the Federated Colonies, whether by means of land carriage or coastal navigation, shall be absolutely free.[16]

No reference to customs duties as such, nor to regulations for the conduct of business: 'absolutely free'. But why should it be assumed that Parkes was responsible for the insertion of this momentous phrase?

Someone had to move resolutions. Parkes, the instigator of the Convention, was necessarily the man. But his original draft had been discussed in a friendly informal conference. Why had it been re-phrased in general and sweeping terms? There is a significant scrap of evidence to begin with. On his copy of Parkes's original Resolutions Griffith wrote, to be inserted at the beginning of the 'trade and intercourse' sentence, the words 'after the establishment of a Fed. tariff'.[17] That the phrase was written in during the informal meeting on 2 March is strongly suggested by Clark's letter, already referred to. No. 3 of his draft Resolutions, set down after the meeting, provided for customs and excise duties to be collected under existing systems until the Federal Parliament should cause uniform duties to be collected. 'I have drafted No. 3', he wrote, 'to meet the objection raised by Gillies that the simple assertion of inter-colonial free trade without any reference to a federal tariff would create misconceptions and dissatisfaction in some quarters'.[18] Thus at that meeting there *had* been a disposition, whether unanimous or not, to include among the resolutions 'the simple assertion of inter-colonial free trade'.

Here let us indulge in speculation. Agreement on the general aim of abolishing all internal customs duties being taken for granted, we can imagine that discussion moved to the form of words required to affirm the principle unambiguously. Parkes had already realized that simply to say that intercolonial trade and intercourse should be 'free from the payment of Customs duties' was not enough; for other charges having the same effect, but not definable as 'Customs duties' might be imposed at the borders. For greater assurance he had therefore added, 'and from all restrictions whatsoever'. But then it had occurred to him, as it probably would to any layman, that some necessary charges, not protective in effect or intention (wharfage, sanitary inspection, quarantine etc.) might thus be ruled out. So, on the analogy of the clause of the American Constitution referring to State inspection laws[19] he had further added, 'except such regulations as may be necessary for the conduct of business'. His was now a complex but rather hesitant Resolution, proceeding from the specific to the completely general and then to an exception. In their draft constitutions the lawyers (Clark, Kingston) had proposed, on the American analogy, to secure internal free trade not by a general statement about intercolonial trade, but as an implication from legislative powers assigned or prohibited. We can suppose that the lawyers found some vagueness about 'such regulations as may be necessary for the conduct of business', but assured Parkes that there was ample precedent in the decisions of the United States Supreme Court for the legality of non-discriminatory fees for services such as wharfage.

We can further suppose that Parkes was nevertheless reluctant to surrender an affirmative form of resolution. Free traders or protectionists, they were all agreed that the fiscal issue, the central question of intercolonial political arguments in 1891, should henceforth be transferred to a Federal Parliament; and his original Resolution showed that he favoured words which should say positively that trade and intercourse within the continent should be free, rather than words which should ensure internal free trade by the prohibition of certain types of taxes. Nor would he, or the other laymen, have been content with the suggestion, borrowed from the American Constitution, that only the Federal Parliament could enact or permit State tariffs or import restrictions; for though Congress had never done so, except in the recent Wilson Act, what they wanted was to remove such power even from a Federal Parliament. On these assumptions, the substance of what Parkes would have said at the meeting of 2 March (or next day, if Clark's attempt at recasting was then submitted to him) would have run rather like this:

'We are concerned to frame general resolutions, expressing principles. We are not framing a Constitution. That will be a task for the committees to be appointed when we have debated, and if necessary, amended the Resolutions which I shall move on Wednesday. You have convinced me that I need not include words expressly to permit reasonable charges for services rendered. I accept the statement of Mr Clark and others that, although the Constitution of the United States mentions only imposts absolutely necessary for executing its inspection laws, other similar charges, if they are not discriminatory, have been upheld as valid by the Supreme Court. What I want my Resolution to secure and affirm is the existing situation in the United States, which, you tell me, is a result not only of the words of the Constitution but of the interpretation of that Constitution by the Supreme Court in the various cases you have mentioned. Why, after American experience, rely on interpretation? My attention was drawn to one of these cases in Melbourne last year, and I referred to it when I moved the principal Resolution at that Conference. This is what I said.

The case seems to set at rest, in the most emphatic manner, what is sometimes disputed—the question of entire freedom throughout the territory of the United States. As the members of the Conference know, she has created a tariff of a very severe, and, in some cases almost prohibitive character against the outside world; but as between New York and Massachusetts, and as between Connecticut and Pennsylvania, there is no custom-house and no tax-collector. Between any two of the States—indeed from one end of the States to the other—the country is as free as the air in which the swallow flies.[20]

All I seek is words to affirm just that, whether mine or others I do not care.'

To return to what can be documented, we do know—from Clark's letter to Griffith—that a 'simple affirmation of inter-colonial free trade' was projected at the meeting; and we do know that what I have imagined Parkes to be asking for was supplied, by himself or another, in the words 'absolutely free'.

As we have seen, Parkes must have been persuaded by the lawyers to include in his motion for the Convention, and more or less in their words, one whole Resolution which had no counterpart in his original draft. If he also agreed to modify and shorten his 'trade and intercourse' Resolution why should he be assumed to be solely responsible for the new sentence? It is simply not plausible to say that the words must have been Parkes's, or adopted by Parkes from another context, on the ground that no lawyer would have used them. After all, a lawyer like Clark had lifted large chunks from the American Constitution, including the prohibition of State taxes on imports 'except what may be absolutely necessary for executing' its inspection laws. The lawyers did not object to 'absolutely'.

It has been suggested that, whoever seized on the phrase in 1891, its origin is obvious. In 1849 a special Committee of the Privy Council, nominally the Committee for Trade and Plantations, reported on the question of constitutions for the Australian colonies. Among reasons for recommending a kind of federal scheme was the desirability of a uniform tariff. Tariff differences were already evident, and the proposed separation of Victoria from New South Wales could add to them. This was a sinful prospect:

So great indeed would be the evil, and such the obstruction of the inter-colonial trade, and so great the check to the development of the resources of each of these colonies, that it seems to us necessary that there should be one tariff common to them all, so that goods might be carried from the one into the other with the same absolute freedom as between any two adjacent counties in England.[21]

Here, then, is 'absolute freedom' in a context referring to free trade between the Australian colonies. If it could be proved, for example by an appropriate reference in the papers of Parkes or Griffith, that this was indeed the source of the words substituted by Parkes on 2–3 March 1891 no historian would be disconcerted. At the same time the charge that 'absolutely free' is laymen's language would be dismissed without further argument, let us hope with costs against the plaintiffs. For who were the members of the Privy Council Committee, and who drafted their Report? Of the five members, three were lawyers—Lord Campbell, author of *Lives of the Lord Chancellors,* Chief Justice of the Queen's Bench 1850, Lord Chancellor 1859; Sir Edward Ryan, ex-Chief Justice of Bengal; and Sir James Stephen, lately Under-Secretary for the Colonies, permanent (legal) Counsel to the Colonial Office and the Board of Trade, 1825–36. It was Stephen who drafted the Report and prepared most of the amendments desired by the Committee.[22] If the Report is the origin of 'absolutely free' then the phrase is beyond question lawyers' language; not indeed, in a formal draftsman's context, but indubitably the words of a lawyer giving reasons for the requirement of internal free trade in a proposed federation.

But there is more to be said. If Parkes did indeed consult or recall the Report at short notice, was it because its phrases had been ringing in his head for over forty years? It is true that he had begun to take an interest in politics before the Report was originally published in New South Wales, and had no doubt read it then. But that was long ago. In his recent utterances about federation he had not referred to Earl Grey's early federal schemes. In 1890 he had even found with gratified surprise that federation was 'the child—the fondled child—of the greatest men we ever had in any of the colonies', and had read for the first time (he said) the Report of Gavan Duffy's Select Committee of 1857 on federation[23] (though in the year it was discussed in the N.S.W. Parliament he had been actively engaged in political journalism and was shortly to re-enter the Assembly).[24] If he did return in 1890 or 1891 to the old Privy Council Committee's Report it could well have been, ironically enough, at the suggestion of a lawyer, Inglis Clark. For Clark had certainly recently been reading in that context. 'I do not think it has been hitherto generally known', he had said in Melbourne,

that when the draft Bill for the better government of the Australian Colonies was first submitted to the Imperial Parliament in 1849, there was a provision in it for the establishment of something like federation, that is to say, for the adoption of a uniform tariff by a central body representing the several colonies.[25]

The Draft Bill was based closely on the Report, and who but Inglis Clark, with his passionate interest in American precedents would have drawn Parkes's attention, a few days earlier, to the judgment in *Guy* v. *Baltimore?*

This is an intriguing possibility and it would be amusing if it turned out to be the case. Yet unless documentary proof appears it may be doubted whether the phrase 'absolutely free' was in fact suggested by the Report of the Privy Council Committee. Of course the nearly identical phraseology about inter-county trade is suggestive; but would the Report have been so readily identified as the origin of Parkes's amended Resolution—an amendment made only on 2 or 3 March 1891—if the revelant phrases had not been quoted in the historical introduction to Quick and Garran's *Annotated Constitution,* and there followed by a sentence from a despatch by Denison, a contemporary Governor, which is a gloss upon them: 'an absolute and unrestricted freedom of intercourse is most advantageous'?[26] The similarity to the phraseology of Section 92 leaps to the eye of a historically-minded constitutional lawyer, and such a man has necessarily read his Quick and Garran. It is strange, however, that while their quotation from Denison suggests that they had not failed to see this, Quick and Garran made no reference to the precedent in their notes on Section 92. They were very careful men. Perhaps it had occurred to them that when you want to make an absolute statement, you are likely to use the word 'absolute' (or 'absolutely') without searching ancient documents for precedents. Suppose Parkes had been convinced by the lawyers that he need not provide for the legality of non-discriminatory charges for

services, but was still worried that a suggestion like Clark's—
'free and exempt from all customs duties whatever'—by itself
might not exclude impositions, not definable as customs duties,
which could have a protective or restrictive effect. Suppose he
had referred to his original phrase, designed presumably to meet
this point ('and [free] from all restrictions whatsoever') and said:
'This is what we want. How shall we say it?' The answer was
available in a much more recent and to some of these men more
familiar, document than the Report of the Privy Council Committee: the Report of their debates in Melbourne a year earlier.
Griffith would merely have had to recall that in *his* opening
speech he had said that while a federation would doubtless in
the end mean a fiscal union, a federation without one would be
better than nothing:

> And there would be this advantage, that under the new arrange-
> ment the absurdity of fighting one another by customs tariffs would
> become so apparent that before very long they would be given up.
> *It has been said that there can be no federation without absolute
> freedom of interchange of products* . . .[27]

Need we look any further? There is no proof that Parkes in-
vented the fatal phrase. There is a strong probability that Griffith
did; and there is absolute proof that in any case he used it, in
the appropriate context, a year before the Convention assembled
in Sydney.

In 1891 'absolutely free' was, to coin a phrase, absolutely free
of legal criticism in open Convention, both in discussion of
Parkes's Resolutions and in Committee of the whole. Its appearance in public may be very briefly summarized. In moving his
Resolutions Parkes said simply that he sought to define 'what
seems to me an absolutely necessary condition of anything like
a perfect federation, that is, that Australia, as Australia, shall be
free—free on the borders, free everywhere—in its trade and intercourse between its own people'. But note that his exemplar was

> that great country to which we must constantly look, the United
> States . . . from one end of the United States to the other there
> is no custom-house office. There is absolute freedom of trade
> throughout the extent of the American union and the high duties
> which the authors of the protectionist tariff are now levying on the

outside world are entirely confined to the federal custom-houses on the sea-coast.[28]

This is almost a paraphrase of what he had said in Melbourne about the the implication of *Guy* v. *Baltimore*. It strengthens the impression that he had not been thinking of English counties in 1849 but of the States of the Great Republic in 1891.

Parkes was followed by Griffith, and all that need be remarked here about the cautious language of that cautious man is that for him the word 'absolute' had a technical meaning to which we shall return: 'Suppose the federal parliament were to consider it desirable that there should be something like absolute free-trade, or as near free-trade as possible, that as small an amount of money be raised by customs as is compatible with the existence of the government'.[29] Munro of Victoria, a layman, was the only speaker to be a little worried, but merely because the Resolution might be interpreted to require intercolonial free trade before the imposition of a federal tariff,[30] a matter that was later attended to by an introductory phrase. Barton took it as 'a matter of course that at some period, and at an early period, after the federation of the colonies, the trade and intercourse, whether by way of land carriage or coastal navigation, shall be absolutely free',[31] and did not linger in comment. For the rest, there was reiterated agreement on the principle (with some Western Australian worries about Western Australia's position) and no objection to the words.

The Resolutions were debated in Committee of the whole when the general speeches had been concluded. After some desultory skirmishing, there was general agreement that detailed amendments of accepted principles were better not pressed, but left for the debate that would follow the framing of a draft Constitution. Parkes's second Resolution was agreed to without discussion, for the vital question of the composition and powers of the Senate was awaiting settlement. Shipwreck on that rock having been avoided, the Convention proceeded to the appointment of committees—Constitutional, Finance, Judiciary—from which, through the Constitutional Committee, a draft bill was to emerge.

The Bill was ready on 31 March. In expounding it as Chairman of the Constitutional Committee, Griffith explained, without elaboration, that 'so soon as uniform duties are imposed, the trade of the Commonwealth by any means is to be absolutely free. Every member of the Convention knows that a provision of that nature must be in the Constitution'.[32] Apart from one irrelevant question, not concerned with phraseology, the Clause, when the time came, was again agreed to without debate.[33] No lawyer, and only faintly one layman on a side-issue, had in public uttered even a squeak about 'absolutely free'.

Griffith was generally acknowledged to be the main architect of the Draft Constitution of 1891. This view may be accepted, if we consider his role not only in drafting but in guiding the draft through the Constitutional Committee and the Convention. More clauses were taken, with little alteration, from Inglis Clark's draft than has been generally realized,[34] but the close and detailed compilation of a new document, using Clark's and other models, and incorporating the specific directions of the Convention and its committees, was mainly Griffith's work. Six years later, when as Chief Justice of Queensland he was beyond the battle, his name was still quoted with awe in the second Convention. Let us follow the dealings of this eminent lawyer with the sentence that became Section 92.

On his copy of Parkes's original Resolutions, as we have seen, he inserted a sentence to require that intercolonial freedom of trade should not begin until a federal tariff was in existence. In the Convention he did not criticize the phraseology of Parkes's actual Resolution incorporating 'absolutely free'. The Resolutions as reported from the Committee of the whole on 18 March left him, as Chairman of the Constitutional and Drafting Committees, with the unaltered sentence, 'That the trade and intercourse between the Federated Colonies, whether by means of land carriage or coastal navigation, shall be absolutely free.' The Finance Committee was instructed especially to consider this Resolution (and that concerned with the exclusive grant of Customs and Excise powers to the Federal Parliament) and to report to the Constitutional Committee. This it did, through its Chairman, James Munro of Victoria, in a Report dated 23 March.[35] The members of this Committee were Munro, Mc-

Millan, McIlwraith, Bray, Burgess, Atkinson and Marmion, the only lawyer among them being Bray. They recommended that a Federal Constitution should provide, *inter alia,* 'That after the establishment of such [i.e. a uniform] Tariff the trade and intercourse between the Federated Colonies, whether by means of internal carriage or coastal [*sic*] navigation, shall be absolutely free.' They recognized that 'one of the main objects of Federation is freedom of Commercial Intercourse between the Colonies'.

The Constitutional Committee referred its Resolutions, and those of the Finance and Judiciary Committees, to a Drafting Committee originally consisting of Griffith, Inglis Clark and Kingston. For this Drafting Committee Griffith, working all day on 24 March to 11 p.m., prepared and sent to the printer a draft Bill.[36] In this the relevant Clause read:

So soon as the Federal Parliament has established uniform duties of Customs and duties of Excise upon goods the subject of Customs duties, and uniform bounties upon the production or export of goods, the following consequences shall ensue:—
(1) The trade and intercourse between the States of the Commonwealth, whether by means of internal carriage or ocean navigation, shall be absolutely free.

It will be noticed that Griffith had changed the original 'coastal' to 'ocean' navigation, so that he had given some thought to the wording. His marginal gloss, added in his hand to the proof of the draft, read: 'On establishment of uniform duties of customs and excise trade, within the Commonwealth to be free.' This first draft of a constitution was worked upon by the Drafting Committee and the revision was submitted on 26 March to the Constitutional Committee for preliminary consideration. Intercolonial free trade now had a clause to itself: 'So soon as the Federal Parliament has established uniform duties of Customs and duties of Excise upon goods the subject of Customs duties, the trade and intercourse between the States of the Commonwealth, whether by means of internal carriage or ocean navigation shall be absolutely free.' With that day's discussions to guide them further the Drafting Committee were then to retire for three days (it was the Easter week-end) to the sanctuary of the steam-yacht *Lucinda* to frame a Bill for submission to the full

Convention. Poor Clark had contracted influenza. He did not join them until Sunday afternoon, and Edmund Barton took his place. For some reason not readily apparent, apart from his legal qualifications and self-confidence, Bernhard Wise was invited or permitted to accompany them, though he was not a member of the Convention. Using the proof discussed by the Constitutional Committee on 26 March, Griffith, Barton and Kingston spent Saturday 28 March in revision. Perhaps the pruning knife of Kingston, a terse draftsman, can be deduced from the more compact clause which now emerged, though the corrections were in Griffith's hand: 'So soon as the Federal Parliament has imposed uniform duties of Customs trade and intercourse throughout the Commonwealth, whether by means of internal carriage or ocean navigation, shall be absolutely free.'[37]

So the Clause stood in the revised proof submitted to a further meeting of the Constitutional Committee on 30 March.[38] Griffith's notes on his copy, used to record the revisions made in that day's discussions, substituted 'Parliament of the Commonwealth' for 'Federal Parliament', and inserted a comma after 'Customs'. In this form it was included in the Draft adopted by the Constitutional Committee on 31 March, in time for the meeting of the full Convention in the afternoon.[39] And in this form, in due course and as we have seen without discussion, it was included in the 'Draft of a Bill to constitute the Commonwealth of Australia', adopted by the National Australasian Convention on 9 April 1891.

Griffith was not to be a member of the Convention which, after the doldrum years from 1891 to 1896, assembled in Adelaide to frame a Constitution which, this time, must necessarily be submitted for approval or rejection by the people of the colonies there represented. But he was not yet finished with the words 'absolutely free'. By mid-1896 the Federal movement had revived. Though Queensland still held back, enabling Acts authorizing elections for a new National Convention had been passed in four of the other colonies, with Western Australia expected to follow suit. Griffith could take no active part but he could be sure that anything he said on the subject would be heard with attention. So in June 1896, as President of the University Extension Council in Queensland, he took the opportunity to deliver an address on 'Some Conditions of Australian Federation'.[40] He traversed generally the nature and alternative systems of federation, before proceeding to a detailed re-consideration of the financial proposals of the Draft Bill of 1891. One of the few clauses of the Bill which he actually quoted—or misquoted—was the provision concerning intercolonial free trade. 'It must be assumed', he said, 'that at a shorter or longer period after the establishment of a Federal Government—and the shorter the better—"trade and intercourse throughout the Federation, whether by land or water will be absolutely free".' We may assume that he was quoting from memory rather than reflecting, as a lawyer, that 'land or ocean' might not perhaps include rivers and lakes; but the significant point is that in such an inaccurate version of the Clause he had re-drafted so frequently, the one absolutely constant element remained absolutely constant.

In July 1896 Griffith made a more formal statement, in response (he wrote) 'to a desire expressed in different parts of Australia that I should write something in the nature of a short statement or exposition of the general subject of Australian Federation', and he added that for the most part the *Notes* expressed views embodied in the Draft Constitution of 1891.[41] What he said on intercolonial free trade is worth close attention:

The most important of the MATERIAL EFFECTS of Federation would probably be those which would follow from making 'trade and commerce [sic] absolutely free' within the Federal Territory, as must inevitably happen when a uniform tariff is established for the whole Federation. This means the abolition of such Customs duties as have the effect of protecting the industries of one Colony against those of another.[42]

He went on to argue that, though this situation would be viewed differently by free traders and protectionists, the net proportion of actually protective duties in existing colonial tariffs was not very great. 'If trade and commerce were absolutely free', Queensland products would enter freely into all other colonies, and vice versa; there would be specialization of production within Australia according to natural advantages or the relative energy of the people. Further, the 'greater facilities for TRAVEL that would be afforded by the abolition of intercolonial Customs barriers might be expected to bring about a large increase of intercourse between the people of the several Colonies.'[43] The question of protection against the rest of the world, he continued, was a different one. There would almost of necessity have to be a federal tariff of sufficient amount to produce a large revenue, and 'whether it was called by the name of a "Revenue Tariff" or a "Protective Tariff" would be of little importance.'

Now this is a vital clue to the original ready acceptance of the phrase 'absolutely free'. It would be almost insulting to document the repeated opinion, in the Conventions of 1891 and 1897–8, that a major reason for federation was the consequent *abolition* of customs houses and customs duties at the borders. But in the great nineteenth-century debate on free trade versus protection, a debate in which the Australian arguments were a mere echo of those familiar in England, continental Europe and America for half a century, 'free trade' as a national policy was *not* incompatible with customs houses and customs duties. Free trade meant the absence of tariff protection, and a revenue tariff could be a free trade tariff provided either that the imports taxed were not, and could not, be produced in the country concerned, or that equal excise duties were imposed on similar goods produced there. The point is well illustrated in a widely-read contemporary *History of the Free Trade Movement in England*,[44] written for general readers. The author was at pains to show that though £20 million of revenue was produced by the British tariff, 'our present short list of articles subject to import duties forms a thoroughly free-trade tariff, in the truest and fullest sense', for it afforded no protection whatsoever to domestic producers.[45]

As we have seen, Griffith in 1891 had been curiously technical about 'absolute free-trade'; it would be approached 'when as small an amount of money should be raised by customs as is compatible with the existence of government'. We are justified in deducing that, in his conception, 'absolute free-trade' would be attained when there was *no* revenue from customs, not even from nonprotective duties.

We can now see why, in a sentence intended to affirm and secure positively a principal aim of federation, it was not merely 'free-trade' between the States which was enjoined, but 'absolute free-trade'. Non-protective duties or imposts of some kind might

still have been compatible with free trade as generally understood: a Tasmanian tax on pineapples, for example, or a Victorian
tax on jarrah timber. 'Absolute free-trade' meant *no duties at all*,
protective or non-protective; a state of affairs existing in no
country of the world, not even in free-trade Britain, but which it
was intended to establish as between the semi-independent
'countries' or States of the federation.

There is no reason then to suppose that up to this time
Griffith thought there could be any legal ambiguity about
'absolutely free'; even the obstacles to 'intercourse' were apparently the vexations of customs inspection and duties. A year later
(June 1897), for the first time, he expressed a doubt. When the
first (Adelaide) draft of the Constitution Bill was available he
submitted his comments and criticisms to the government of
Queensland. What he had to say about Clause (or Section) 89,
as the predecessor of Section 92 was then numbered, will best
be considered when we have seen what the new Convention
had made of it.

By the accident of Clark's bout of influenza in 1891 Edmund
Barton became the only member common to the Drafting Committees of both Conventions. When the second Convention was
dissolved in Melbourne on 17 March 1898 he had more close
scrutinizing experience with the wording of Section 92 than any
other man concerned with the drafting of the Constitution. The
last, the very last, alteration in its wording had been inserted as a
drafting amendment in his own hand. We must now trace his
dealings with words which he (like Griffith) would be required
to interpret in future years as a judge of the High Court.

When the Convention assembled in Adelaide in March 1897
Barton was legally simply one of the delegates from New South
Wales, though in fame as a federal leader he stood first among
them. Private meetings and plots before the formal opening on
22 March secured the appointment of Kingston as President.
There were similar private discussions and apparently similar
differences of opinion about the method of procedure. That it
was Barton who rose to move for the appointment of a Select
Committee, two members from each colony, to frame Resolutions for the Convention, did reflect the general assumption that

he would play a leading part; but the debate which followed, led by Turner, also indicated a pre-arrangement, perhaps not unanimous, that Barton alone should be asked to present Resolutions, and take charge of business as Leader. This apparently being accepted, Barton modestly revealed that he had in fact already made a draft of 'resolutions based very much upon those adopted at the Convention in 1891' and had even had some copies printed.[46] He moved these on the same day. The third affirmed that sole power to impose duties of customs and excise should be vested in the Federal Parliament; the fifth read:

That the trade and intercourse between the Federated Colonies, whether by land or sea, shall become and remain absolutely free.[47]

In introducing the Resolutions he added nothing in detail: 'Clearly we could not have border duties. We should have free intercourse by sea, as well as by land, between one colony and another.' For the next week before the Resolutions were referred to select committees, the statesmen of Australia poured out opinions and oratory. Some of them quoted the words of the fifth of Barton's Resolutions, others referred to the principle it embodied; but this was not the stage for detail and if any one had reservations about the form of the words he kept them to himself. Some argued that to secure absolutely free trade it would be necessary for the Federal Parliament to control the railways, so that differential charges might be prevented, but none lingered on definitions. 'It is a universal admission that one of our main motives for Federation is the destruction of our intercolonial fiscal boundaries', said Reid,[48] and that was enough. There were no quotation marks in Deakin's voice when he prophesied that 'with a common tariff and absolute intercolonial free-trade'[49] Australia's resources would be vastly developed.

On 31 March three select committees—Constitutional, Finance and Judiciary—were appointed. Every delegate had a place on one or other of them. The Finance Committee was required to report specially to the Constitutional Committee on the Resolutions concerning customs duties and intercolonial free trade. It did not have a single lawyer among its members, apart from the ex-officio membership of all premiers, of whom those in some sense legally qualified were Turner, a solicitor, and Reid, a barrister. The Chairman was McMillan, a merchant, formerly Treasurer of New South Wales.

The Finance Committee's Report, dated 9 April, recommended that a number of Resolutions be provided for in a Federal Constitution. Among these was, unchanged, Clause 8 of Chapter IV of the Draft Bill of 1891: 'so soon as the Parliament of the Commonwealth has imposed uniform duties of Customs, trade and intercourse throughout the Commonwealth, whether by means of internal carriage or ocean navigation, shall be absolutely free.'[50] But McMillan also wrote privately to Barton, reporting suggestions made by various members of the Finance Committee. In their formal Resolutions, he said, the original Clauses of 1891 appeared, and it was thought better to make suggestions informally than to interfere with these. The last 'suggestion' was this:

'Absolutely free' at the end of the clause is considered to be possibly misleading—How does it affect Wharfage & Tonnage rates &c? Rates of Harbour Boards &c?[51]

So the laymen had returned to the doubts which had affected Parkes. The lawyers, looking to the United States, could dispel these without difficulty, and happily retain unsullied the simple phrase 'absolutely free'.

And so they did. Latitude could be granted to Barton, in framing his original Resolutions, to express general affirmations based on those of 1891. But when he and his well qualified legal colleagues of the Drafting Committee, Sir John Downer and Richard O'Connor, framed a draft Bill for the Convention they were solemnly acting as constitutional lawyers. Certainly they were following as closely as possible the Bill of 1891, subject to such modifications as the select Committees had recommended, and apart from the query raised in McMillan's private note no change had been recommended in what now stood as Clause 86 in their draft. But they had looked closely at the wording. The Clause now read, 'So soon as uniform duties of customs have been imposed trade and intercourse throughout the Commonwealth whether by means of internal carriage or ocean navigation, shall be absolutely free.'[52] Barton's 'by land or sea' had not been preferred to Parkes's original phrase; wharfage and similar dues did not perturb those who knew their American judgments; and their tinkering simply made smoother the passage to the resounding conclusion. If this was not by now technical lawyers' language it is difficult to know how one could ever obtain an affiliation order against a lawyer. There is one last resort: to see what its legal sponsors said when the phrase was attacked.

In Committee of the whole Convention Clause 86 was reached on 19 April. In the earlier discussion of the powers of the Federal Parliament Deakin had wished to move an amendment to ensure that the federal power to regulate trade and commerce under Clause 50 (later 51) did not prevent the States from restricting or prohibiting within their borders the import or sale of alcohol and opium; but Barton had told him that the point would more properly be raised under the Clause dealing with freedom of trade.[53] Accordingly he now moved an amendment to this effect. Turner intervened to ask a question. He had been a suburban solicitor and would have disclaimed constitutional learning. Still, it is fair to point out that formally he could be described as a lawyer. He drew attention to the words 'absolutely free'.

I can understand that [trade and intercourse] should be absolutely free from any duty on importations. These words are about the largest that could be possibly used, and might include all charges for tolls, wharfage dues, and other matters like that. We ought to be careful about using words which may have a wider interpretation than was originally intended. I will ask Mr Barton to tell us what the words mean, for the desire of the Committee is that when we have a uniform tariff as against the outside world, as between State and State there should not be any Customs tariff.[54]

Good for Turner! Glynn, a barrister, remarked that it would be better to strike out the Clause, which went further than was intended. Reid interjected: 'This clause is a financial peroration.' There was some interchange until Barton got a word in. He began by admitting a howler, 'I was under the impression that these words were in the American Constitution', but conceded that they were not. Then he attempted to answer Turner:

It was thought in 1891 that this clause should be as absolute in its terms as possible. If there is to be any exception to absolute freedom of trade and intercourse from end to end of the Commonwealth it should be expressed by way of exception. We take it that if we are to make provision for this or that, as the necessity arises, and that this thing shall not be charged with Customs while that shall be, we may have prolonged attempts to make things definite. Make them indefinite and the best way for the protection of the Commonwealth, which is the object aimed at in this clause, is to prescribe definitely that all trade and intercourse may be absolutely free except with regard to these derogations or exceptions which the Constitution imposes. That was the view with which the clause was drawn now and in 1891 . . .[55]

He disposed firmly of the view that the Clause could rule out payment for services rendered. Every ordinary service—postage for example—would have to be paid for, but subject to this, 'trade and intercourse is to be absolutely free. We had better leave the clause in its present form.' The rest of the discussion concerned Deakin's specific amendment; as there seemed to be some concern about his wording, his motion for the postponement of the whole Clause was agreed to.

Barton's explanation is instructive. First, it is clear that at this time his mind was fixed on customs duties only. Secondly, it never occurred to him to place the onus of the original words on Parkes, or to apologize for them as laymen's language. As a draftsman, 'now and in 1891', he accepted them without question as appropriate. Thirdly, he appeared to think that once the laymen's difficulties about charges for services were removed, there was nothing more to be said. Of course Barton, unlike some of the laymen, was always conscious that the Constitution would have to be interpreted as a whole, and he knew that the Clause would need to be read with others that might modify its wide terms. But he was quite unable to see any technical objection to its actual words.

Discussion of the postponed Clause was resumed on 22 April when Deakin moved a revised version of his amendment relating to opium and alcohol. His motion was lost on this occasion, but it was to be revived at the next session of the Convention. The main interest of the discussion is that for the first time in this context heavy artillery was brought to bear against the Drafting Committee, and that the fire was returned. The Clause as it stands, said Isaacs, a learned barrister, 'is not only unnecessary, but it is very dangerous. It goes much further than it is intended, and there are some expressions which, taken in connection with other portions of the Bill, are extremely large and alarming.'[56] He proceeded to expand this. Taken literally, it meant 'free of everything, even of a licence'. American Supreme Court decisions had given trade and commerce the widest possible meaning, and the general power of the Commonwealth to regulate them under Clause 50 was ample. The Clause was really pointed at the border duties. 'We know what we intend, but these provisions are to be subject to judicial interpretation hereafter.' Barton, now interested, began to ask questions about its applicability to types of imposts; Isaacs was ready with replies. He insisted that there was enough power in other Clauses, expressly or by implication, to achieve the object of this Clause, and again the future judge of the High Court spoke as a prophet: 'There is not the slightest doubt that these words will be tested hereafter'.[57]

In reply another future judge of the High Court fired an equally heavy shell:

I do not think [said O'Connor] there is a more necessary provision in the whole Constitution than this, because it contains on the face of it, immediately after the law [sic] regarding the imposition of uniform duties, a declaration that trade and intercourse shall be absolutely free when these uniform duties have been once imposed.

Without the Clause, he said, there could be no prohibition of *octroi* duties. (It must be remembered that 'throughout the Commonwealth' still stood.) For the rest, he utterly repudiated any possibility of interpretations such as Isaacs had foreshadowed. 'This is a mere declaration, and the meaning of it is that the passing commerce of a State shall be absolutely free.'[58] And that was that. As a member of the Drafting Committee he spoke firmly: 'I take it that the Committee [of the whole Convention] will not be in favour of disturbing the section in the words in which it stands now.' Nor was it. The Clause was agreed to without division.

On 23 April 1897, after approving a first draft of a Constitution, the Convention adjourned, with the intention of re-assembling in Sydney on 2 September. In the interval the premiers were to proceed to the pageantry and junketings of the Diamond Jubilee in London. In accordance with the enabling Acts which had authorized the Convention, the Draft Constitution was next to be submitted to the colonial parliaments, whose suggestions for amendment would be considered at the next session of the Convention. Copies were also formally to be sent to the Governor of South Australia so that they might officially reach the Colonial Office.

During this interval, Clause 89 (formerly 86) did not escape attention. Presumably because it did not appear to affect the interests, either of 'the empire' or of British bondholders, it was passed over without comment in the intensive and frequently hostile examination to which the Draft Bill was subjected in the Colonial Office in June and July.[59] In the colonial parliaments discussion ranged far and wide over the whole question of federation, embracing both the wildest general attacks on the principle and detailed technical criticism of the clauses of the Draft Bill[60] but with two exceptions no amendments to Clause 89 were suggested. The parliaments were agreed in suggesting amendments along the lines of Deakin's motion regarding the preservation of State powers to regulate the import and sale of opium and alcoholic liquors, as a proviso either to the renumbered Clause 52 (powers of the Commonwealth) or to Clause 89. Curiously, the one formal 'suggestion' about Clause 89 that otherwise emerged from their discussions came from the newest and most remote parliament, that of Western Australia. When the Legislative Assembly, sitting in Committee, came to Clause 89 the Attorney-General Septimus Burt (not a delegate to the Convention) moved that the phrase 'throughout the Commonwealth' be replaced by 'between the States'. Though he may not have known it, this was a return to Parkes's original Resolution in 1891. 'Throughout the Commonwealth' had first appeared in the Drafting Committee's revisions of Griffith's preliminary draft, and had survived to the end, to be embodied in the Bill of 1891. In the Adelaide session of the present Convention Isaacs had suggested 'among the States',[61] probably without consciously returning to Parkes's Resolution, since the point arose from his own general argument. Burt said simply that he had got the idea from reading the debates of the Parliament in Sydney, where it had been pointed out that if commerce were to be absolutely free throughout the Commonwealth, the States would be debarred even from dealing with such matters as the licensing of hawkers.[62] Walter James, a barrister, asked what the clause meant now. He received no answer. The suggested amendment was passed on the voices, to be duly presented for the consideration of the Convention.

There was, of course, much public and unofficial discussion of the Adelaide Draft Bill but, because of his singular authority, only one commentator need be noticed here. Queensland was unrepresented at the Convention. Its Parliament had no official concern with the outcome of the proceedings in Adelaide. But there was a natural curiosity about a Constitution which, if adopted by the other colonies, would probably apply to Queensland at some time in the future, and there were still active hopes that the colony might yet be represented when the adjourned Convention met in Sydney. Griffith resolved, or was prompted, to draw up for the government some *Notes* on the Draft Constitution, which were published as a Parliamentary Paper.[63] It was likely that at least the lawyer-members of the Convention would read them with close attention.

The *Notes* compared the new Bill with that of 1891, praised it in general terms, and made a number of suggestions for consideration in the tone of 'a most friendly critic of the work of the Convention'. After discussing the finance Clauses, and those referring to an Inter-State Commission concerned with trade and commerce by rail and river, Griffith wrote:

I venture, before passing from this subject, to suggest a doubt whether the words of s.89 (which are the same as in the Draft Bill of 1891) are, in their modern sense, quite apt to express the meaning intended to be conveyed. It is, clearly, not proposed to interfere with the internal regulation of trade by means of licenses, nor to prevent the imposition of reasonable rates on State Railways. I apprehend that the real meaning is that the *free course of trade and commerce* between the different parts of the Commonwealth *is not to be restricted or interfered with* by any taxes, charges, or imposts. Would it not be better to use these or similar words? If it is also intended to prohibit such interference by the imposition of preferential or differential rates on railways or rivers, suitable words should be added. The following are submitted for consideration . . .[64]

His suggested lengthy extension of the main proposition, to meet explicitly the case of differential railway and river charges, may be neglected; it arose from doubts about the colonies' willingness to leave supervision of these matters to a Federal Inter-State Commission. But on the main proposition itself, it will be noticed that Griffith had changed his mind. He had never, through all the stages of the Bill of 1891, criticized the original 'absolutely free'; and, as we have seen, writing five years later, he had quoted the words in two separate, published essays without any comment on their adequacy as a definition. He now proposed that the wide, 'absolute' statement should be replaced by the specific, and negative, injunction that between the different parts of the Commonwealth 'the free course of trade and commerce is not to be restricted or interfered with by any taxes, charges or imposts.' It seems significant that he suggested a doubt whether, *in their modern sense*, the words were quite apt. Surely this was to safeguard himself? Since he, the great constitutional authority in charge of the Bill of 1891, had never before criticized them, and may indeed have been responsible for them, he was shrewd enough to imply that they had been appropriate at the earlier date, though in the interval the 'sense' of the words had changed. But why had this revelation come to him between June 1896 and June 1897?

The answer appears to be obvious. He was writing after 'a careful reading of the Official Record of the Debates of the Convention',[65] and he must have thought twice about what Turner, and more particularly Isaacs, had said in the discussion of Clause 86 (89 in the final Adelaide Draft). He must have noticed that Isaacs had been doubtful about 'throughout the Commonwealth' in that Clause and would have confined the phrase to Clause 50 (52 in the final Adelaide Draft; later 51) in the proviso about uniformity of customs, excise and bounties. He must also have noticed Isaacs's opinion that the sentence 'no tax or duty shall be imposed on any goods exported from one State to another', if read with other Clauses forbidding States to tax imports or exports, and forbidding either Commonwealth or States to derogate from freedom of trade or commerce, was sufficient to secure the *intention* of 'absolutely free', while avoiding its dangers. Isaacs was no layman. His argument must have

impressed Griffith, in the isolation of Brisbane, more than it had
Barton and O'Connor in Adelaide, sensitive in defence of their
own words and particularly against the technical criticisms of
Isaacs; for a plot, though not of their making, had excluded him
from the Drafting Committee on which he had a just claim to
serve.[66] Whether Isaacs's argument would gain additional authority now that Griffith had endorsed it remained to be seen.
Meanwhile Barton and O'Connor themselves had read Griffith's
Notes, and had second thoughts about the arguments they had
dismissed in Adelaide.

The Convention duly re-assembled in Sydney on 2 September
1897. The first business was the formal presentation of amendments to the Adelaide Draft suggested by the various colonial
legislatures. These were ordered to be printed. On Barton's
motion, chapter 4 of the Draft Constitution—'Finance and
Trade', which included Clause 89—was referred for consideration and report to a select committee of the premiers with one
other representative of each colony. The membership of the
Drafting Committee—Barton, O'Connor and Downer—was then
discussed. It had originally been a sub-committee elected by the
Constitutional Committee, and this was the first time its membership had been open to discussion by the full Convention.
Though Barton said they would welcome assistance, he hinted
strongly that the existing Committee was large enough. Walter
James moved that Kingston, Symon and Isaacs be added to it.
Isaacs, while stating clearly that he thought a membership of
three was desirable, did not decline the nomination. The motion
was narrowly lost, by 20 to 21. The relevance of the incident
here is that a second rebuff may well have had some effect in
causing Isaacs (and for that matter Symon) to press technical
criticisms in open Convention, in a manner which provoked the
Drafting Committee into resisting them. Something like this was
to be evident in the last stage of the history of Section 92.

The Sydney session of the Convention did not deal directly
with Clause 89. It had a fairly strict time limit. Turner and other
Victorian ministers and members of Parliament would need to
return home early for an impending election, and substantial
decisions without Victorian participation were unthinkable. The

amendments suggested by the legislatures had been considered only as far as Clause 70, and the Finance Committee had not yet reported, when the Convention adjourned on 24 September to meet next in Melbourne.

But the matter was raised indirectly. Deakin's former amendment concerning State regulation of opium and alcohol was now discussed as a 'suggestion' of the Parliament of Victoria in connection with Clause 52 (later 51) which affirmed the Federal Parliament's power to regulate trade and commerce among the States. In arguing for an express provision to permit States to prohibit the sale of alcoholic liquors within their boundaries, Isaacs pointed out that internal free trade in the United States could be upset at any moment by Congress, which could legislate to permit such restrictions, and in this matter had done so by the Wilson Act. But, unless a provision were inserted in the Commonwealth Constitution, 'a subsequent Clause 89, saying that inter-state commerce shall be absolutely free, would prevent even the Commonwealth parliament from making such a provision as is now suggested. Therefore it is necessary, if we retain Clause 89'.[67] Thus Isaacs had apparently resolved to renew the battle on that Clause when the opportunity should occur. O'Connor thought he was making too much fuss about American precedents on the question of alcoholic liquors and that the matter was one for federal legislation rather than for embodiment in the Constitution; but he then said something very significant, if we recall his clash with Isaacs in Adelaide:

The only thing that prevents the federal government from dealing with the question in this way is the prohibition which may be implied from the clause relating generally to freedom of trade—clause 89. I have always thought that the words in that clause are very much too general. It was pointed out in Adelaide, and having thought over the matter since, I have come round to the view, that we should state our meaning there more definitely. There is nothing more dangerous in the Constitution than vague general words, the meaning of which we do not at present know ourselves. We ought to be very careful not to leave anything in the constitution which may be seized on by-and-by to wrest its meaning to something different to what we intended.[68]

Isaacs, his main point thus amply conceded, exclaimed that the only way to give the Federal Parliament express power to

permit State control of liquor would be to strike out Clause 89.
O'Connor replied 'No'; and quoted an amendment 'which has
been suggested': this was a literal quotation from Griffith's
Notes of the previous June. 'That will be very dangerous!', said
Reid. Isaacs was still not satisfied, but the discussion was
diverted away from Clause 89 to the principal matter, the retention of State powers over liquor. Some members wished to post-
pone the discussion until Clause 89 was reached. Barton said
that he proposed to amend Clause 89, 'so as to prevent the commonwealth parliament from being denuded of the powers it
would otherwise have',[69] but did not give details. His request
that the matter be postponed for the Drafting Committee to
consider was nevertheless denied. The States' power to regulate
liquor was agreed to as a proviso to the Commonwealth's power
to regulate trade and commerce.[70]

This was not the end of the matter. Cockburn (South Australia) raised a similar question concerning a State's power to
prohibit the introduction of diseased animals or plants. Higgins
saw what was worrying him: 'if clause 89 remains as it is the
states of the Australasian commonwealth will have no such
power'. And then Barton, like O'Connor before him, intimated
that he intended to propose a specific amendment to Clause 89
to make it read as Griffith had suggested, namely: 'So soon as
uniform duties of customs have been imposed, trade and intercourse throughout the commonwealth is not to be restricted or
interfered with by any taxes, charges or imposts'.[71] Here, it could
seem to a reader who has followed this complicated story so
far, is the death-knell of 'absolutely free'.

He knows it was not so; but it is indeed apparent that in the
final days of the Sydney session 'absolutely free' was in greater
peril than at any other time in the history of the Convention.
The control of liquor was an intensely 'political' or 'electoral'
issue. The colonial parliaments had asked for amendments which
should secure the continuance of power to the States; and behind
them stood churches and temperance societies, with their hardly-
won Local Option Acts. Barton had asked that the amendment
be negatived, promising that the whole matter would be recon-
sidered in Melbourne in the context of his proposed revision of
Clause 89. But Holder—a Methodist lay preacher, total abstainer

and lecturer on abstinence—had strongly opposed this course; it might be procedural in intention, but it would be misunderstood by the temperance societies, and 'make them antifederationists'. Others made the same point. So the amendment was passed, with the three members of the Drafting Committee among the minority; and two of these, O'Connor and Barton, had explicitly stated their intention of proposing an amendment of Clause 89 to confine it to freedom from 'taxes, charges or imposts', a phrase that, apparently, they assumed would permit federal legislation to authorize the States possibly to prohibit, certainly to license liquor sales. Thus it was that in Melbourne Clause 89 was not to be considered in immediate proximity to the touchy issue of liquor regulation by the States; the urge to revise it for this purpose had gone, since the purpose had been achieved; and Barton was becoming testy about proposals to permit this or that exception to the requirement of internal free trade. There was no further discussion of the liquor question. The removal of the amendment from the Clause concerning the powers of the Commonwealth (now Section 51) to a Clause (now Section 113) of its own, and some verbal changes in it, were later drafting procedures. The most serious threat to the original wording of Clause 89 had disappeared before that Clause was re-considered in Melbourne.

When the delegates met on 20 January 1898 they knew that this must be the last session, and that they must continue until they had finished their task. The weariness and edginess that became evident before the Convention was dissolved nearly two months later is not irrelevant to the present subject.

In the ordinary course of procedure, Clause 89 would not come up for further discussion until the Report of the Finance Committee appointed in Sydney was available. There was a preliminary skirmish on 7 February, when Cockburn, still anxious about phylloxera and the South Australian vineyards, asked whether there was any power in the State or the Commonwealth to prohibit all imports from a diseased area, in view of the words of Clause 89. He recalled the amendment foreshadowed by Barton in Sydney, and found him sympathetic about the immediate question of leaving such powers with the States, but inclined to suggest a specific amendment for the purpose.[72] Two days later the Report of the Finance Committee was presented by Reid, and Barton also made available suggestions of the Drafting Committee about the order in which the financial Clauses should be taken.[73] The Finance Committee suggested no change in the fundamental sentence of Clause 89, though they wished to add a paragraph concerning the transitional period before the imposition of uniform customs duties, a matter irrelevant here.

The discussion, a week later, did at last make a dint in Clause 89. Isaacs supported the Western Australian suggestion to substitute 'between the States' for 'throughout the Commonwealth'. He referred to Griffith's *Notes*, and again warned about the largeness of the words 'absolutely free'. 'Free of what? Free of everything'.[74] Though he agreed that with these words charges for services would be legitimate, he thought licence-fees would not. What they wanted was to establish free trade between the States, and they should look carefully at the words expressing it. Barton, as in Sydney, was impressed; he favoured Isaacs's view; but he wished to hear further discussion. Quick supported Isaacs; but Downer lent his authority as a member of the Drafting Committee to the view that the Clause should stand unaltered. Authorize licences as an exception, he said, but 'do not alter this provision, which contains a cardinal principle of our Commonwealth in favour of absolute free-trade within its borders'.[75] This was a strong Clause, 'a broad central declaration'. Other provisions in the Constitution would show its intention. At no point did this eminent lawyer object to the actual words 'absolutely free'; on the contrary he emphasized their propriety. But the matter immediately before them was Isaacs's amendment, which Barton again commended, and this was agreed to without a division. Then, curiously, 'absolutely free', to which Cockburn had again objected, was passed by. Discussion moved on to a merely transitional proviso suggested by the Finance Committee.

The Convention next proceeded to discuss the finance Clauses and the special position of Western Australia, and then got bogged down in the long, long debate over Clause 95 (now 99) forbidding any law of commerce or revenue giving preference to one State over another. The main point at issue was the effect upon the systems of differential railway rates by which New South Wales and Victoria (or rather Sydney and Melbourne) sought to attract the traffic of the Riverina. The discussion necessarily involved reference to the meaning and effect of the various Clauses concerned with the regulation of commerce, and with free trade between the States. Clause 89 was frequently mentioned, but in effect as one of the noises off. Its wording had been settled for the time being and was taken for granted. Discussion ranged round its implication for the practice of special railway rates intended to attract traffic across State boundaries, and as Professor Beasley has shown, it is important as an elucidation of the *meaning* of Clause 89 in the minds of a number of delegates. But it need not be followed here because the actual wording of Clause 89 was not before the Convention.[76]

Weeks later, in the long business of reconsideration and recommittal, Clause 89 was specifically discussed for the last time, though that was not quite the end of it. Isaacs, again quoting the authority of Griffith, moved that after 'free' there be added 'from taxation or restriction'.[77] His arguments were familiar; it was dangerous to leave the Clause as it stood, and his words expressed the Convention's intention. By 'restrictions' he meant 'restrictions on entry into a colony of persons or goods'. Lyne became suspicious; he wanted Barton to tell them whether the addition would affect differential long-distance railway charges. Reid intervened, and strongly defending the Clause as it stood, uttered historic words: 'It is a little bit of laymen's language which comes in here very well.'[78] Isaacs's amendment was lost by ten votes to twenty.

But he had one more chance, on the motion that the Clause stand part of the Bill. Again he warned them. The Clause might mean that Victoria's differential railway rates for Riverina traffic would be invalid even before an Inter-State Commission could consider them. What Barton said in reply sounds very odd, when we recall his acknowledgment in Sydney that he had doubts about the language of Clause 89, and would propose an amendment of the kind suggested by Griffith and Isaacs; so odd that it seems to require explanation. It was now midnight after an all day's sitting; they were in fact to continue until 4 a.m., and had sat until after eleven on the previous night. When most delegates were in bed, when even his fellow-members of the Drafting Committee had had enough, Barton in these closing days and nights had been working away at the drafts with the secretary, Robert Garran, who recalled that they 'would carry on till at four or five in the morning I could persuade him to call it a day.'[79] He must have been tired; and they had just returned from supper. He had respected Isaacs's learned assistance on some points, but here was Isaacs once again pressing objections, and even, abandoning his more general arguments, harping on some possible but obscure disadvantage to Victoria. Only by some such combination of weariness and irritation can we explain Barton's firm refusal to see a point which in Sydney he had seen clearly enough. For he now said: 'I cannot see any particular difficulty about this matter . . . I cannot apprehend the difficulty my honorable and learned friend seems to be suffering under'. He quoted Clause 89:

Do we mean that, or do we not? Do we mean that trade and intercourse is to be absolutely free, or is it to be free only *sub modo*? . . . I do not know why intercolonial free-trade, if it is essential to federation, should be objected to when it is provided in the Constitution in so many words. Why should we have all these qualifications?

He swept aside Isaacs's (and Griffith's) suggested words, forgetting that earlier he had looked on them favourably, and again asserted his failure to comprehend the point: 'I am unable to see why words of this kind . . . should be waived or whittled away, or why they should be made subject to any qualification or restriction.'[80]

Isaacs, fairly enough, disclaimed any intention to cut down the doctrine of intercolonial free trade. Some other Victorians began to see his point about railway rates: that special rates to attract the Riverina traffic would, for New South Wales, affect trade entirely within its own boundaries, but for Victoria might be held to affect trade between the States, and so infringe Clause 89. Deakin, at the very end of the second Convention he had attended, now actually suggested that the Drafting Committee would never by itself have used the words 'absolutely free'; they had merely taken them over from the Bill of 1891, like other phrases which the present Convention had since qualified. He asked Barton to consider them carefully, in relation to Isaacs's argument; and again Barton said that he could not see the point but promised to read the report of the debate, and to suggest an amendment if he were convinced.[81] Then Clause 89 was agreed to. In its last appearance, discussion had been clouded by Isaacs's confining his argument to a debatable legal point which Victoria alone could have an interest in clearing up; but Barton's tenacious defence of 'absolutely free' was still curiously obstinate and inconsistent with his (and O'Connor's) views as expressed at Sydney. And in the voting on Isaacs's amendment, which was more or less in the terms they had earlier favoured, they had both been against him.

The draftsmen still had some work to do. One of four hundred or so drafting amendments gave Clause 89 the number known to later generations, 92. Another inserted the word 'commerce'. Another altered 'So soon as uniform duties of customs have been imposed', to 'On the imposition of uniform duties'. And there were some minor changes in the wording of the second (transitional) paragraph. On the last business day of the Convention these with other Clauses, were agreed to without discussion. Section 92, in its final form, survived unscathed until the Commonwealth of Australia Constitution Act received the Royal assent on 9 July 1900. Its future lay with the High Court and the Privy Council. The lawyers who had nourished it and defended it were now absolutely free to say what it meant.

3

THE COLONIAL OFFICE AND THE
COMMONWEALTH CONSTITUTION BILL

B. K. de Garis

In March 1897 fifty delegates representing five colonies gathered in Adelaide for the opening of the National Australasian Convention, charged with the responsibility of framing a new constitution which it was hoped would provide a basis for the federal union of the Australian colonies. The first session lasted for four weeks and broke up on 23 April, in time for the premiers of the colonies concerned to sail for England to participate in the celebration of Queen Victoria's Jubilee and to attend the associated Colonial Conference. By that time the first draft of a constitution had been completed, and this was referred to the parliaments of the participating colonies for consideration.[1]

The four month adjournment also gave the Colonial Office in London an opportunity to scrutinize the Draft Bill and to decide what part the British government should play in the constitution-making process. For several decades the staff of the Colonial Office and successive Secretaries of State for the Colonies had watched the fitful progress of the federal movement with keen interest. From 12,000 miles away the jealousies and rivalries which preoccupied the colonists seemed trivial compared with the benefits which federation would confer upon the colonies, and those who were responsible for British colonial policy and administration were uniformly anxious that Australia should be united. Memories of the failure of Grey's attempt to federate Australia and Carnarvon's attempt to confederate South Africa, together with the notorious touchiness of colonial leaders, made the British officials reluctant to interfere, but they lost no oppor-

94

tunity to encourage any spontaneous movement in Australia towards federation.[2]

In 1890–1 the Colonial Office followed the proceedings of the Federal Conference in Melbourne and the National Convention in Sydney with close attention. The Draft Commonwealth Constitution Bill of 1891 was analysed and there was some discussion of how to 'bring the Imperial factor into play' to help the Australians work out their federation.[3] The Permanent Under-Secretary, Sir Robert Herbert, suggested that it would probably be necessary for the colonies to send delegates to London to settle their own differences of opinion and to hear any imperial objections, but he warned that 'no chickens are hatched yet on the other side'.[4] Herbert's pessimism soon proved all too justified. The colonists temporarily lost interest in federation and nothing further came of the 1891 Bill. Curiously enough, although Herbert retired not long after writing this minute, he made a temporary return to the Colonial Office nine years later and had thus to participate in negotiations with Australian delegates along the lines he had foreseen.

As reports of the proceedings of the 1897 Convention reached London, the Colonial Office began once again to consider how it could hasten the consummation of the federal movement, and in this it received some encouragement from Australia. Alfred Deakin, who had done his most valuable work at the Convention behind the scenes as a mediator between conflicting groups, carried on with this role in a wider setting. Evidently fearful that the smaller colonies would not accept the limitations which had been placed on the financial powers of the Senate, Deakin wrote to two former Governors of his colony, Sir Henry (now Lord) Loch and Lord Hopetoun, now both resident in England, asking them to exert their influence to convince the Premiers of Western Australia, Tasmania, and Queensland of the necessity for this arrangement.[5] Loch and Hopetoun both forwarded Deakin's letter to Joseph Chamberlain, the Secretary of State for the Colonies, with strong recommendations that he should attempt to influence the Premiers as Deakin requested and offers of their own help if it could be useful.[6] A despatch from the Governor of Western Australia, Sir Gerard Smith, also prompted the

Colonial Office to consider what use might be made of the visit to London of the colonial premiers. In the previous year Smith had hinted that the only certain way to arouse enthusiasm for federation in his colony would be a personal visit by the Secretary of State.[7] He now suggested that the attitude towards federation of the Premier of Western Australia, Sir John Forrest, was swinging in the balance and would rest largely upon the arguments which Chamberlain might address to him when he visited London.[8] In his minute on this despatch John Anderson of the Australasian Department at the Office doubted the wisdom of putting pressure on individual premiers but suggested that some good might be done by emphasizing to them as a group that their position was weakened by their disunity and lack of a strong central authority.[9]

Further discussion was sparked off by the arrival at the Colonial Office of a copy of the Draft Constitution Bill as it stood at the end of the Adelaide session of the Convention; in a series of minutes a number of possible amendments were canvassed, but there was no agreement as to how these should be brought to the attention of the Australians.

Sir John Bramston, the Assistant Under-Secretary in charge of Australasian affairs, noted that prior to the passing of the British North America Act and the creation of the Canadian Dominion, a constitutional conference of colonial and imperial delegates had been held in London under the presidency of the Secretary of State for the Colonies.[10] It would be desirable to repeat this procedure, Bramston felt, 'in order that the Colonial Governments might understand how far they can go without infringing on the essential attributes of H[er] M[ajesty] and her Government here', but he reluctantly concluded that the great distance between England and Australia made the scheme impracticable. As an alternative he urged that an eminent constitutional lawyer such as Lord Herschell, the Lord Chancellor, or Sir Henry Jenkyn or Sir Courtenay Ilbert, the Parliamentary Draftsmen, should be sent out to explain the views of the British government to the next session of the Convention. Unless some action along these lines was taken, Bramston warned, there was likely to be trouble later when the Constitution Bill was sent 'home' for submission to Parliament. It is significant that the idea

of a conference like that which had preceded the confederation of Canada was not taken up by Bramston's superiors; quite apart from the practical difficulties involved, it is unlikely that the colonists would have been willing to participate. However both the Permanent and Parliamentary Under-Secretaries, Sir Edward Wingfield and Lord Selborne, were impressed by the suggestion that a constitutional authority should be sent out to the Convention. Wingfield proposed that the premiers should be sounded out whilst in London to ascertain whether this would be acceptable to them, and whether the colonies would be willing to meet the expenses of the mission.[11] The only alternative, he felt, was to embody the views of Her Majesty's government in a despatch which might be laid before the Convention. Selborne deprecated the idea that the colonies should be asked to bear the costs involved, but he warmly supported the plan to send out a representative and suggested Sir Robert Finlay, the Solicitor-General, as another possibility.[12]

All these proposals were weighed up by Chamberlain, who concluded that the Solicitor-General could not be spared, and that in any case it would be useless to send anyone of lesser standing than Lord Herschell, who was unlikely to be available.[13] Nevertheless Chamberlain instructed his staff to prepare two memoranda; one firmly expressing the views of Her Majesty's government on aspects of the Draft Constitution which affected the rights of the imperial Parliament and the unity of the Empire; the other containing friendly suggestions which it seemed useful to make towards improving the Constitution on matters which were of no direct relevance to imperial interests. These memoranda could then be given to the premiers or used as a brief for a delegate to the Convention, as seemed best. In either case, Chamberlain pointed out, even if the Australians did not accept the advice of Her Majesty's government, they would be acquainted with its views and prepared for argument if a protest was subsequently necessary.

Following this instruction not two but three memoranda were prepared in the Colonial Office, with the assistance of the Crown Law Officers.[14] Memorandum A contained a list of suggested amendments to the Draft Constitution on matters concerning imperial interests; Memorandum B gave reasons for these sug-

gestions; and Memorandum C contained all the other criticisms
of the Bill which had occurred to those examining it. When the
memoranda had been completed Chamberlain departed from
both his earlier plans for using them and passed them on in strict
confidence to the Premier of New South Wales, George Reid,
whilst Reid and his fellow Premiers were in London for the Jubilee celebrations. Having first sounded Reid out in conversation,
Chamberlain forwarded the memoranda to him with a personal
letter in which he pointed out that the first two were the important ones so far as Her Majesty's government was concerned.
Unless the Bill was amended along the lines suggested, objections to it might be raised when the imperial Parliament was
asked to confirm it, Chamberlain hinted. He added:

I must earnestly ask you for your personal attention to these two
papers, as I am anxious to avoid the possibility of friction hereafter.
I do not think that any of the amendments are important from your
point of view, and if so it may be possible beforehand to deal with
them and so to prevent any questions being raised in the British
Parliament.
Memorandum C contains what I may call friendly suggestions
which have occurred to our draftsmen in the course of their examination of the Bill. They may be useful to you in repairing omissions,
or making difficult points clear, but they are forwarded for your
private and independent consideration and with no desire on our
part to press you to adopt them if they do not need this to your own
judgement.[15]

Chamberlain obviously hoped that Reid would be able to secure
a fair proportion of the changes to the Constitution desired by
Her Majesty's government, without the risk of imperial affront
to colonial susceptibilities which a more open intervention would
have run.

The choice of intermediary was in some respects a clever one;
Reid was Premier of the senior Australasian colony and the immediate initiator of the 1897 Convention, so that any suggestions
he put forward for the amendment of the Constitution would
receive serious attention, but he did not belong to the inner circle
of committed federalists who might be expected to resent any
British criticism of their Bill. Chamberlain's decision to take
Reid into his confidence may also have been influenced by the
thought that apart from the cumbersome and potentially ex-

plosive possibility of sending an imperial delegate to the Convention, the most obvious alternative was to act through Charles Cameron Kingston, who was not only Premier of South Australia, but President of the Federal Convention. Kingston was also in London for the Jubilee and was the logical person to bear any formal communication between the British government and the Convention, but he was a fiery radical and vehement nationalist who was greatly distrusted in the Colonial Office. A few years earlier the Governor of South Australia had warned in a despatch that 'in dealing with Kingston you are dealing with an able but absolutely unscrupulous man. His character is of the worst; he is black hearted and entirely *disloyal*'.[16] It seems unlikely that Chamberlain would have relished asking a man with a reputation of this kind to help the British government influence the shaping of an Australian constitution.

On the other hand the great disadvantage of working secretly through Reid was that the Convention as a whole, and the Australian public, were not made aware of the objections held by the British government to some provisions of the Constitution. Chamberlain had previously stressed the importance of preparing the ground for future intervention, if such became necessary, by openly expressing the views of Her Majesty's government now; the course of action he decided upon threw away this chance, and he paid the price three years later.

Chamberlain appears to have made only one other serious approach to the Australian premiers about the Draft Constitution Bill. In his opening statement to the Colonial Conference which followed the Jubilee celebrations he alluded briefly to the restrictions on appeals to the Judicial Committee of the Privy Council contemplated by the Adelaide session of the Convention, and urged that uniformity of law throughout the Empire ought to be preserved by an unrestricted right of appeal to this common tribunal.[17] This lead was not taken up until late in the Conference, when Sir Edward Braddon of Tasmania proposed that Privy Council appeals should be discussed.[18] Reid immediately countered with the opinion that any discussion of the subject by the Conference might be seen as an attempt to influence the Convention sitting in Australia;[19] his view prevailed, and the discussion trailed off into an inconclusive debate about the possible reorganization of the Judicial Committee. This argument comes strangely from a man who, at much the same time as he expressed it, accepted a secret brief from the British government to influence the Convention on their behalf, but clearly few of the Australian premiers were anxious to discuss the matter and Chamberlain did not press it. The general question of Australian federation was also discussed by the Conference in connection with imperial federation and the political relations of England and the self-governing colonies. The movement for federation in Australia was applauded by Chamberlain, though he disclaimed any desire to interfere unless asked,[20] and a Resolution was passed in favour of the federal union of any groups of colonies which were geographically united.[21] There is no evidence to suggest that Chamberlain made any other attempt to influence the attitudes of the premiers towards the federal movement, though no doubt there must have been some informal discussion of the subject at the multifarious festivities associated with the Jubilee and the Colonial Conference. The Secretary of State was evidently content to wait and see how successful Reid's un-official activities on behalf of the Colonial Office would be.

The memoranda entrusted to Reid represented a very thorough review of the Draft Commonwealth Constitution Bill as it stood at the end of the Adelaide session of the Convention. In Memo-randum A seventeen amendments were listed, all of them related to provisions in which the imperial government felt entitled to take an interest. These suggested amendments were explained and justified in Memorandum B.[22] Some of the seventeen were clearly intended to protect the prerogatives of the Queen and her representatives; some to preserve uniformity of law and prac-tice throughout the Empire; some to protect the interests of private individuals and groups in Britain or other parts of the Empire. In a few instances the Colonial Office apparently wished to bring the Australian Constitution into conformity with Cana-dian precedents or to eliminate what were considered to be un-duly 'American' provisions. However in most cases an assortment of justifications was offered, and it is difficult to classify the sug-gested amendments in terms of motive or effect.

The first amendment suggested was the deletion of the pro-vision that all treaties made by the Commonwealth should be binding on the courts and people of all States, even where contrary to the laws of the States, from the seventh covering Clause, which defined the extent of the operation of the Constitution and laws of the Commonwealth. It was pointed out that this provision had probably been copied from the American Constitution but was not applicable in British countries where treaties technically were made by the Crown rather than the State, and did not have the force of statute law unless specific legislation was passed. The last section of the same covering Clause extended the operation of Commonwealth laws and treaties to all British ships 'whose last port of clearance or whose port of destination' was in the Commonwealth. Notwithstanding the fact that an almost identical provision had been inserted as an amendment in the Federal Council Act of 1885 by the imperial government itself, the omission of the provision was now urged on the grounds that British ships throughout the Empire were covered by the Imperial Merchant Shipping Act of 1894. The preservation of uniformity of shipping laws was alleged to be a matter of great importance to all connected with the trade. Moreover it was argued that the imperial government was responsible for maintaining the privileges and exacting fulfilment of the duties associated with the British flag, and ought therefore to have legal control over all British ships.

The first amendment proposed to the Constitution proper, as distinct from the preliminary covering Clauses, was the omission of Clause 2 respecting the appointment of a Governor-General, on the grounds that this was adequately provided for elsewhere in the Constitution. Not only was the Clause unnecessary, and without parallel in the British North America Act, it was asserted, but it was likely to arouse objections when it came before the British Parliament by purporting to give the Queen powers she already possessed, and to compel her to act constitutionally when she must already do so. The British North America Act was also invoked in support of an amendment to Clause 8, regarding the powers of the Commonwealth Parliament, which were to be equivalent to those of the House of Commons until such time as it declared its own powers. The Colonial Office memoranda proposed that, following the Canadian precedent, words should be inserted in the Clause to specify that even then the Commonwealth should not give itself greater powers than those possessed by the House of Commons at the time of the declaration.

A rather more important point was raised in connection with Clauses 52 and 53 in which the powers of the Commonwealth were enumerated. Clause 52 gave the Commonwealth full power to make laws on thirty-seven different subjects, Clause 53 gave exclusive powers to make laws on four more; but included in these lists were several matters such as external affairs and treaties, or fisheries beyond territorial limits, which were still imperial concerns, since the imperial government was responsible for the relations of the Empire with foreign powers. It was believed in the Colonial Office that the form of these Clauses had been borrowed from the American Constitution and that their purpose was to specify the division of powers between the Federal and State Parliaments. However Australia, unlike the United States, was a part of the Empire and the use of words like 'full' and 'exclusive' in connection with powers over external affairs might be taken to limit the powers of the imperial Parliament. To remove any possibility of confusion on this point, it was recommended that the opening phrases of each of the two Clauses should be reworded to make it clear that the powers listed were conferred only as between the Commonwealth and the States.

Another thorny problem arose in connection with the exercise by the Governor-General on behalf of the Queen of the power of Royal Assent to Bills passed by Parliament. There had been much debate between the British and Canadian governments as to whether the Governor-General must always exercise this power on the advice of his ministers, or whether in exceptional cases he might act in accordance with instructions from the Queen. The upshot of this was that the Governor-General in practice always followed the advice of the local government, but that the door remained open to instructions from the Queen. In the Australian Draft Bill, however, the relevant Clause, number 57, followed the British North America Act in the main but omitted the phrase which directed that the Assent should be exercised subject to instructions from the Queen. The Colonial Office scented in this alteration an attempt to make the Governor-General a local rather than an imperial officer, and proposed the addition of the appropriate phrase to make the Australian Constitution follow the Canadian example. If the Governor-General could not be instructed by the imperial government to withhold assent from any proposed law, the more extreme and unpopular power of disallowance of Commonwealth Acts would be used more freely, it was argued, and the risk of friction between the governments would be increased. For similar reasons an increase from one year to two years in the period during which a law assented to by the Governor-General might be disallowed by the Queen-in-Council was suggested. Otherwise the imperial government might be forced to disallow an Act where some other arrangement might have been reached had more time been available for negotiation between the governments.

The ninth and tenth amendments suggested in the memoranda were of a largely formal character and concerned Clauses 60 and 68, both relating to the powers of the Governor-General as the Queen's representative. In each case a change of wording was requested to make the Clauses purely declaratory of the existing powers of the Queen and to avoid any inference that the ability of the Queen to exercise her powers through the Governor-General depended upon statute. With regard to Clause 60 it was also submitted that the Clause as it stood created unnecessary confusion between the military powers of the Governor-General and of the General Officer Commanding; these were matters which would be better regulated through the Queen's commissions and instructions.

One important general aim of the Draft Bill was of course to transfer to the new Federal government control over various matters which had hitherto come under the jurisdiction of the separate colonies. Hence in Clause 70 it was provided that any powers regarding these matters which were vested in the governor of a colony with or without the advice of his council, should be transferred at the establishment of the Commonwealth to the Governor-General with the advice of the federal Executive Council. Here once again the Colonial Office suspected an attempt to change the nature of the office of governor, for there was no provision for the Governor-General to act without the advice of his council. Yet, if the Governor-General was to be an imperial officer, there clearly must be some occasions when he would have to do so, for example when dismissing a ministry. The memoranda therefore proposed the amendment of the Clause to restore the Governor-General to a constitutional position comparable with that of colonial governors. 'The constitutional rule that the Governor must, in almost all cases, act by the advice of his Council, is sufficient without a statutory enunciation of the rule', it was argued.

The twelfth and fourteenth amendments proposed in Memorandum A were relatively straightforward suggestions that the words 'public ministers, consuls, or other representatives' in Clauses 73 and 77 should be replaced by 'consuls or other agents', as the latter was a more correct description of those classes of foreign officials who were in the colonies. Though these were put forward as technical corrections requiring no further justification, they were of course based on the assumption that Britain would continue indefinitely to handle diplomatic matters on Australia's behalf.

Vastly more significant than these were the proposals contained in the memoranda for the alteration of Clause 75 regarding appeals from Australian courts to the Judicial Committee of the Privy Council, the only issue about which Chamberlain had openly spoken at the Colonial Conference. Chapter 3 of the Draft Constitution provided for the creation of a Commonwealth High Court, competent to decide appeals from other federal and State courts. Dissatisfaction had long been felt in the colonies with the expense and the long delays attendant upon Privy Council appeals, and the new court appeared to provide a convenient opportunity for ending these. After several close divisions the Adelaide Convention had thus resolved to abolish Privy Council appeals as of right, and to allow them only by special leave of the Queen, in cases involving the 'public interests of the Commonwealth, or of any state, or of any other part of Her dominions'. This change was quite unacceptable to the British government, and a completely re-drafted Clause 75 was proposed, leaving open the possibility of appeals in all types of cases from the High Court, or any State or federal court from which there was an appeal to the High Court, by leave of the High Court itself or the Queen-in-Council. Even this would mean the end of automatic appeals to the Privy Council, but it was a great deal less restrictive than the Australian draft.

In support of its amendment the Colonial Office quoted extensively from two earlier self-justifications prepared by the Privy Council in response to criticism of the appeal system in Australia in 1871 and in Canada in 1875. The right of every subject of Her Majesty to approach the Throne for redress of grievances was stressed, as was the value of uniformity of legal interpretation. The value of the Privy Council as a tie binding the Empire together was also emphasized. In addition to these arguments borrowed from the Privy Council itself, several new ones were advanced by the Colonial Office, notably that a continued right of appeal was a necessary form of protection to the investors of British capital in Australia against judicial decisions influenced by 'local prepossessions'. With what reads as something almost like a threat, Memorandum B pointed out that: 'It cannot be for the benefit of the colonies to alarm those investors. They are also very numerous and powerful and the amount invested is very large. They will no doubt oppose any proposal to abolish the appeal to the Queen in Council.' It was also stressed that leave to appeal would be granted only in cases where there was an important issue of principle at stake, or where there were *prima facie* reasons for believing that there had been a miscarriage of justice.

Protection of the British investor was also a major reason for the amendments which were suggested to Clauses 82 and 98, regarding the transfer of customs and excise revenue to the Commonwealth. These duties had always provided the lion's share of the revenue of each colonial government and might be regarded as the main security for their respective public debts. The Colonial Office therefore proposed that these Clauses should be amended to ensure that, despite the transfer of customs and excise duties to the Commonwealth, the holders of the public debt of each colony should continue, if necessary, to have a prior charge upon them. The memoranda contended that, although there was little practical danger that the stockholders' rights would be impaired, it was desirable to protect the credit of the colonies by clarifying the point.

Finally, a very minor alteration was suggested to Clause 102, which dealt with the powers which would be retained by the governors of the States after the establishment of the Commonwealth. The purpose of the amendment was to avoid any confusion between the powers vested in a governor by the laws of a State and those vested in him by the Queen's Letters Patent.

These then were the seventeen amendments suggested in Memorandum A and explained in Memorandum B. In addition, Memorandum C contained criticisms of five of the eight covering clauses and seventy-five of the one hundred and twenty-one clauses of the Constitution proper. A preamble to this memorandum explained:

The following criticisms are made on the draft Bill on the same lines as they would be made upon a Bill which had passed through a hard fight in the House of Commons and was beginning its course in the House of Lords.

Many points are no doubt the result of a fight or a compromise and cannot well be altered, and their effect must be left to the course of events.

In other cases, especially where the difficulties will arise before the Federal Government and Parliament are fully constituted, amendments are required.[23]

Very few of the criticisms or suggestions in this memorandum directly concerned matters of policy or principle; almost all of them were intended to clarify the meaning of clauses in the Constitution, or to improve the machinery which the Constitution was to set up. Many examples of imprecise or inconsistent use of terminology were pointed out; some Clauses, numbers 12, 16, 25, 48 and 111, for example, were alleged to contradict or cut across others. In covering Clause 7 and Clauses 86, 108 and 110 instances were discovered of phraseology borrowed from the Constitution of the United States which was technically inappropriate in its new context. Another common criticism, made of Clauses 6, 9, 10, 41, 50 and 63 among others, was that many of the general arrangements covering different aspects of elections, ministries, and parliaments, did not provide adequately for the special circumstances which might arise at the inauguration of the Commonwealth.

Perhaps the most important part of Memorandum C was its preamble, in which the form in which the Constitution should be presented to the imperial Parliament was discussed. As the Bill stood at the end of the Adelaide session, the first eight Clauses were numbered separately from the Clauses of the Constitution itself; these covering Clauses were clearly intended for enactment by the imperial Parliament and defined some important terms used in the Constitution, as well as describing the character and purpose of the Bill, the extent of its operation, and its relationship with previous legislation. It was not clear, however, whether the Constitution itself was to be a schedule to the Bill, in the manner of the Australian Constitution Acts of 1855 and 1890, or a part of the Bill, in the manner of the British North America Act of 1867. The difference between these alternative procedures was of more than nominal significance, for in the latter case every clause in the Constitution would be open to amendment by the imperial Parliament, and the Colonial Office was of the opinion that changes would almost certainly be made. However, if the Bill consisted of the eight initial covering clauses with the Constitution scheduled to it, it would be more difficult for Parliament to make amendments. The Colonial Office therefore recommended that further thought should be given to the form of presentation of the Bill.

Whilst the Colonial Office busied itself preparing its three memoranda and deciding how they should be used, the Draft Constitution was also under close scrutiny in Australia. By the time the Convention assembled in Sydney on 2 September 1897 for its second session, the premiers had returned from London and the parliaments of the five participating colonies had considered the draft and suggested amendments to it. Altogether some 286 amendments had been proposed,[24] and though many of these overlapped or cancelled each other out, it was considered essential that the Convention should give due attention to all of them so that none of the parliaments could feel affronted. Almost at once it became apparent that the business could not be completed in time for the Victorian delegation to return home for the general election which was pending, and arrangements were made for a third session, to be held in Melbourne early in 1898. The Sydney session therefore confined itself to dealing with the amendments proposed to the first seventy clauses of the Draft Bill, and to particular consideration of the composition and powers of the Senate and the solution of deadlocks between the two houses. The remaining clauses and the amendments proposed to them, together with all other unresolved questions, were

dealt with in Melbourne at the last and longest meeting of the
Convention, which began on 20 January 1898 and did not end
until 17 March. By the conclusion of the Melbourne session
finality had been reached, and a Bill to Constitute the Commonwealth of Australia was ready to be submitted for the approval
of the Australian people through a referendum.

During the Sydney and Melbourne sessions a number of the
amendments desired by the Colonial Office were unobtrusively
incorporated into the Constitution, and it is clear that Reid must
have made use of the memoranda which Chamberlain had entrusted to him. So discreetly did he do this however, that the
other members of the Convention were quite unaware of what
was going on. The secret did not come out until 1900, when
delegates from the colonies went to London for further negotiations with Chamberlain prior to the enactment of the Constitution Bill. Even then the matter was kept as quiet as possible
and an impression created that the memoranda had dealt only
with the Privy Council appeal question, so that the episode
remained shrouded in obscurity. Few memoirs or histories of
the federal movement mention the Colonial Office memoranda,
none give details; such references to them as there are seem generally to be based on the limited disclosures made in 1900, rather
than on any direct knowledge of the original memoranda of
1897.

For example, Quick and Garran note in their comprehensive
narrative of the federal movement that in 1897 Chamberlain
gave Reid a 'confidential memorandum of the criticisms of the
Crown Law Officers which included an objection to the almost
total abolition of Privy Council appeals', and cite as evidence
the limited extract made public in 1900.[25] Their account goes
on to say that the memorandum was handed by Reid to the
Drafting Committee and that as a result several amendments
were made, the Privy Council appeal Clause in particular being
considerably modified. Few could be in a better position to know
the facts than Garran, for he attended the Conventions as private
secretary to Reid, who lent his services to the Drafting Committee; but there are several surprising features about this account.
The memoranda are not mentioned by Quick and Garran in
connection with the Convention, but only in the context of the

negotiations in London in 1900. Only one memorandum is referred to rather than three, and no indication is given of its content other than the objection to the abolition of Privy Council appeals. Also the alterations made to the appeal Clause at the later sessions of the Convention are attributed to the influence of the memorandum, which is almost certainly untrue.

There are thus reasons for doubting whether Quick and Garran had much first hand knowledge of the memoranda, but they are probably correct in suggesting that Reid passed them on to the Drafting Committee. The most direct evidence on this point arises out of the visit of the Australian delegates to London in 1900 to see the Constitution Bill through the imperial Parliament. Edmund Barton, the former Leader of the National Convention and Chairman of the Drafting Committee, was appointed as the New South Wales delegate, and he sailed for England in company with two of the delegates from other colonies. Fearing that Chamberlain had asked for a delegation to be sent only because he intended to tamper with the Bill, Barton took with him the Colonial Office memoranda given to Reid three years before, so that he and his colleagues could study them during the voyage for clues to the objections which might now be raised.

Barton appears to have led the others to believe that the documents were as new to him as to them. In writing from Colombo to Sir Samuel Griffith, the Queensland delegate, Dickson, mentioned the memoranda and expressed regret that he had not seen them earlier, but added that 'even Barton did not get them till he was leaving'.[26] However, in a letter to the Victorian delegate, Alfred Deakin, who had gone ahead by an earlier ship, Barton himself had bemoaned the fact that if only they had travelled together they could have discussed 'the many questions we may be expected to answer, as to some of which I possess important information which was confidential at one time, but which our position as colleagues would have entitled us to examine together'.[27] The implication that Barton had had the memoranda for some time but had not been at liberty to show them to Deakin is reinforced by the tone of some notes on them which Barton made at this time.[28] In regard to one suggested amendment he commented that 'The Drafting Committee could not imagine how this extraordinary suspicion was generated.'[29] Of another he wrote that 'In redrafting the clause the Drafting Committee embodied the suggestion made for the avoidance of discussion.'[30] The weight of evidence is thus clearly in favour of the view that Reid not only made use of the Colonial Office memoranda himself at the later sessions of the Convention, but that he passed them on to Barton and the Drafting Committee. In misleading some of his fellow delegates on this point in 1900, Barton was only maintaining the secrecy which Reid had established from the beginning.

An examination of the Convention Debates and of the changes made in the Constitution at Sydney and Melbourne strengthens this conclusion. The first amendment requested by the Colonial Office, the deletion of the words 'and all treaties made by the Commonwealth' from the seventh covering Clause, had also been suggested by the Legislative Council of New South Wales, and as a member of that House Barton formally moved it in the Convention, though without much personal enthusiasm.[31] Reid then supported the amendment strongly and advanced in its favour precisely the same arguments as had been used by the Colonial Office.[32] The amendment was then passed without further debate. Later in the Convention Reid himself moved the amendment to Clause 60 desired by the Colonial Office, a simple matter of substituting the word 'exercisable' for 'exercised' to make the Clause declaratory in form, and secured this without debate.[33] Similarly, Reid was successful in amending Clause 70 to enable the Governor-General to act with or without the advice of his Executive Council, rather than always with it as the Adelaide draft required, in exercising powers transferred to him from the governors of the colonies.[34]

More controversy was aroused by the second amendment to covering Clause 7 suggested by the Colonial Office, that is the complete omission of the provision extending the operation of the laws and Constitution of the Commonwealth to all British ships visiting Australia. Reid moved this amendment and argued for it at some length,[35] although his understanding of the arguments put in his mouth by Memorandum B was somewhat imperfect and he was not well acquainted with the background to the Clause. The main reasons he gave for his amendment were

precisely those of the memorandum, that shipping throughout
the Empire was already covered uniformly by the Imperial Merchant Shipping Act, and that the phrase 'whose last port of
clearance or whose port of destination' was so wide as to require
the application of Australian laws to a ship not simply whilst in
Australian waters but throughout the whole of its voyage to
and from Australia. Unless this Clause was expunged, Reid
assured an interjector, the Constitution would never be accepted
by the imperial Parliament.

Most members of the Convention found this claim very difficult to believe, and one speaker after another reminded Reid
that the Clause he wished to delete was exactly the same as a
Clause inserted in the Federal Council Act of 1885 by the imperial Parliament itself. Sir John Downer went so far as to suggest that as the imperial Parliament had forced the Clause upon
the colonies in 1885, it was far more likely to object to the deletion of the Clause than to its retention.[36] In the course of discussion Reid was led into a revealing exchange:

Reid   May I tell hon. members that I do not speak idly in the
remarks I am making. I hope hon. members will give me credit for
making these observations knowing what I mean. I tell the Committee that these words will be a source of embarrassment in the
consideration of the bill, that they conflict with the laws of the
British Empire, and seek to establish a jurisdiction which we shall
not get, a jurisdiction beyond our limits.
Fysh   We have got it already in regard to beche-de-mer fishing for
instance!
Reid   I do not know whether beche-de-mer fishing comes within the
limit of the general navigation law. It may be so. I have nothing
more to say, except that I speak advisedly.
Clark   Has the right hon. gentleman been talking with 'Joe'
[Chamberlain]?
Reid   My hon. friend is entirely wrong: but I have taken advantage
of my visit to the mother country to get all the information I can
with reference to matters of this kind, and I shall tell the Committee
advisedly that difficulty may arise if these words are left in the
clause.[37]

It was an exasperating situation for Reid, since he was unable to
convince the Convention that he had correctly gauged Chamberlain's views short of disclosing that he had been briefed by him,
and this he was not free to do. When challenged directly he was

forced into an oblique lie, but it is obvious that he had been using the Colonial Office memoranda. Eventually Reid withdrew his motion to omit the entire provision and accepted amendments changing the application of the Clause from ships 'whose last port of clearance or whose port of destination is in the Commonwealth' to those whose 'first port of clearance and whose port of destination are in the Commonwealth', and completely excepting naval vessels.[38] This compromise went some distance towards meeting the objections expressed in Memorandum B, but did not do so entirely.

Only a few hours after this incident Reid laid before the Convention the objections of the Colonial Office to another Clause, number 8, which allowed the future Commonwealth Parliament to confer upon itself powers greater than those of the House of Commons. This time however, Reid was careful to avoid any suggestion that he had inside information, indeed he did not move any amendment but contented himself with pointing out the possibility of making a change.[39] The suggestion was ignored and the Clause passed as it stood.

The other British suggestions and arguments for them do not appear to have been brought forward publicly by Reid. An amendment to Clause 57 identical to that proposed in the memoranda had been suggested by the Legislative Assembly of Victoria, but Reid remained silent when it was discussed, and the amendment was negatived.[40] When Clauses 82 and 98 were under consideration, Reid not only refrained from putting the British case for giving the bondholders of the colonies a charge upon the customs revenue collected by the Commonwealth, but expressed views on the Clauses which were incompatible with the wishes of the Colonial Office.[41] On the all important Privy Council appeal question too, Reid took up a position rather different from that advocated at such length in the memoranda,[42] though he was not so strongly opposed to appeals as he had been at Adelaide. This Clause was the subject of some of the fiercest battles of the Convention, the chief protagonists being Sir George Turner, Sir Joseph Abbott and J. H. Symon, rather than Reid or Barton. After many amendments and counter-amendments the final version of the Clause was considerably less restrictive than it had been after the Adelaide session, though it still did not meet the wishes of the British government.

The remaining amendments suggested in Memoranda A and B were of a relatively trivial character, and in most cases the Clauses concerned or the relevant parts of them were not discussed at all by the Convention. Nevertheless by the time the Constitution Bill was completed at the end of the Melbourne session, several more of the amendments had been wholly or partially included in it. This was no doubt the work of the Drafting Committee, which from time to time presented the Convention with long lists of small changes, most of which were accepted without challenge by blanket Resolution. In this way the words 'public ministers, consuls, or other representatives' were replaced in Clauses 73 and 77 by 'consuls or other representatives', and Clauses 60 and 68 were made declaratory, though other suggested modifications to them were not made. Clause 102, which the Colonial Office had claimed could be interpreted in a misleading way, did not appear at all in the final version.[43]

Of the seventeen amendments advocated in the first two British memoranda Reid had argued for five, with complete success in three instances and partial success in a fourth; five more of the desired changes were introduced by drafting action. In three instances Reid expressed views tending towards incompatibility with British proposals, and four suggestions were neither mentioned in debate nor otherwise effected. In sum, approximately half the suggested amendments had found their way into the Constitution by the end of the Convention; on all the more important questions at least some concessions to British wishes had been made. It is clear that the memoranda were largely responsible for this.

Virtually all of the many criticisms, queries and suggestions contained in Memorandum C were of a technical character, more suited to consideration by the draftsmen than debate by the Convention. Reid was more interested in broad principles than technical minutiae and does not seem to have brought any of these proposals before the Convention, though on a few occasions members of the Drafting Committee did. For example, O'Connor successfully moved to extend from six months to a year the period after the enactment of the Bill within which the Queen was to proclaim the establishment of the Commonwealth.[44] At least thirty-five or forty similar small changes were made by the Drafting Committee without challenge or discussion.

Many other suggestions contained in the memorandum were not taken up. The Australians were much less concerned than the imperial authorities about the inapplicability of some general regulations to the inaugural period, preferring to trust to the good sense of the first cabinet and Governor-General rather than to clutter up the Constitution with complicated special provisos. Barton and his colleagues were also unrepentant about their use of phrases, borrowed from the American Constitution, which their British critics felt to be unsuited to a British country. In some cases valid points of good draftsmanship made in the memorandum had to give way to political considerations; in others the Colonial Office and British Law Officers had misunderstood the Adelaide draft or were unaware of the way phrases were commonly used in the colonies. However, when due allowance is made for all these limitations, it is clear that the British memoranda were not only used by the Drafting Committee, but were of value to them. The imperial intervention in the constitution-making process did not affect the basic character of the Constitution, but it did help to make it a better Constitution.

The Draft Bill, as it stood at the end of the final session of the Convention, had next to be submitted to a referendum, and New South Wales, Victoria, South Australia and Tasmania agreed to hold this in early June 1898. In each colony groups and individuals at once began to campaign for and against the Bill.[45] In the three southern colonies those who supported the Bill were more numerous and better organized than those who opposed it, but in New South Wales the 'Billites' and the 'Anti-Billites' were evenly matched, and the equivocal attitude of the Premier accentuated this. Reid announced that as the immediate initiator of the federal movement and a member of the Convention he intended to vote for the Bill, but that as the Premier of New South Wales he must express doubts as to whether the interests of the colony were safeguarded adequately.[46] Federalists in all colonies were alarmed by Reid's declaration, and this led to a further curious minor episode involving the Colonial Office. The Chief Justice of Victoria, Sir John Madden, who was administering the colony in the absence of the Governor, cabled to Chamberlain the novel suggestion that the Colonial Office should ask the Premiers of Canada and South Africa to send the Premier of New South Wales their good wishes for the success of the Federal Bill. 'The Premier of New South Wales himself and the Colony are doubtful supporters, and it is believed that the cause both in New South Wales and elsewhere would be greatly helped by what I suggest', Madden cabled.[47]

In the Colonial Office, John Anderson deprecated the idea of coercing Reid and New South Wales, but felt that it would do no harm to pass Madden's cable on to the Governors of Canada and South Africa without any endorsement. The Permanent Under-Secretary, Wingfield, and Chamberlain himself, both accepted this suggestion and the message was duly passed on,[48] though it does not appear to have evoked any response.

The result of the referendum was an anti-climax. The Bill was approved by Victoria, Tasmania and South Australia, but in New South Wales the affirmative vote, though a majority, did not reach the quota required by the Enabling Act for the colony to federate. However, after a delay of a few months a Premiers' Conference in Melbourne agreed to make a few amendments to the Bill to meet the wishes of New South Wales, and the Bill thus revised was submitted to a further referendum. This time Reid supported it in a less ambiguous fashion and the referendum was carried in each of the four south-eastern colonies. At this stage Queensland, which had not been represented at the Convention, decided to give its people an opportunity to vote on the Constitution Bill, and here too an affirmative majority was recorded. Western Australia still could not make up its mind, but by the end of 1899 the other five colonies had requested the British government to submit to the imperial Parliament their Bill for the Constitution of an Australian Commonwealth.

In the meantime the Colonial Office had followed the deliberations of 1897–9 with close attention. As reports of the proceedings of the Sydney and Melbourne sessions of the Convention reached London, they were analysed by the clerks of the Department responsible for Australasia; variations from the Adelaide draft were noted, particularly in those Clauses to which the British government had suggested amendments. After the Sydney session John Anderson wrote approvingly, 'They appear to be trying to meet us to some extent',[49] and on receipt of the proceedings of the final session he minuted, 'nearly all the vital amendments put before Mr. Reid have been carried—a strong proof of the commanding position acquired by him amongst Australians'.[50] In October 1899 a confidential memorandum was prepared analysing the extent to which the objections made in 1897 were met by the final Draft Bill, and summing up the views of the Colonial Office at that stage.[51]

The prevailing tone of this document was one of restrained satisfaction. The covering Clauses, which had formerly contained the 'most serious blots', were held to be innocuous in their revised form except for the latter part of Clause 5, regarding the powers of the Commonwealth over British shipping. The partial improvement of this provision secured by Reid was judged insufficient and further amendment was suggested. The memorandum also questioned whether the Colonial Laws Validity Act would apply to Commonwealth laws as things stood. Numerous doubts and queries were voiced about Clause 74, the Privy Council appeal Clause, but the final verdict was that the jealousy of the colonists towards imperial interference made it useless to offer further objection on this matter. A few other points were raised when the memorandum came before the senior officials in the Office, but no final decisions were reached.

The Parliamentary Draftsman and the Crown Law Officers were also invited to examine the Bill and their comments reinforced the doubts already expressed about the power of the Commonwealth over British shipping, the status of Commonwealth legislation, and judicial appeals, as well as opening up several other issues. However, the Law Officers were careful to state that, although they regarded at least five amendments as desirable, it was up to the Colonial Office to decide whether or not it was expedient to press these.[52]

The process of examining the Bill proceeded desultorily for some months whilst the colonies were busy with their referenda, but by the end of 1899 it became necessary to decide what should be done.

The general consensus of opinion among Chamberlain's advisers seems to have been that, although the Bill was much better than it had been when the 1897 memoranda had been drawn up and it would be unwise to irritate the colonists by interfering at such a late stage in proceedings, it would probably be necessary to make one or two alterations before the Constitution was enacted. To facilitate this, it was suggested that the colonies should be invited to send delegates to explain the Bill, though it was recognized that since the Constitution had been ratified by popular referendum, such delegates might claim that they had no authority to accept alterations. Nevertheless, Chamberlain decided after a conference with his senior officials to broach the question of delegates with the colonial governments.[53]

The telegraphic despatch which followed this decision did not directly invite or command the sending of delegates, nor did it indicate that amendments to the Bill were under consideration. Instead, the hope was expressed that it was true as reported that delegates would be sent to England 'to assist and explain when Parliament is considering the Federation Bill'. Consultation between delegates and the Crown Law Officers on constitutional and legal questions might, it was stated, 'avoid any protracted discussion and opposition on technical points in Parliament'.[54] This less than candid 'invitation' was received in Australia with a good deal of suspicion but after some intercolonial wrangling five delegates were appointed: Edmund Barton from New South Wales, Alfred Deakin from Victoria, Charles Kingston from South Australia, James Dickson from Queensland, and Phillip Fysh from Tasmania. As noted above, Barton anticipated that the Colonial Office would try to introduce amendments to the Constitution and went armed with the memoranda of 1897, which he thought might give some insight into Chamberlain's intentions. In due course these forebodings proved entirely justified, for although the officials at the Colonial Office finally came to the conclusion that, of the many alterations to the Australian Bill which might be desirable, only two were essential, Chamberlain informed the delegates that four amendments would be necessary. In particular, he insisted on the retention of an unrestricted right of appeal from Australian courts to the Privy Council. A protracted battle followed before a compromise was at last reached and the Constitution Bill enacted. That battle, and the reasons for Chamberlain's insistence on amending the Bill more severely than his advisers deemed wise, form a separate story. What should be noted here is the manner in which the means adopted by Chamberlain in 1897 to influence the shaping of the Australian Constitution rebounded on him in 1900.

When the Adelaide Draft Bill was first under consideration in the Colonial Office, Chamberlain himself stressed that Her Majesty's government should state its views plainly on matters of imperial concern, so that if it later became necessary to press for alterations, the ground would be prepared. However, by confiding his views only to Reid, Chamberlain failed to heed his own advice. Apart from Reid and the three members of the Drafting Committee none of the Convention delegates, nor the colonial governments, had any inkling that the British government was not entirely happy with their Draft Constitution, apart from Chamberlain's passing reference to Privy Council appeals at the 1897 Colonial Conference. Thus, when the idea that delegates should be sent to London to discuss the Bill was brought forward, at the very moment when it seemed that the last obstacle to federation had been overcome, the leaders of the federal movement were outraged.

A few months before this Sir Charles Dilke, an erstwhile colleague of Chamberlain with an interest in colonial affairs and many friends in Australia, had warned Alfred Deakin that an attempt to amend the Commonwealth Bill was probable, especially in regard to judicial appeals.[55] Deakin replied indignantly that if the British government objected to any of the provisions of the Constitution, it ought to have said so while the Convention was sitting. The premiers had visited London after the Adelaide session, Deakin pointed out, but nothing had been said to them. Deakin went on to say,

we have been permitted to draft our own Constitution in our own way in perfect freedom and without even the assistance of suggestions from any Imperial authority unless Mr. Reid in the early part of the Sydney session referred to some such hint when supporting an alteration which was at once made on the control proposed to be vested in the Commonwealth over British ships trading to and from Australia. Under these circumstances to alter our work after we have finished it (without giving us the opportunity of knowing of any objections and of meeting them as we probably should have done most cordially) by a mere exercise of overlordship would be an inconsiderate, impolite and offensive act of supremacy. There ought not now to be the least tampering with a measure which has run such a gauntlet of criticism and secured at last such an overwhelming verdict in its favour from our Parliaments and peoples.[56]

This outburst was typical of the reaction of leading federalists in all colonies when Chamberlain's cable regarding delegates, guarded though it was, was made public. J. H. Symon, a South Australian Convention delegate who had had much to do with the shaping of the judicial appeal Clause, wrote directly to Lord Selborne, Chamberlain's Parliamentary Under-Secretary, to say that the suggestion that delegates should be sent was unfortunate and inopportune, as any amendment of the Bill would make another referendum necessary and play into the hands of those who were opposed to federation.[57]

In the course of the negotiations in London the point was repeatedly thrown at Chamberlain that he ought to have voiced his objections to the Draft Constitution much earlier, and eventually the secret trickled out that the Colonial Office had in fact prepared a memorandum on the subject in 1897 and that this had been confidentially entrusted to the Premier of New South Wales. In his speech introducing the Commonwealth Bill in the House of Commons, Chamberlain explained that during the Jubilee celebrations of 1897 he had discussed the Draft Constitution with the premiers, and had handed to Reid, as the 'Dean of the representatives from Australia', a memorandum on the amendments desired by Her Majesty's government.[58] Following this disclosure Chamberlain was asked to table the memorandum in the House, and in response he produced an extract from Memoranda A and B dealing with the question of judicial appeals.[59]

Chamberlain's explanation was summarily dismissed by Sir Henry Campbell-Bannerman, the Leader of the Opposition, who took the Secretary of State to task for proposing amendments to the Bill at such a late state in proceedings:

If what is proposed was to be done, it surely is not now, it should have been done, but two or three years ago. A prudent and careful Minister would have set himself to bring about a harmonious understanding and arrangement upon the points of difference which existed. The right honourable Gentleman spoke of conferences in the Jubilee year, and quoted from a memorandum, but that is not enough. Negotiations went on in Australia, conventions were held, and proceedings were reported at great length, draft Bills were published, different amendments were published, and the arguments by which they were supported or rejected were published, and everyone knew all about it, but the Government did nothing. They reserved action until the people of Australia had committed themselves by solemn plebiscite to the provisions of the Bill, and then they insist on a change, thus—in effect, though I agree not in intention—giving an open rebuff to the Australian people.[60]

Outside Parliament the Australian delegates added fuel to the flames. Kingston was particularly scathing about the secrecy with which Chamberlain had cloaked his attempt to secure amendments to the Constitution. In a strongly worded letter to *The Times* the South Australian delegate rhetorically enquired of his readers whether it would be believed that, despite his position as a colonial Premier and as President of the Convention, he had never heard of the Colonial Office memoranda until after his departure for England in 1900. Much of this was merely the froth and bubble of political controversy, but it is clear that the means Chamberlain had chosen in 1897 of seeking to ensure that the Australian Constitution would be satisfactory to the imperial government seriously weakened his position in 1900.

In retrospect it does seem that Chamberlain would have been wiser and more prudent to have discussed the Draft Constitution with the Australian premiers, openly and in detail, while they were in London for the Jubilee, or alternatively to have informed the Convention by despatch of the views of Her Majesty's government. Of course such a move would probably have evoked howls of protests from some Australian nationalists. Despite Deakin's assertion to Dilke that if Chamberlain had announced his objections earlier they would have been met most cordially, Deakin's own relations with the Colonial Office were never smooth, and some of the other federalists were a good deal more aggressive than he. But any friction which might have been caused by a frank approach to the question from the beginning, could not have been greater than that which was aroused by the indirect procedure which was, in fact, adopted. That Chamberlain should have employed such backdoor tactics is perhaps an indication of the exaggerated fear which many British officials in the late nineteenth century had of colonial nationalism.

The incident is also interesting for the light it throws on George Reid and his relationship to the federal movement, though the evidence can no doubt be interpreted in different ways. To those who see Reid as an unprincipled opportunist, his acceptance of a secret brief from Chamberlain might be explained as an attempt to curry favour with the imperial authorities, perhaps with an eye to selection as the first prime minister of the Commonwealth; his deception of the Convention as yet another example of his devious untrustworthiness. Those who take a more favourable view of Reid might argue that he was but performing his duty to the Queen and her advisers in seeking to reconcile local and imperial interests, and his duty to the federal movement in smoothing the way for a ready acceptance of the Constitution when the time came for its enactment. Throughout his association with the federal movement Reid had difficulty in reconciling conflicts of loyalty. It can now been seen that at the Convention that conflict was even more complex than has previously been recognized. It must be said in his favour that although he co-operated with the Colonial Office to the extent of moving a number of their amendments, and laying their memoranda before the Drafting Committee, he did not compromise with his own views on any important question.

4

THE AUSTRALIAN NATIVES' ASSOCIATION
AND FEDERATION IN SOUTH AUSTRALIA

Janet Pettman

The Australian Natives' Association (A.N.A.) of South Australia was established on 1 December 1887 as a national association whose chosen role was to stimulate national consciousness and to work for the federation of the Australian colonies. It was an expression of nationalism and of nativism (the pride of the Australian-born in their assumed superiority to immigrants) and operated through a private organization using pressure and publicity in an attempt to influence public opinion and government action.

The traditional view of the A.N.A.'s role in the federal movement treats the A.N.A. on an Australia-wide basis, generalizing from Victorian experience, without specific investigation of that role in South Australia. This tradition gives the A.N.A. credit for the 'popularization' of the federation movement after the 1891 Federal Bill lapsed. This image rightly belongs to the Victorian A.N.A., but not to the South Australian body, where the order was reversed. The A.N.A. in South Australia began its efforts at the same time as Parkes made his early moves, and both the A.N.A. and Parkes had similar aims: to co-operate with intercolonial counterparts to define a scheme of federal government, and to plan action to achieve it. The Intercolonial A.N.A. Federal Conference in January 1890 initiated the popular, or non-parliamentary activity before the official conferences and conventions. But Native leadership in the federal movement in South Australia lapsed in 1891, the only significant contribution after this date being the formation of the Australasian Federation League in South Australia. The formation of this League was decisive for the federal movement, but fatal for the A.N.A. for the movement was now organized by the League, and the public and many Natives by-passed the A.N.A. In the vital years, 1897–9, the A.N.A. almost died, at the very time when tradition has it acting to win South Australians to the federal cause.

Generalizations from A.N.A. experience in the eastern colonies fail to take into account the contrasts between the South Australian A.N.A. and its Victorian counterpart. Established in 1871, the Victorian A.N.A. at first confined itself to its friendly society and mutual improvement activities, interpreting its 'non-party' nature as 'non-political'.[1] Only in 1890 did it accept an active role in politics. Once it had entered the political arena, however, its large membership (19,000 in 1891)[2] and the influence of its leaders on the wider colonial scene, ensured that the Association was the most important non-governmental force in Victorian politics.

In South Australia, the A.N.A. was first established as a national association, with the intention of exercising its influence on political issues. Only later was the friendly society aspect added, to attract members and to bind them more closely to the Association. The main conditions for membership were native birth and good moral character. The entry of members was through a process of nomination, seconding and election, which helped restrict membership to those of 'approved' character and standing.

The A.N.A. was governed by a Board of Directors, a powerful executive responsible only through the re-election and censorship powers of the Annual Conference of the A.N.A. Branches of the Association held fortnightly meetings, and sent delegates to the Annual Conference. But the development of branches was far more troubled, and progress on a much smaller scale, than in Victoria.

The Adelaide Branch and the Board of Directors were established in December 1887. The Mount Gambier Branch (formerly under Victorian control) and the Broken Hill Branch (formerly under New South Wales) soon joined the South Australian body, and a new branch was established at Port Adelaide. A ladies' branch, the Wattle Blossom League, was opened to native-born ladies and to non-native wives of Natives.

In January 1890 the Adelaide Branch claimed a membership of 286,[3] and the South Australian membership totalled 600. But in the early 1890s the A.N.A. entered a period of depression which was to leave the Board and the Adelaide Branch as the only effective representatives of the A.N.A. in South Australia during the vital years which witnessed the popularization of the federal movement. The Mount Gambier Branch suspended meetings in 1892, and remained dormant until 1899. The Port Adelaide Branch finally closed down in 1893, after two years without regular meetings. The Broken Hill Branch was suspended in December 1892 for failure to pay dues, and after that date the only proof of its existence was the angry exchange of letters between the S.A. Board and the former secretary of the Branch. Even the ladies collapsed—in June 1893 the Wattle Blossom League decided to disband.

The Adelaide Branch continued fortnightly general meetings until 1896. The majority of meetings were addressed by leading public figures, and attended by a small but notable group of men. In September 1895 the search for increased membership led to the adoption of a resolution that non-native males be admitted as associates, but even this radical modification of the A.N.A.'s nativist principles attracted few additional members. In 1897 there was a heavy fall-off in active membership, as key Natives turned their attention elsewhere, including to federalist bodies then active in the national cause. The official membership figure in January 1899 was only 150.[4] Only in 1900 did attendance at meetings increase again, but the A.N.A. remained more a social than a national club, with smoke socials, musical and literary evenings, and euchre predominating. In 1902, however, general meetings approached the early 1890s pattern, where national and patriotic activities outweighed the social, and the A.N.A. was revived as a political forum of importance. After 1900, too, the A.N.A. spread over South Australia, with new branches opening up in both city and country areas. Membership increased from 261 in February 1901[5] to 578 benefit members six years later.[6]

Thus the A.N.A. in South Australia was struggling for its life during the vital years of the federal movement, and its rapid revival reached its peak after federation had been achieved.

However, even in the depths of its depression the A.N.A. attracted attention, received considerable and sympathetic press coverage, and was addressed by speakers of the highest standing within the colonial setting. This paradox can be explained in terms of the members themselves, for the Natives were of sufficient importance to make the A.N.A. significant simply by belonging to it. It was not the A.N.A. which enabled members to exert authority in the colony; it was rather that members who had already established their right to authority co-operated through the organization of the A.N.A. The Natives all belonged, by birth or adoption, to the restricted colonial élite of the time. Their influence reached throughout political, commercial, financial and professional spheres in an all-embracing and interlacing pattern of connections.[7]

A number of leading Natives had been educated at secondary and/or tertiary level in England, including two at Eton, one at Harrow, and a number who took low degrees at Cambridge University. Those educated in South Australia had usually attended establishment schools, notably St Peter's Collegiate School and John L. Young's school. Very few Natives left school at an early age. Many then went to university or directly into business or financial institutions. Some went onto family properties, and some were cadetted as journalists (in a number of cases, with the family newspaper).

By the time these men became associated with the A.N.A., they had considerably widened and diversified their interests. Lawyers were the largest professional group, journalists and editors a close second—a powerful combination of the most vocal sections of the community. The Natives had considerable and varied business, mining, pastoral, financial and commercial interests. They held high positions in many bodies such as the Chamber of Manufactures, the Chamber of Commerce, the Royal Society of St George, the Freemasons, the Druids, the Foresters, Oddfellows, the Adelaide Club, the Y.M.C.A. and church organizations.

The Natives were active in politics, both municipal and colonial. In 1887–1902 their ranks included eleven Justices of the Peace, fourteen local councillors, five suburban mayors and four mayors of Adelaide. These four (L. Cohen, F. W. Bullock,

C. Willcox and C. Tucker) were in office for the whole period 1890 to 1898.

Twenty-one Natives were members of Parliament during these years. They included two Presidents of the Legislative Council (Sir Richard Chaffey Baker and Sir J. S. Stirling), two Speakers of the House of Assembly (Sir John Cox Bray and Sir Jenkin Cobs), four Premiers (F. W. Holder, Sir John Downer, C. C. Kingston and V. L. Solomon), and a number of cabinet ministers. Since these figures cover those active within the A.N.A. at a time when effective membership was little over 100 men, this is an impressive line-up.

The closed nature of the A.N.A. in South Australia, and its connections with 'the Establishment', are in contrast with membership patterns in Victoria. There, membership was not only on a much larger scale, but also followed a different, far more diverse pattern, drawing extensively on middle-class and working-class areas, and including a number of large branches in the industrial suburbs of Melbourne, like Fitzroy, Brunswick and Carlton.

The A.N.A. in South Australia was officially non-secular and non-partisan, essential if it were to fulfil its chosen role, to stimulate a patriotic nationalism amongst all Australians. All shades of political opinion were represented, but the vast majority of Natives belonged to the liberal-progressive grouping, which dominated Native pronouncements and actions. Links between the labour movement and the Natives were few, weak and restricted to parliamentary politics, while the A.N.A. had almost no contact with the trade unions or the workers themselves.

The Native concept of the future Australian nation rejected both the imperial federalism of conservatives and loyalists, and the egalitarian republic of the radicals. The Natives would sometimes ridicule everything British as a reaction to British criticism of Australia—but only as a defence mechanism when under attack.[8] For the most part, Anglo-Saxonism, race pride and close attachment to the Queen abounded.[9] Love of Empire could reach almost hysterical heights, as evidenced by A.N.A. activities in South Australia during the Boer War. However, the A.N.A. did act as a spearhead to national consciousness and

Australian sentiment—simply because it attracted those already converted to its cause. The A.N.A. thought, talked, and occasionally acted within a national frame of reference, and so helped to articulate the increasing attachment to Australia, and resentment of colonial status, among fellow Australians. Its attitude to the rest of the world was defensive.

The Natives wished to isolate Australia from outside threats, to build a new nation in freedom, to make Australia great. To these ends, the Natives supported a White Australia policy to keep out 'cheap and nasty labour', a high external tariff to keep out the products of the cheap and nasty labour and a strong defence force to back up these policies, with force if necessary. All these things would be secured by federation, and would, in turn, make possible the building of a great nation which could assert its authority abroad, and secure the ideal society at home. Without federation, this Australia could not come into being. This assumption dominated the Natives' thinking throughout the early years of the A.N.A.

The South Australian A.N.A. played a role very different from that of its Victorian counterpart. Its first contribution was its initiation of the Intercolonial A.N.A. Federal Conference. Taking advantage of the opportunity provided by Major General Edwards's report on colonial defence, the New South Wales Board sent a telegram to the South Australian Board, reading, 'Our Association desires hearty co-operation of yours in successfully pressing the rising federal sentiment.'[10] As a result, the South Australian Board resolved that President Sir John Cox Bray telegraph intercolonial counterparts suggesting an Australian conference of A.N.A. delegates 'to consider the best scheme of federal government'.[11] The Board presumed that the A.N.A.'s chosen role in nationality gave it the right to consider this question with authority.

A South Australian Board meeting on 21 November 1888 was told that the Conference had been approved. The Board then prepared the following series of resolutions to be submitted to the Conference:[12]

1. That the time has come when it is desirable to provide for the establishment of a Federal Parliament for Australasia.
2. That the Federal Parliament should be empowered to deal with

national questions, leaving to the Parliament of each colony all legislation affecting local affairs.

3. That the members of the Federal Parliament should consist of an equal number of representatives of each colony, to be elected by the people of each colony.

4. That the Federal Parliament should be empowered to raise the necessary revenue for the purposes of the Federal Government.

The Adelaide Branch considered the Board's resolutions, but concluded that Australia was not yet ready for federation.[13] It recognized the advantages of federation, however, and so decided to support the establishment of a Federal Parliament, with equal numbers from each colony, elected by the people, as the first step towards effective union. Its hesitancy was disguised in a resolution endorsing the Board's actions, but few Natives expected concrete results from the Conference.

The Conference was held in Melbourne early in January 1890, with the South Australian President, Bray, presiding. It concluded that 'the time has now arrived for the federation of the Australian colonies',[14] a statement which the South Australian A.N.A. had earlier doubted. The Conference's federal formula included a Governor-General; two houses of Parliament, one elected by the people, and the other, in which each colony would be equally represented, appointed by the State legislatures; and the transfer to the Federal government of those duties for which the colonies had proven themselves inadequate, including defence, customs and railways.[15] This Federal government was to operate within the framework of the British Empire, provided for by a Governor-General, the Queen's representative in Australia, and acting head of state. The Natives thus rejected the radical vision of a republic, the American system of presidential executive, and the British system of unitary government. It accepted the British model of cabinet government, modified by some aspects copied from the United States, as a model for federalism.

The Conference aimed at 'crystallising the floating sentiment and placing something definite before the people' with regard to federation,[16] and this is what it did. It publicized the issue of union itself, and articulated a particular concept of what form that union should take. The form of union envisaged was considerably stronger than that seen in the Federal Council, but stopped short of unitary government. The autonomy of the colonies was to be preserved in many spheres, partly because the colonies were already in existence, and would be difficult to liquidate; and partly because the Natives did not wish to abandon their own standing and interests, which were so closely bound up with a colony-centred élite.

The press reacted cautiously to the Natives' Conference, regarding it as of little practical significance, but not being prepared to ridicule Sir John Cox Bray and other respected delegates. The *Chronicle* noted that 'There has been some good natured chaffing at the expense of the association for the assumption that a large amount of importance attaches to the Conference', and warned the Natives against 'premature' self-confidence.[17] The *Observer* implied that the A.N.A. could be using the excuse of a common birthplace to drink and make merry, the 'exhilarating influence of champagne' featuring in activities.[18] Perhaps more indicative of the attitude of the press, however, was the fact that although the Conference proceedings were reported in some detail, no paper felt its decisions warranted scrutiny and editorial comment. Post-Conference reports were limited to noting Bray's return to Adelaide, and quoting him as satisfied with Conference results. The public either ignored the whole episode, or else rejected the Natives' assumption that they had something to say and the right to say it. One old colonist referred to the Conference 'at which certain resolutions were held up for discussion, which for barefaced impudence beggars any attempt yet made in the same direction', and to the Natives as 'young men wanting to play at parliament'.[19] Another critic resented nativism as such, noting that 'the men who have interests other than given by accident or birth are the men to settle national questions, not the boys whose one aim in life is play of some kind or another'. He concluded by condemning the Natives' 'gas and blow . . . like porpoises flopping about and playing with a very big noise'.[20]

Such hostility, coupled with A.N.A. publicity and descriptive, if not editorial, press coverage, did draw some attention to the Conference. But its impact on the general public, in South Australia at least, was negligible. How, then, could Sowden claim, one year after the Conference, that it had 'by the propagandist work then authorized proceeded in precipitating federation from the clouds in which it has been suspended, and in removing from the federal paths lions that . . . were hopelessly obstructing the advance towards union'?[21]

Sowden was clearly exaggerating, for the Conference failed to rally the general public, and was unlikely by itself to convert colonial statesmen to its own federal concept. However, a number of leading colonial delegates to the 1891 Convention, such as Alfred Deakin and Sir John Cox Bray, were men who had already, in their personal and group capacity, attended the A.N.A. Conference and participated in its work. Other delegates were also Natives, and so were familiar with Conference resolutions, and sympathetic towards them. South Australian Natives at this Federal Convention included (in addition to Bray) Hons R. C. Baker, Sir J. W. Downer and C. C. Kingston. The A.N.A. proposals also had the advantage of being concrete, which gave them strength over formulae less published and less imposed upon delegates' minds before the Convention.

Ten of the twelve proposals of the A.N.A. Conference were embodied in the 1891 Bill, including the provision, abandoned by later conventions, that the Senate should be elected by State legislatives. The *Observer* recalled in 1899 the A.N.A. Conference, and stated that 'in many important respects the Bill placed before the Federal Convention was a copy of the Association measure'.[22] However, it is impossible to give full credit to the A.N.A. for this achievement, since the men at both the A.N.A. Conference and the 1891 Federal Convention represented broadly the same colonial groups and ideas. Writers on the Federal Convention name C. C. Kingston as the delegate most representative of labour, but even he was more representative of Nativist nationalism than the radical republicanism of other elements of society. Thus it is difficult to say whether the A.N.A. Conference, by articulating and publicizing the moderate formula of federation, began a new trend in the federal movement or simply indicated a wider trend which was already in operation.

While claiming to have given impetus to the federal movement, the Natives in South Australia seemed content to leave the furthering of that movement to the politicians and interest groups, and withdrew from its leadership within months of the A.N.A. Conference. One such instance was revealed by the Board, in reply to a letter from Mr B. R. Wise, requesting A.N.A. support for a paper devoted to federation. The Board refused the request, on the grounds that 'The public press offer a better medium for the expression of their views in favour of Federation than any periodical specifically created for that purpose.'[23]

In mid-1891, after many months' silence on the question of federation, the Board asked its branches to consider, endorse and publicize the 1891 Federal Bill. There was a marked lack of enthusiasm among branch members, but it was felt that some gesture was necessary, so the Board decided to organize meetings on four successive nights to explain the Bill to all those interested. However, no further reference to these meetings appeared in the press or in A.N.A. minutes, so the planned meetings may not have eventuated.

On 23 October 1893 the General Meeting of the Adelaide Branch announced that it had been invited to send delegates to the proposed Federation League Conference in Melbourne. However, at the next meeting, a letter from the Prahran Branch (Victoria) explained that the invitation had been sent 'by mistake'.[24] The Natives felt insulted and left out, as indeed they were. There were no South Australian delegates at the Corowa Conference organized by the A.N.A. and other groups in 1893, and in July 1894 the Adelaide General Meeting suffered another rebuke, and decided to write to the Victorian A.N.A. 'expressing regret that this Branch has not been invited to send delegates to the Federation Conference'.[25] Later, in 1896, the South Australian A.N.A. was invited to send delegates to the Bathurst People's Federal Convention, but no delegates were sent. Thus the A.N.A. in South Australia played no part in the major non-parliamentary contributions which helped popularize federation in the mid-1890s.

The reason for the Victorian A.N.A.'s lack of fraternal feeling towards the South Australian Association is not clear, but some factors may be suggested. The South Australian body was very small and its activity in the federal movement after 1891 was negligible; many of the Natives supported a federation of States which benefited the smaller States at the expense of the larger; South Australia was founded later than the eastern colonies and many of its 'elder statesmen' were colonists, not Natives, so the A.N.A.'s nativism was a hindrance, not a help, in the federal movement in South Australia.

The South Australian A.N.A. did make a brief but significant reappearance in the federal movement. On 24 October 1894 a letter was read before an Adelaide General Meeting from the Victorian Australasian Federation League, urging the A.N.A. to establish a branch of the League in South Australia. The Natives, still smarting under the slights from the Natives of the eastern colonies, appointed a sub-committee to establish the League in the colony.[26] This sub-committee contacted commercial and political groups interested in federation, and these groups sent representatives to an A.N.A. Adelaide General Meeting on 3 December 1894. At this meeting, Sowden moved 'that it is desirable to establish an Australasian Federation League in South Australia'.[27] The motion was seconded by L. A. Jessop, Vice-President of the Chamber of Commerce, and supported by L. Grayson, President of the Chamber of Commerce, Hon. D. M. Charleston, representing the Fabian Society, G. Thompson, Vice-President of the Bimetallic League, F. Dowsett of the Democratic Club, and E. H. Bakewell of the Young Patriotic Association. This meeting appointed a Provisional Committee to draw up the rules of the League. No representatives of the Trades and Labour Council or the Labour Party were present, because the A.N.A. had not thought to contact them. The Provisional Committee was later embarrassed by Labour indignation, and resolved, 'That an official explanation be forwarded to the Trades and Labour Council for the oversight in omitting to send an invitation for a delegate to attend the meetings of the Provisional Committee.'[28] The Labour Party was later sent an invitation to be represented in the League.

The Provisional Committee's main task was to draw up a constitution for the League. For its first three meetings, no secretary was appointed and no record kept.[29] Then, on 18 January 1895, Mr F. H. Stokes, a Native, was appointed Honorary Secretary of the Provisional Committee. At this same meeting it was decided to ask Sir J. H. Symon Q.C. to accept the presidency of the League. The constitution listed the objects of the League in its role in the federal campaign:

(a) to secure, irrespective of class or political party, a general organisation of all who wish to advance Australian federation.
(b) to assist with energy all Parliamentary action designed or calculated to further the Federal cause.
(c) to urge all the colonies to favour in the future such measures of legislation and administration as will tend to lessen the difficulties in the way of commercial, political and social union of Australia.
(d) to advocate, and to promote practically, a Federal Union of Australia on such lines as may be constitutionally approved by the Colonies concerned, after further deliberation and report by assembled representatives of each, and
(e) to defend the union when established.[30]

The Australasian Federation League in South Australia successfully united such federalist groups as the Patriotic Association and the Chamber of Commerce, but failed to convince the colony's various labour organizations. Labour remained suspicious, and felt out of place in a League supporting a federal formula for which it had little enthusiasm. Labour criticism of parts of the Bill resulting from the 1897 Convention threatened to tie the hands of the League at a time when it most needed to be active to persuade the public to support federation in the referendum. So the Commonwealth League was formed, to overcome Labour opposition, and to unify the campaigning among those groups favouring the Bill.

The establishment of the Australasian Federation League in South Australia was an important contribution to the federal cause. The League facilitated co-operation between Native federalists and non-Native federalists such as J. H. Symon. The A.N.A. itself had a reputation for exclusivism; it was identified with the call of 'Australia for the Australians', and so could have divided the federal movement and hampered its progress. At this time, too, the A.N.A. was small, lacking momentum and importance, and so was unable to lead the campaign by itself. The League then took over the leadership of the federal movement, and played the part in the popular movement towards federation, which is usually accredited to the A.N.A. itself. In early 1897, before the Federal Convention elections, the League organized a large number of public meetings and sought to influence the delegates to that Convention.[31] But the public was generally apathetic and public meetings were rarely well attended. South Australian figures reveal that only 30.4 per cent of those eligible to vote took part in the 1897 Convention elections,[32] while 39.47 per cent of those eligible voted at the first referendum.[33] At the second referendum, there was less apathy, but more organized opposition. 61.59 per cent of eligible voters took part, but over 10,000 informal votes were cast,[34] partly the result of apathy and confusion arising from the simultaneous holding, with the federation referendum, of the general elections and another referendum. However, the Australasian Federation League had helped organize the federal effort, and had successfully challenged the 'Anti-Billites', the *Daily Herald*, organized labour, and the Single Tax Leagues.

The A.N.A. could claim credit for establishing the League, but by so doing it had superseded itself, and the federal movement passed out of Native hands, into the hands of the League, presided over by non-Native Sir Josiah H. Symon Q.C. Leading Natives, too, by-passed the A.N.A. to work through the League and its partner, the Commonwealth League. Attendance at A.N.A. functions dropped heavily, and in 1897–9 the A.N.A. almost died, at the very time when tradition has it acting to convince South Australians to accept the Bill.

A few convinced and active federalists used the existing organization of the A.N.A. to further their cause, as for example when A.N.A. members C. C. Kingston, F. W. Holder and J. W. Downer addressed appeals for assistance in the federal campaign to fellow members. However, the A.N.A. as such had almost ceased to exist, and was a mere shell of an organization: even A.N.A. 'general meetings' consisted only of a committee, with one or two other Natives adding to their number. The main contribution to federation had been made by other bodies, including the Australasian Federation League and the Commonwealth League, while the A.N.A. was often forgotten.

In 1900, after the battle for federation had been won, the A.N.A. witnessed a revival. This revival resulted partly from activities of the Natives themselves, and partly from a coincidence of favourable circumstances.

The Board and the Adelaide Branch of the Association embarked on an intensive publicity campaign in 1899 and 1900, printing and distributing circulars, inviting the press to attend Board meetings, establishing a multitude of personal and institutional contacts, and consciously cultivating war veterans, federation delegates, and surburban mayors and councillors. The A.N.A. was assisted in this campaign by the fact that several loyal Natives became mayors in 1899 and 1900, and so were well-placed to organize local meetings to win new members to the A.N.A. Even more significant, however, was the coincidence between A.N.A. office bearers and the medium which could make or break the A.N.A. in the eyes of the public—the press. William Sowden, perhaps the most consistently dedicated Native in South Australia, was part proprietor and editor of the *Register* from 1899 on. He was a member of the Board in 1900, and President of the A.N.A. from 1901 to 1905. The *Register*'s editorial on 21 March 1900 expresses Sowden's view that 'National unity was brought within the realm of practical politics by this body of ardent and intelligent young patriots [the A.N.A.] . . . making the question essentially one for the people, and thus bringing to earth the federation which had been so long in the air'.

Another coincidence occurred in the person of J. Lavington Bonython, who worked closely with his father in the management of the *Advertiser* from the late 1890s onward. During this time, he was an Adelaide Branch committee member, was Vice-President of that Branch in 1900 and President in 1901, then in 1902 was elected to the Board of Directors. During this period, considerable and enthusiastic press coverage drew attention to the A.N.A. and reinforced its recently acquired image for nation-building.

But perhaps the most important reason for the A.N.A.'s revival was its ability to take advantage of the rising national and patriotic feeling. Two events at the end of the century stimulated this feeling: South Australia's involvement in the Boer War, and the achievement of federation.

'Our brothers in South Africa' made a great impression on the A.N.A., delighted by the opportunity to prove Australia's manhood, and to gain experience which would be of value in forming the new federal army. The A.N.A. joined the jingoism of the time without reservation, and won publicity through participating in send-offs, returns, patriotic funds, national memorial plans, and even a smoke social for members of the first contingent who had returned invalided from South Africa. But its biggest 'patriotic contribution' was the formation of two A.N.A. rifle companies, in February and March 1900. The Natives' application for a third corps was refused, since the size of the South Australian defence forces had reached its limit.

In South Australia, the A.N.A.'s role with regard to federation was again reversed. Far from strengthening the federal movement, the A.N.A. was itself strengthened by that movement. The excitement, patriotism and 'Australian' thinking made the public more receptive to A.N.A. advances, especially when it was remembered that the A.N.A. had first initiated the 'popular' non-parliamentary participation in federation, and had defined the federal form which had now become a reality. The A.N.A. was now identified in the public mind with federation, an identification strengthened by the fact that a number of important federalists were also Natives, and by the application to South Australia of generalizations referring to the A.N.A.'s leading part in the federal movement of the eastern colonies. This identification was underlined at the A.N.A. annual banquet in March 1901, attended by some of South Australia's 'most eloquent and representative men'. The banquet was the public recognition of the A.N.A. myth as nation-maker and people-inspirer, and at it Symon handed back to the A.N.A. the trusts committed to the Australasian Federation League, leaving the A.N.A. unchallenged claimant of the title of 'nation-preserver', now that the nation had become a political reality. However, the driving force and purpose of the A.N.A., the twin aims of nationality and union, had been achieved, and now it remained to be seen whether the Natives could find a new role, and so ensure their continued existence in the twentieth century.

5

ECONOMIC INFLUENCES ON THE 1898
SOUTH AUSTRALIAN FEDERATION
REFERENDUM

R. Norris

In June 1898 referenda on the Commonwealth Bill, which had emerged from the Melbourne Convention, were held in New South Wales, Victoria, Tasmania and South Australia. Although the general histories tell us that the colonies federated for reasons such as the desire to control immigration and properly organize defence, little detailed research appears to have been done to explain what motivated voters when the issue of federation was put to the popular test: the pioneer articles by Professor R. S. Parker and Geoffrey Blainey[1] were by nature exploratory and sought more to stimulate questions than to supply answers.

It is of course very difficult to determine what influences voters. For example, had skilled opinion pollsters conducted exhaustive surveys in 1898, then even under these most favourable conditions it would not be possible to prove conclusively the real motivation. Rather, reasoned conjectures, based on the issues the campaigners stressed or neglected, contemporary opinions on the merits of federation, and on analysis of the interests involved and the voting returns, are all that can be made.

Clearly a detailed study of the twenty-seven South Australian electorates is beyond the scope of an article. Instead, several electorates and areas will be considered here so that the influence of the campaign appeals and of other factors may be observed more closely. The credibility of appeals would seem to depend mainly on the soundness of their factual bases. However, as conflicting appeals were made on the same issues, and as no one really knew what would happen after federation, then credibility would depend partly on who was saying what to whom. Hence, it is necessary not only to show what electors were made aware of and concerned about, but also to consider the political, social, and economic make-up of the campaigners and their audiences.

For the Bill

The most active and influential campaigners were South Australia's Convention delegates, the colony's leading parliamentarians, lawyers and businessmen. Powerful support was provided by a number of organizations co-ordinated by the Commonwealth Bill League, and by the large majority of newspapers.

One of the more persistent themes used by the delegates to persuade the apathetic and disarm opponents was that of the progressive character of the proposed Constitution. Thus the radical liberal, Charles Kingston, who acclaimed it 'the most democratic measure ever framed'[2] was joined by the diehard conservative, R. C. Baker, who exclaimed: 'never . . . has a more democratic Constitution been submitted for the approval of any people'.[3] Again, a variety of vague, brief, and rare references were made to the theory of federalism, common citizenship, defence, nationhood and destiny. However, topics such as these served essentially as background to the great appeals on which the campaign was founded. These concentrated on the immense financial and commercial benefits federation and intercolonial free trade would bring to the geographically central colony; and, conversely, on the perilous position that might follow if the small, sparsely populated South Australia should fail to federate and thereby become an isolated 'foreign' state, or should no union occur at all and New South Wales go protectionist.

This 'business aspect' was frankly termed 'the most important to South Australia'.[4] As J. H. Gordon put it, the magnificent Spencer Gulf made Port Augusta the 'natural' port for large regions of New South Wales, Queensland and Western Australia. Riparian rights would be assured and 'cut-throat' railway rates, which caused Murray steamers to rot on 'our great River' and prevented Kingston from becoming the port for a 'big slice of Victoria', would be swept away. 'Above all', one-third of the 'enormous' rail revenue derived from the Barrier traffic was threatened by the very strong New South Wales party which favoured constructing a line, 'charging preferential rates and imposing an export duty on ores to prevent the trade coming down from Broken Hill'. Gordon exhorted his audience to look at the map, and they would realize that when trade got into the 'proper' course its revival would 'astonish the world'.

Fear of Lyne and the protectionists was also evident in the further claim that exports, especially primary produce to Broken Hill, would be retained or expanded. The delegates' manifesto declared that federation would open up 'unrestricted markets of nearly 4,000,000 customers instead of a restricted market dependent upon the goodwill or caprice of your neighbours'.[5]

Finally, the delegates reassured the colony that federation would replenish, not deplete, the public purse. Treasurer F. W. Holder, a member of the Convention Finance Committee, announced four 'dividends'[6] to offset the one new expense of £30,000—the colony's share of the cost of the new federal machinery. These were £10,000 of savings on redirected rail traffic, the return of River Trade Revenue, release from the 'burdens' of the Northern Territory, and £40,000 gained through the consolidation of loans. In this way an apparent deficit was converted into a potential asset.

Whilst the delegates attempted to broaden their appeals, the Leagues and newspapers paid little heed to peripheral issues and aimed their propaganda straight at the pocket. The Conservative Party's National League manifesto began: 'The advantages to be gained by South Australia as a producing country by inter-colonial free trade will be very great.'[7] The nature of the Commonwealth League's appeal is illustrated by their notice which was inserted in country papers. As may be seen, seven of the points, occupying about 80 per cent of the space—numbers 1, 2, 4, 5, 6, 9, 11—are directly economic, and two others, 3 and 10, are related. No mention is made of defence or immigration.

Adelaide's *Register*, the free trader champion of the landed interests, provided massive news and editorial support. Its tone is suggested by an early editorial that began: 'The oratorical fripperies ought to be as the mere trimmings are to the substantial dish. Federation has come down out of the air, and federal orators should descend from the clouds. The people are invited to make a business bargain.'[8]

The Commonwealth League

BENEFITS OF
FEDERATION.

1. To promote the prosperity of Australia in general and South Australia in particular. Without Federation South Australia never can become great or populous. She is now stationary and depressed.

2. To secure more abundant and permanent Employment to the Workers.

3. To give better opportunities to our children to make homes for themselves without sending them out of South Australia.

4. To give Cheaper food and Clothing.

5. To develope the Resources, Trade, and Manufactures of South Australia.

6. To encourage the expenditure of Capital to stock and develope our abandoned Pastoral Country.

7. To make yourself a Citizen of an Australian Nation—one flag and one people.

8. To create United Australia.

9. Our share of the expense of Federation cannot exceed £33,000; but against that we shall have extra Railway Revenue (£10,000 per annum) Savings—Agent Generals Office, reduction of cost of Local Parliament, Ministers, Government House, and others. Besides, there will be a direct gain of at least £40,000 per annum by Federalising the South Australian Debt. Federation will, therefore, cost South Australia nothing.

10. The terms now offered are specially favorable to South Australia. If we reject them we shall never again get terms so favorable to the smaller Colonies.

11. If the larger Colonies Federate without us, we shall be powerless against such a combination which may ruin our trade and manufactures and diminish our revenue, and we shall ultimately be forced to join them on almost any terms they choose to dictate:

———

Vote "YES" for the Commonwealth Bill on June 4th,
and
ADVANCE AUSTRALIA!

JOHN MOULE,
Secretary,
Adelaide, May 21st, 1898.

Advertisement from the *Orroroo Enterprise*, 27 May 1898
(By courtesy of the State Library of South Australia)

The twenty-two of the twenty-seven rural papers supporting the Bill also added little that was new, but gave the economic pleadings a distinct local flavour. In the upper north, 'when our people remember how Port Augusta has been robbed of the Queensland trade and the consequent decadence of this port, it will be a hard task indeed to convince them that we have no interest in the proposed union'.[9] Port Pirie and Petersburg owed 'their prosperity, almost their existence, to the Barrier trade'.[10] In the remote south-east where people 'have tasted the sweets of a free Border' any 'man or woman . . . who will vote against federation might just as well cut their own throats [*sic*]'.[11]

However, one new idea was propagated by the urban and rural press. Voters were urged to 'act on the advice of the men in whom they have reposed sufficient confidence to entrust the task of drawing up this deed'.[12]

Against the Bill

This campaign was conducted by the Labour organizations, a number of prominent non-Labour politicians and businessmen, the Free Trade Association and the Single Taxers, a co-ordinating body called the Anti-Commonwealth Bill League, and a very small minority of newspapers.

The appeals in defence of the *status quo* were essentially negative, seeking to refute the claims of the Billites: as Labourites supplied the bulk of organized opposition the campaign reflected their views. Thus it was said that the likely conservative Senate and the amendment procedures made the Constitution 'undemocratic' and 'cast-iron'. The High Court was denounced as 'superior to Parliament'[13] and an 'oppression to the people'. Labour preferred a unitary system with majority rule but the Bill was a 'mongrel—it was neither Federation nor unification'.[14]

However, these major themes were undermined by fellow campaigners and glaring inconsistencies. The Adelaide *Advertiser*, radical rag of the day, opposed the Bill but none the less regarded it as 'beyond all question . . . a great victory for democratic opinion.'[15] Again, despite fear of the Senate and preference for unitary government, Labour's future leader warned that federal legislation could be controlled by the more populous States and, with the Senate 'powerless to interfere', 'Home Rule' would be abrogated. On the other hand one Labour M.P. liked the Senate as it 'had no power' whilst the Hon. John Warren, the Longwood Conservative, abused it as a 'House of Review without power to act':[16] the latter held that property had no control over the revenue it had provided but 'the most debased of either sex will have the same power as managing Australia as the most worthy colonist.' Finally, the free traders deplored the Bill as 'it was not a federation bill; it was a unification measure'.[17]

Only the economic issues united the Anti-Billites for a concerted opposition. Hugh R. Dixson, Chairman of the Anti-Bill League, himself pointed out at the inaugural meeting that although the various parties present had diverse opinions, they all opposed the financial clauses.

Perhaps the most repeated counter-appeal, based on the calculations of Coghlan, the New South Wales statistician, was that the additional annual cost of the Federal government would be a 'step towards insolvency or additional taxation'.[18] In Labour's view extra taxation, especially the socially indirect customs, 'would tell heavily on the working classes';[19] to Warren property would pay the piper but not call the tune; to the Single Taxers all except land-taxes were invalid and these were precluded; and to the free traders all customs taxation was abhorrent.

A similar near consensus was held on the question of intercolonial free trade. This principle was so widely accepted that while it was firmly predicted that Adelaide's factories would be doomed without protection, the case was not so much that intercolonial free trade as such was undesirable but rather that the Bill would not in fact permit trade to find its natural outlets. First, to counter the strong appeals on the Barrier traffic, Labour's railway unionists and former employees devised a plausible argument: as the Bill outlawed preferential but allowed long-haulage development rates within State boundaries then if New South Wales constructed a line to Broken Hill 'S.A. would be in a position at present to compete with them by means of the preferential rates; but if anything of the kind took place under federation, that colony could take advantage of the development rates and so carry off the trade from S.A.'[20] Secondly, as to riparian rights, the colony was 'worse off than if the Convention had left the matter alone':[21] J. H. Symon's own Convention verdict was quoted—'Gentlemen, you have given us the rivers, but you have taken away the water.'[22]

In all, because of the prohibitive cost of federal government, the unsatisfactory rail and river provisions, and the threat to Adelaide's protected factories, the Anti-Billites prophesied higher taxation, State bankruptcy, depopulation to the eastern States, 'reduction in wages in most industries, and the overthrow of the local boot, furniture, rope, glass . . . and other manufactures.'[23]

Conclusions

Some interesting observations may be made on the campaign in South Australia. Few appeals, for instance, were made to federate for purposes of defence. Several papers feared cruiser raids on Newcastle and Darwin, where danger loomed largest; the *Northern Territory Times* worried lest 'a speculative freebooter might drop in here and rob us of every penny in or out of the banks'.[24] Kingston and Holder mentioned the topic once or twice, and P. McM. Glynn referred in early speeches to the 'young and militant' Japan. However, the fact is that by the campaign's end the subject was played down: Glynn who in April had written of 'the momentous issue of national defence'[25] failed to include it in his final appeal.

The explanation seems to be that defence served as an Achilles heel for the Anti-Billites to attack, partly with class prejudice against standing armies, but chiefly on grounds of expense. It was charged there would be 'no limits'[26] to expenditure on forces and also that 'we shall be compelled to take over the debt of thousands spent on the now obsolete defences of Victoria':[27] even one of the Bill's supporters warned that 'extravagance by the Federal Parliament in the matter of defence . . . seems to be the only danger which now presents itself.'[28] These were telling points as the colony's concern during the nineties was for economy in defence: expenditure had fallen from £52,169 in 1890 to £21,786 in 1898 and Kingston himself had attempted to reduce the estimate to £8,500 in 1895. Therefore, when defence proved vulnerable, it was considered prudent to deny its importance. Thus Holder said, 'it was not owing to any threatened danger that they were called to federate the colonies':[29] on the very eve of the referendum he criticized the Sydney estimate of £75,000 as it assumed present defences were inadequate. 'This,' he said, 'is very much open to argument, but it is clear that if more defence is required than we have now it is not the result of Federation.'[30]

Significantly, appeals on behalf of immigration control were conspicuously absent. There appear to have been but two, both by Kingston: one of which mentioned the impossibility of effective local legislation against coloured races and declared that the Federal government, acting for all Australia, would provide 'immigration restricted or prohibited as a white Australia requires'.[31] The few other references to immigration were extraordinary. Holder, in seeking to refute the argument that the Commonwealth would not relieve South Australia of the Northern Territory, told of a syndicate which was prepared to pay all the debt 'if it were given permission to bring in colored labor'.[32] Therefore, if the Commonwealth refused to take it over, 'they could easily bring them to their bearings by telling them that unless they did the offer of the syndicate would be accepted.' King O'Malley spoke in a similar vein.

These curious statements imply one of two things. Either Holder and O'Malley seriously believed a federated South Australia would still be able to admit Asiatics—which suggests that federation was seen to have little to do with immigration control; or, their arguments were sheer political expediency to counter the cost factor—which shows that immigration was less important than the £70,000 p.a. the colony hoped to save. In either event it says little for the mass appeal of immigration control as such in South Australia at the time of the referendum.

Two illustrations confirm that a White Australia and the campaign on the Bill were not generally related. First, the Northern Territory had about three-quarters of all Chinese in the electorates: it was, in April 1898, concerned about their competition in trade, industry, pearling and mining. But the *Times* made no appeal to federate to control immigration. Secondly, two weeks before the referendum the first case of leprosy was detected in Adelaide: the 'leper',[33] a Chinese hawker, aroused anti-Asian sentiments. Yet not one paper, delegate, or League related the incident to the Bill.

In contrast to defence and immigration much was made of the Constitution's democratic character. It seems most unlikely, however, that this issue would have had much impact, partly because the Kingston Ministry had made South Australia into the most progressive colony—as Gordon admitted, 'the colony had little to gain in the matter of political freedom',[34] and partly because the campaign both for and against the Bill cut completely across current political allegiances.

On the one hand the Liberal delegates were the bitter political rivals of their Conservative counterparts, and on other issues were deadly foes. Kingston, for example, was attempting to storm the Legislative Council, the Conservative stronghold of which Baker was President. His attempted duel with Baker in 1892 was common knowledge, and Symon's public correspondence with Kingston 'would have justified half a dozen duels'.[35] Sir John Downer and V. L. Solomon led the Assembly Opposition. The joint advocacy of such men for the Bill as a democratic advance did not inspire confidence: as one cartoon suggested they were 'Strange Bedfellows'.

On the other hand, the young Labour Party, the government's staunch ally, opposed the Bill and so too did a number of Independent ministry supporters and Liberals, who deserted their leaders. An extreme case was T. H. Brooker, Liberal member for West Torrens, who was appointed government Whip in April. Conservatives, who generally dissociated themselves from their adversaries in the Anti-Bill League, were also present. Further, Labour's inconsistent stance on political and constitutional grounds was undercut by the *Advertiser*.

Paradoxically, however, the very hostility between the delegates strengthened their claims to be acting for the welfare and survival of the colony: they were 'diametrically opposed to each other some being democrats and some conservatives, and yet they all recommended the adoption of this Bill.'[36] Premiers and Treasurers, past and present, backed by leaders in commerce and industry, pleaded that federation and the introduction of internal free trade (promised by Kingston as the Federal Parliament's first duty) would guarantee the colony's revenue and trade. Their opponents, spearheaded by an unprecedented alliance of Labourites and certain factory owners, were clearly united only on economic issues. They pleaded that federation would be to the financial and commercial detriment of the colony and would ensure the extinction of certain factories.

Undoubtedly, therefore, the issues of finance and free trade not only dominated the campaign, but they also provided the degree of unanimity within the protagonists necessary for coherent and credible appeals. Is it possible, however, and this is the crucial test, to relate the implied economic motivation to the actual voting response?

SOME CASE STUDIES

The Dissenting Electorates

Only West Adelaide, Kingston's own constituency, and West Torrens rejected the Bill. There are two important reasons for believing that these districts were particularly susceptible to the economic forebodings of the Anti-Billites. First, of the colony's electorates West Adelaide had the second highest percentage—29 per cent—and West Torrens the highest—35 per cent—of employed residents engaged in manufacturing.[37] Secondly, they were the twin centres of what the 1891 Royal Commission on Intercolonial Free Trade termed important 'features of dissent' (boot and shoe, tannery, tobacco, furniture, coachbuilding and tinware)[38] to its call for free trade.

Three of these protected manufactures were based in West Adelaide. Dixson, the Anti-Billite Chairman, operated the largest tobacco factory there. Malcolm Reid, probably the major furniture manufacturer, was most notable of the twenty-two proprietors listed by Directories as being in the electorate; this was the highest number for any electorate, and almost one-third of the colony's total.[39] Nineteen of the sixty-five coachbuilding and trimming works, more than double the number in any other electorate, were situated in the district.[40]

The two closely related industries of tanning and boot manufacturing were based in the townships of West Torrens. Alexander Dowie's tannery and boot factory, the colony's largest, was amongst the concentration here of thirty-one of the colony's thirty-three tanneries and fellmongeries.[41] The voting returns were Hindmarsh 594 Yes to 1,145 No, Thebarton 203 to 463, and York 82 to 197. These were the major places of opposition, and the Hindmarsh return was the highest negative vote recorded at any polling booth in the colony.

Further, not only were the dissenting industries firmly sited in the dissenting electorates, but there is abundant evidence to show that owners, workers, and union representatives were actively opposed to federation. Dixson threatened at the Chamber of Manufactures and in letters to newspapers to close his factory if the Bill was passed, and it was alleged that he had given his men notice to take effect in that event: at the Tobacco Twisters' Union meeting, which declared against federation, one member held the measure would 'ruin the tobacco industry in South Australia'.[42] Reid also threatened to discharge fifty-odd carpenters 'as our colony cannot compete with Victoria'.[43] Finally, although James Duncan, Chairman of the Commonwealth League, was joined by another West Adelaide coachbuilder in calling for free trade, there is little doubt which of the two sides workers would believe on the subject of wages; Labour's W. H. Robinson, M.L.C., a prominent Anti-Billite who helped draft their manifesto, was a coachtrimmer by trade and a delegate of the Coachmakers' Society.

A similar situation existed in West Torrens. Dowie reiterated his 1891 opposition to free trade and forecast a 'disastrous effect on local manufactures';[44] the Operative Bootmakers' Union was unanimous that 'a considerable amount of work would be imported from the eastern colonies that is now made in the colony'.[45] The tanners' attitude was even more extreme because, far from desiring free trade, they wanted export duties placed on raw hides; the West Torrens Working Men's Association was to urge the government 'to take steps to keep the work of handling hides in the colony'.[46]

Moreover, the majority of these industries had well founded fears of free competition for, protection notwithstanding, they already had large adverse balances of trade with the eastern colonies. For example, South Australia in 1898 imported £19,031 of cigars and manufactured tobacco from New South Wales and Victoria against the grand total of £5 exported to *all* markets:[47] imports of furniture, doors and sashes from the two rivals totalled £11,039 compared with exports to *all* colonies of

£5,955:[48] combined imports of boots and shoes were £23,310 against £8,281 exports to *all* colonial markets.[49]

In addition to these 'features of dissent', West Adelaide and West Torrens were closely involved in a second major debate: the question of railways and federation. Apart from the issue of rail traffic, another, more localized, focused attention on the Islington railway workshops in West Torrens. This was the predicted effect of free trade on the workshops following the government's decision in March to begin there the State manufacture of locomotives. The good news—the shops were on reduced time —immediately provoked strong anti-federal feeling. Tom Price, a Labour M.P., spoke of those who wanted Islington to remain a patching shop, and to force manufactures out of the colony as 'the clique [who] howled for free trade, and damned everything else.'[50]

Once more the Anti-Billites were well placed to command respect. H. Adams, Labour M.L.C. for the districts, and E. L. Batchelor, joint secretaries of the Anti-Billite League, were officials of the Railway Service Mutual Association, Adams as a founder council member in 1887, and Batchelor as President for many years. The latter, who in 1893 had relegated the mighty Kingston to the junior position in West Adelaide, and kept him there, was also between 1889 and 1890 four times President of the Amalgamated Engineers. Price and Batchelor were former Islington employees.

It is not possible to determine the electoral distribution of the 220 tobacco workers, 325 cabinet-makers, 342 coachbuilders, 287 tanners, 949 bootmakers, and 643 railway mechanics in Locomotive Construction and Maintenance Departments, listed in the *Statistical Register*. However, it seems reasonable to assume that the dissenting electorates had a very high proportion. First, along with the highest percentage of residents engaged in manufacturing there was the heavy siting—in some the near total—in these districts of the 'features of dissent'. Secondly, the two electorates had, except for the major seaport areas, the highest proportions of population occupied in transport, and both had long and close connection with railways. West Adelaide possessed the province's main station and offices, goods yards and sheds, carters and carriers. The workshops had been situated at Bowden until

1869 and West Adelaide until 1883, when the Islington works were erected.

Furthermore, apart from the men (and their dependents)[51] directly involved with the threatened industries, it seems unlikely that other electors could fail to be influenced by the fears of redundancy, depopulation and lower wages. West Adelaide's local traders and shopkeepers, for instance, could hardly have been pleased with Dixson's declared intention to close up and sack.

So too with West Torrens. There the repercussions of unemployment in the tanneries in March, because of the export of raw hides to New South Wales, must have been widely felt already. It was reported that 'Hindmarsh is now unusually slack and men are out of employment . . . Large tanneries may have to reduce hands, small ones close',[52] and reference was made to the fellmongeries which had been recently decimated by sheepskin exports. Indeed the local town councils opposed the Bill. One Hindmarsh councillor (a tanner) declared: 'federation would crush a large number of manufactures at Hindmarsh and elsewhere':[53] the Council unanimously approved the stand of Councillor Hourigan (Labour M.P. and founder President of the Tanners' Union) against the Municipal Association's resolution in support of the Bill. The Mayor of Thebarton explained that as the ratepayers believed they would not derive any benefit from the Bill, and were therefore 'dead against it'[54] he had opposed the resolution: the Council endorsed his action.

In pressing the view that the vote in these electorates reflected a regional economic interest, it is necessary to counter an alternative explanation: that it was primarily a working-class response to a campaign in which working-class leaders were prominent. Had this been the case, other working-class areas might also have been expected to defeat the Bill outright, and handsomely. But Port Adelaide, the only electorate with two Labour members, narrowly approved it and Port Pirie voted 711 to 344. It is interesting to note that as the first and second seaports of the colony, and with industries such as flour manufacturing and smelting, they were, unlike the dissenters, highly susceptible to the heavy Billite propaganda on the benefits of free trade.

Undoubtedly the best illustration of the secondary importance of this factor is provided by Wallaroo, probably the strongest working-class electorate. The mining and smelting company employed 1,067 men at its Wallaroo works and 759 at the Moonta copper mines. The Bill was opposed by the district's two sitting members and by the Amalgamated Miners' Association, whose President, John Verran, said that the Bill 'was not going to benefit the laboring classes in any way: on the other hand Federation . . . would be a decided blow to labor and labor representation.'[55] But all three mining towns approved the Bill; Wallaroo voted 207 to 77, Moonta 482 to 298, and Kadina 302 to 67.

Now clearly these returns ran counter to political and class sentiments. They did not, however, oppose economic self-interest, as Verran's appeal was immediately undermined by the company's decision to borrow £100,000 in order to extend their Wallaroo works to smelt Barrier concentrates and to construct a sulphuric acid plant. Baker, a director of the company, and with, as he put it, 'comparatively to my means a large stake in this company',[56] campaigned hard in the area. He pointed to his personal interest and to the employment the new works would provide, conditional on the supply of ores being guaranteed by federation. Holder also pressed this issue which 'could not be done without intercolonial free trade'.[57] The *Plain Dealer* asked whether 'any localite' could 'afford to vote against the Bill,'[58] and later explained that the miners had seen through the 'game of the knaves who sent round that Federation meant a reduction in wages.' Indeed one can almost sense the miners saying to themselves that in Baker there was at least one delegate who was prepared to put his money where his mouth was.

This is not to deny the influence of class sentiments. On the contrary they would make the appeals of their leaders more credible. But where class and regional interests clashed, the latter triumphed. In short, West Adelaide and West Torrens were for good reason fearful of intercolonial free trade and it seems fair to conclude that they voted No primarily on the grounds of economic interest.

The Wine Industry

We have noted how electorates rejecting federation possessed industries most vocal against free trade. It is useful to ask now, by way of contrast, whether regions dependent on industry which called for free trade were abnormally pro-federal.

Winemaking was one such industry, anxiously seeking free colonial markets for its increased production: in 1891, 12,314 acres were under vine and 801,835 gallons of wine were produced; by 1898, 18,761 acres produced 1,283,094 gallons. The great question was: 'What shall we do with our Mataros?'[59]

Care was of course taken to ensure that the producers were well aware of the advantages of free trade. For example, the leading winemaker, Thomas Hardy, who had told Dixson that the wine industry's 'enormous expansion' would make up for 'all their tobacco factories',[60] was an active campaigner. At the Vintage Sports in McLaren Vale he appealed for a vote of Yes as federation would extend markets and benefit the district. Asking his manager 'what is to become of all these boys and girls?' he observed how 'dreams of federation . . . come as a consolation'.[61]

Hardy's influence would have been particularly strong in McLaren Vale where the disused hotel was converted into a home for employees, the deserted flour mill into the Mill Cellars, and where he produced the bulk of his wine. However, it would not have been limited to the growers because, as a delegation from the Chamber of Manufactures observed, the 'astonishing' advance in winegrowing brought benefits not only to the producer, 'but also to the business parts of the townships'.[62] Nor would his influence have been confined to this one area. Hardy had toured extensively with Symon for nearly a decade extolling the virtues of free trade: as a past President of both the Vignerons' and the Winegrowers' Associations his views must have commanded respect in all the wine areas.

What were these areas and how did they vote? There were the Barossa Valley, founded by Seppelt, the 'South' rehabilitated by Hardy, and the Clare-Auburn area. Between them the three districts had two-thirds of the acreage under vine in the colony. The Barossa, the major grower, cast 1,053 Yes and 98 No votes; that is 91.5 per cent favoured the Bill. The South, the second area, registered 82.4 per cent support, and Clare-Auburn, the third, 84.4 per cent. Seppelt's Tanunda voted 226 to 14, Hardy's McLaren Vale 132 to 14, and overall 2,503 out of 2,889 formal votes endorsed the measure. Thus in the wine

areas an average of 86.6 per cent approved federation compared
with 67.4 per cent for the colony as a whole and 75.2 per cent
for the rural electorates.

In sum, federation and free trade were synonymous: it was,
as the circular of the Winegrowers' Association put it, 'the duty
of every member'[63] to vote for federation. The wine regions were
indeed abnormally pro-federal.

The Adelaide Hills

Although the Billites proclaimed that no producers stood to
gain more than South Australians, they did concede occasionally
that some farmers might be adversely affected. The few unfor-
tunates (orchardists, potato growers and dairymen) were con-
gregated in the gardens and farms of the Adelaide Hills. It
seems no coincidence that the Hills electorates of Onkaparinga
and Mount Barker, which voted only 60.6 per cent and 62.3
per cent in support, were the least enthusiastic rural supporters
of federation.

It is not surprising that potato and dairy interests should have
been hesitant about free trade; in 1891 they had expressed mis-
givings and in 1898 both had had large adverse trade balances
and suffered from intercolonial competition. However, as Hills
orchardists had staunchly supported free trade in 1891, an explanation of the changed circumstances is required. What happened was that their important Barrier market for apples and
pears had actually been lost to them in March 1898, when New
South Wales enforced regulations prohibiting the entry of fruit
infected by codlin moth. Hills growers and shippers were
reported to be 'up in arms' and delegations tried unsuccessfully
to get the regulations modified; later the home government was
petitioned to alter their own provisions to permit the sale of
infested fruit on the local market. Hence, federation, which
until three months before the referendum had promised to
guarantee continued access to Broken Hill as a dumping ground
for diseased fruit, had abruptly lost its appeal. Yet, at the same
time, whilst it was acknowledged that federation could do nothing to remedy the situation, the Bill allowed free entry of rival
colonial produce. Thus it had become a positive threat to the
Hills orchardists, who, ever conscious of such imports, were
of necessity turning their attention to the home market.

The National League became so alarmed by agitation against the Bill that a special meeting of the various Hills branches was convened at Uraidla to dispel the 'false impressions' circulating about the effects of federation. Baker, the League's founder, admitted that under certain conditions imports from Victoria and Tasmania lowered the value of Hills produce. But, as on average a favourable trade balance existed, if colonial markets were lost and the local producers had sole control of the local markets 'they would still not be the losers'.[64]

However, several factors militated against Baker's special pleading. First, he ignored the fact that the Hills orchard fruit, devastated by the codlin moth, could no longer be exported. Secondly, he based his averages on the outdated figures of 1894–5–6; but by 1898 fresh fruit imports *exceeded* exports. Thirdly, he neglected to mention potato and dairy interests which were being seriously menaced by imports. Finally, by far his best example, hay and chaff, was singularly inapplicable to the Hills; little was produced there and not one District Council in the two electorates appeared in the first thirty-four for the colony.

By direct contrast, in terms of orchard acreage, four of the colony's first six District Councils—East Torrens, Onkaparinga, Stirling, Crafers—were in the Hills, and the first two headed the colony.[65] Again, three of the top eight potato districts—Crafers, Kondoparinga, Onaunga—were in the electorates. Mount Barker and Onkaparinga District Councils, encircled by rich dairy land abounding in milch cows, were the two leading producers of butter and cheese.

In all, six areas rejected the Bill. Certainly the best illustration of the connection between economic interests and opposition to federation was in the Crafers-Stirling region which straddled the two electorates. Crafers, despite its mere thirteen-square miles area, still managed to be amongst the leading districts for orchards and potatoes. So too did the slightly larger Stirling. The voting at townships in this region was Stirling East 100 to 99, Uraidla 61 to 105, Stirling West 75 to 92, Mylor 23 to 35.

Nor can this relatively rare rural opposition be explained by political or class influence. In 1896 Onkaparinga returned two candidates of the conservative National League, which had strong branches throughout the Hills. The senior member, W. H. Duncan (incidentally, like Baker, a director of the Wallaroo and

Moonta Mining Company) had topped the poll at Stirling West and Uraidla, which voted No. In Mount Barker the delegate Dr J. A. Cockburn was the senior member; but Stirling East and Mylor where he led the poll were centres of opposition. At Woodchester, which rejected the Bill 22 to 52, the League's President, B. A. Moulden, secured the most votes.

Rather, orchardists obviously believed that 'the people ought to be satisfied to eat home-grown food'[66] even if much of it was diseased. Potato farmers did not see eye to eye with Baker, for as a commercial note put it 'the business doing in potatoes is not brisk on account of the decreased demand caused by the influx of Tasmanians into Adelaide'.[67] Many dairymen doubtless agreed with 'Producer' who emphatically declared: 'no one interested in the dairy industry should support Federation, as he has something to lose and nothing to gain.'[68]

The Wheatlands

If the lukewarm response of Hills electorates may be attributed to a unique set of circumstances which threatened specific primary producers there, *protection*, not free trade, was overwhelmingly regarded in the countryside at large as the block to prosperity. This common belief in part answers one major point made by Geoffrey Blainey, who noted the very strong support in electorates such as Yorke Peninsula in the northern wheatlands. Blainey argued that as South Australian markets for wheat had been lost through growing self sufficiency in the other colonies, 'The wheat industry could, and did, gain little from the removal of colonial tariffs. Here is 40 per cent of the colony's federal vote awaiting a sound explanation in terms of economic interest.'[69] Now the question of what actually happened to wheat exports after federation is not relevant. What is relevant, is what was thought likely to happen at the time of the referendum.

It had long been anticipated that with a return to free trade 'South Australia would be the granary and vineyard of Australia, but eventually the manufactures would gravitate towards the coal mines'[70] of the eastern colonies. The *Register* considered the colony 'essentially adapted for the production of grain'.[71] The Arden Vale and Wyaca Farmers' Club (near Quorn) carried a resolution favouring federation. The *Port Augusta Dispatch* bluntly asserted: 'the fact is that this province is a producing and not a manufacturing community'.[72] Even Labour campaigners predicted that 'South Australia without doubt would occupy premier place with respect to wheat, vine, fruit, and such like products'.[73] Dixson, the only Anti-Billite persistently to challenge these convictions could not raise the bogy of intercolonial imports as wheat was already on the free list. In any event, he had been thoroughly discredited in the country because of his blatant self-interest in protection.

Moreover, though little wheat was exported in 1898 to any market, colonial or overseas, flour was third in the export of South Australian produce. It was the highest of all to colonial markets, and totalled £201,583 in that year;[74] New South Wales was the main customer. One leading miller blamed the tariff war with Queensland—formerly 'one of our best markets for bread-stuffs'— for causing mills to be established there. Sixteen millers, the second largest group in the area, signed the manufacturers' letter to the Commonwealth League in support of free trade.

Again, 'wheatlands' was something of a misnomer as other primary industries, especially pastoral, were well represented in these electorates. Pastoralists, along with agriculturists, had been even more in favour of free trade in 1891 than the mercantile classes; Warren was commonly regarded as a black sheep. The largest hay districts were also north of Adelaide, and sizeable and expanding exports of hay and chaff went to New South Wales: one merchant addressed a notice in the *Register* to the 'Hay-growers of South Australia . . . Federation will remove the restrictions under which you now suffer and give you Larger Markets and Better Prices.'[75] The salt industry in Yorke Peninsula eagerly awaited the abolition of tariffs and the *Port Augusta Dispatch* reported that people there claimed that 'under the present Bill they can export £100,000 worth of salt annually'.[76] Augusta itself, together with other northern towns such as Petersburgh and the Burra, looked to their total rehabilitation and more. The Barossa winegrowers were near-intoxicated with free trade.

Further, the upper and lower north was heavily canvassed by the delegates, three of whom—Holder, Downer, Howe—represented districts there. On their platforms sat most of the northern politicians, themselves farmers, graziers, millers; past and present Ministers of Agriculture were among their number. They eulogized the delegates, endorsed their views, proposed votes of thanks, and called for three cheers. Several, such as the members for Yorke Peninsula, campaigned independently.

In short, it was an ingrained article of faith that the colony was destined to regain her position as the granary and garden of the continent: wheat, flour, and other industries in the northern electorates had good economic *motives* for federating, motives which were made all the more credible by virtue of the wholehearted advocacy of the country papers, the rural-based Leagues, and the countryside's own delegates and politicians.

The South-east

At the colony's opposite extremity in the south-east, where people had 'tasted the sweets of a free Border', the referendum result was considered a foregone conclusion. Even Dixson admitted he was on difficult ground there. At Mount Gambier he said he knew he addressed 'an audience that was suffering constant annoyance and trouble from these Border duties; and if the South-Eastern people were [asked] they would say "Away with these duties".'[77]

The response did not disappoint the Billites. The electorate of Victoria voted 1,863 to 572 and the adjacent border regions of Albert 1,348 to 158; in all, 81.5 per cent favoured federation. One of the greatest majorities was recorded at Kingston, where issues of trade had been stressed in propaganda appeals. Its potential as a port was first reported in 1866 by James Cooke, formerly a Liverpool shipping employee and promoter of railways and Kingston's founder. Cooke's report was referred to by the local M.P., A. H. Peake, twenty years clerk of the Naracoorte District Council. The railways would tap the Wimmera and Kingston would become the 'Liverpool of Australia'. But 'hostile tariffs had starved it'.[78] Kingston voted 171 to 19, 95 per cent for the Bill.

It is noteworthy that the south-east's two comparatively hostile votes, recorded by Millicent (223 to 166) and near-by Tantanoola (46 to 36) can readily be explained as reflections of regional economic interests. Millicent-Tantanoola was a leading

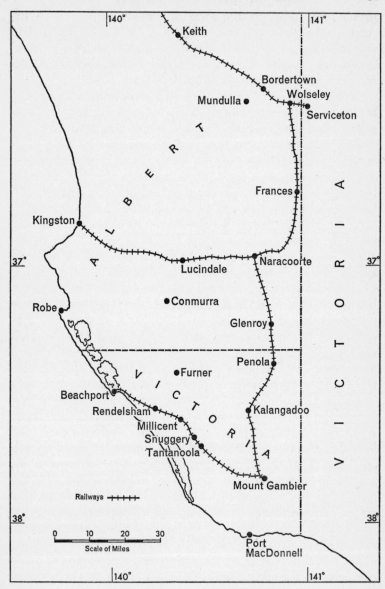

The south-east of South Australia

potato area, to which the same arguments applied as in the Adelaide Hills: 'Spuds and Federation', as Gordon termed it, was therefore a big issue in the Victoria electorate. By contrast, in adjoining south-eastern Albert, there was little potato production and the question did not arise.[79]

Again, towns like Naracoorte which were much closer to the border had felt restrictions such as the stock tax keenly. Some graziers had land in both colonies, and it was even suggested that the area be made federal territory, and thereby bring to an end the lengthy dispute over the actual demarcation of the boundary. Every witness at the 1891 Commission strongly advocated free trade, and one claimed that as a result of duties depopulation had occurred and 'half our trade has gone'.[80] By comparison, Millicent was divided on the question. The clerk of the District Council, unlike his counterpart Peake, supported the border duties, and a landowner-grazier, a free trader, said, 'I believe I am not backed up by the majority of the people in this district'.[81]

Divergent economic interests can also explain the difference between Millicent and Mount Gambier (vote 1,149 to 287) even though both had potato and stock industries in common. The stock tax, for instance, was seen in 1891 and 1898 to limit severely the price and quantity of fat cattle and sheep exported to Victoria. But Millicent could do little trade of this type for two related reasons. First, because of poor land her stock were 'stores' and therefore unfit for butchering; second, Millicent kept her sheep for wool, not meat. Mount Gambier, however, was a very large exporter of fat stock, grazed her sheep for meat, and looked to a nearer and freer Melbourne market. Special appeals on the stock tax would have had less impact in Millicent which was more dependent on vulnerable industries: besides, the grazier free trader, on his own evidence, had little influence. Rail figures confirm that potatoes and wool, as opposed to livestock, were relatively more important to the small Millicent region than to the large Mount Gambier. Thus, in 1897–8, Mount Gambier dispatched thirty-five times more cattle and sheep than the Millicent area; on the other hand the potato tonnage was only eleven times greater and the wool five times less.

Furthermore, whereas the commercial capital of the south-east aspired, like Naracoorte, to become the federal capital, one more

Millicent industry opposed free trade. In 1891 chicory farmers favoured the retention of protective tariffs as cheaper produce was grown in the large peat areas of Gippsland and the Dandenongs; without protection, one declared, he would 'have to go out of business at once'.[82] Some fifty men were employed at the time, and it was then described as a fast growing industry. Although no mention of this very local issue is recorded in the 1898 campaign, the farmers concerned still resided at Rendelsham and the protective tariff still remained on chicory.

To conclude, the south-east border region taken as a whole did what Dixson feared and said, 'Away with these duties'; as the *Naracoorte Herald* declared, federation without intercolonial free trade would be like 'Hamlet without the ghost'. The few discrepancies were but variations on the regional economic theme; Millicent which had *relatively* less to gain was *relatively* less in favour of federation.

The River Murray Trade

Finally, to complete these test cases, how did the Murray towns respond to the strong appeals to federate in order to recapture the river trade?

This question cannot be answered by simply treating every place on the river system as an actual or potential interstate trader. Blainey, for example, noted that Meningie (34 to 98), Victor Harbor (110 to 73), and Murray Bridge (116 to 94) recorded 'surprisingly' strong No votes and that overall twenty river towns voted only 1,173 to 511. Therefore, though he conceded Morgan (156 to 5) and Goolwa (218 to 30) sensed prosperity, he argued that if the towns 'believed they would recapture the river trade, they gave no confident indication of it in the 1898 poll.'[83]

But surely, in terms of *recapturing* the trade lost to the eastern colonies, only river towns which were, or perhaps could be, engaged in interstate trade need be counted. Meningie, on the remotest part of Lake Albert, had nothing whatever to do with this trade; instead the interests of the farmers there would be paramount. So too with the majority of settlements which were neither engaged in nor competing for interstate trade and therefore had no special reason to be enticed by this particular appeal.

The River men had sayings for such places and their inhabitants. The towns 'turned their backs on the river'; the settlers 'believe the river comes out of a hole half a mile above and disappears into a hole half a mile below'.[84] Evidence at the Inter-State Royal Commission on the Murray shows that in the 1890s the river towns which served as ports were those with *strategic positions and railheads* on the river. In order of importance they were: Morgan on the upper reaches; Goolwa at the mouth; and Murray Bridge in the centre.[85] Thus only the latter and Victor Harbor, the Encounter Bay seaport associated with Goolwa, were not strongly pro-federal.

There seems to be a twofold explanation for Murray Bridge's vote. First, not only was it a minor port to the others, but it was very much less concerned with interstate trade. Wool was the chief import from New South Wales and Victoria, but in 1898 Murray Bridge handled £213 worth to Morgan's £86,000 and Goolwa's £37,376.[86] The largest item at Murray Bridge was £17,266 of dried fruit. But no dried fruit was imported from the eastern colonies via the Murray.[87] Presumably then this was South Australian produce, and an 1893 report does in fact establish that it handled the greatest amount of local down river trade and more South Australian trade in both directions than the others combined.[88] The pattern of trade therefore was: interstate wool for overseas export to Morgan or Goolwa, and *intrastate* produce for Adelaide to Murray Bridge. Secondly, the town, laid out in 1883, was still basically a rail centre; it had for instance a branch of the Railway Service Association and it was a Labour stronghold to boot. Therefore the residents of the town proper would have been susceptible to the Anti-Billite case on railways and river.

Victor Harbor's below average support is perhaps more difficult to account for, but it should be realized that its undoubted decline was at least in part caused by factors which federation could not rectify: the navigation problems at the river mouth and the construction of the colony's own rail to Morgan in 1878. Moreover, even at its very peak in the late seventies Victor Harbor had few residents engaged in transport; in the whole district of Encounter Bay only nine persons were employed on waterways and railways compared with the 123 tenant farmers and labourers. By contrast Goolwa was the true river port; there some thirty-six were employed in water transport and trades and only seven in agriculture.[89] Again, at Victor Harbor in 1896, the Labour candidate achieved his one major triumph over King O'Malley: the position was reversed at Goolwa.

Finally, it is worth remembering that in the region west of the lower Murray the eastern slopes of the Lofty Ranges ran to the lakes and river. There, and on the eastern run of the lakes as well, mixed farming with emphasis on dairying was carried on. Victor Harbor had a butter factory, and the near-by district of Bremer, where Milang (vote 71 to 62) was situated, was the largest manufacturer of butter outside Adelaide. The Milang *Lakeside* factory also operated the Meningie *Lakeside* creamery. It is very possible that the general area fed milk and cream to Milang and Murray Bridge—itself in the Hills Onkaparinga electorate—for manufacture or railing to Adelaide.

Goolwa therefore was an exceptional town and its 87.9 per cent support contrasts with the electorate's 72.4 per cent: Morgan's 96.9 per cent too was considerably higher than the 82.9 per cent for the wheatland Light. Hence voting variations corresponded once more to economic interest, and the interstate traders Goolwa, the oldest, and Morgan, the busiest, responded magnificently to this particular appeal.

ALTERNATIVE INFLUENCES

The importance of economic factors must, of course, be weighed against the influence of others. An attempt has already been made to assess the relative impact of some possible alternatives such as political and class sentiments, and two old standards, defence and immigration have been considered. However, two fresh and interesting ideas were suggested by Blainey as alternatives or mitigating factors to the economic. These were an application of Turner's frontier thesis to the referendum, and the influence of the churches in the campaign.

Briefly, the first idea was that the migratory tendencies of Burra and Moonta miners and farmers 'would tend to make them indifferent to state rights and boundaries, and, mixing with "t'other siders", to become more Australian-minded'.[90] As it happens this particular aspect of the thesis is not really applicable to

South Australia as the migrants were *leaving* the colony for others where their votes would be registered. But it should be noted in passing that an abnormal indifference, rather than a special enthusiasm, for federation was evident on the fringes of civilization. By far the least densely populated electorates were the Northern Territory and Flinders. But a mere 22.1 per cent and 26.6 per cent of electors even bothered to vote. These were the lowest rates of all and well below the country average.

It is true that the Territory's voters polled Yes very strongly, but they had unique regional motives—'those many adjuncts to advancement which South Australia has denied her'[91]—to break away from the colony proper. Flinders, on the other hand, recorded third lowest of rural votes in support of the Bill.

Moreover, the next most thinly populated area was the electorate of Albert, excluding the established south-east border region. But the great Murray-Mallee area voted 208 to 249 and rejected federation: four of the six small Village Settlements, whose settlers really were pioneering, defeated the Bill.

It would seem more probable, therefore, that in South Australia the greater support in the rural areas in general reflected not the frontier influence or disdain for boundaries as such, but rather the conflict between protection for Adelaide's secondary industries and free trade for primary producers. The 'exotic' factories were to be sacrificed for the good of the country which would 'reap' the benefits.

As to Blainey's other suggestion, federation was referred to at the Anglican Synod, and the Council of Churches, despite some division of opinion about mentioning the subject from the pulpit, did issue advice 'to constitute May 29th a Federal Sunday'. In the event, however, a Protestant paper reported that 'as was anticipated, very few of the Churches took part in the Federal Sunday movement'.[92] Newspapers reported only six sermons in Adelaide and only four could be traced in the country. Nevertheless, though apparently very few sermons were delivered there is no doubt where the Protestant sympathies lay. The church dignitaries—the Presidents of the Wesleyan and Primitive Methodist Conferences, the Moderator of the Presbyterian Assembly and the Bishop of Adelaide—chorused their approval and officially blessed the Bill.

The Roman Catholic Church was less inhibited on the issue. The *Southern Cross* reported the Melbourne Convention, solicited advice from the Catholic Glynn on the progress there, and commended him for getting God mentioned in the Constitution's preamble. In the pre-referendum edition delegates were given space for their final appeals and the Archbishop of Adelaide was quoted as 'unreservedly in favour of federation'.

However, this very Protestant-Catholic unanimity makes it difficult to assess the influence of the churches. It is possible that their common front raised the margin of victory, but it could not account for the regional variations. But in fact it appears more probable that the churches had little effect, quite apart from the 'very few' sermons. For example, the sole cleric to preach against the Bill was the Anglican vicar of St Bede's in Semaphore. He apparently failed to convert many of his flock as Semaphore, which was about 45 per cent Anglican to the colony's overall 29.5 per cent, voted 496 to 205. The only other reported opposition was that of Labour's Tom Price, who spoke about federation at the Queenstown Primitive Methodist Church. Alberton, the nearest polling place, returned 136 to 43. These two votes were the very ones which prevented the Port Adelaide electorate from narrowly defeating the Bill.

Great significance may also be accorded to the lack of influence of the Catholic Church on the faithful. West Adelaide, though a small electorate, had the highest number and percentage of Catholics; it was 29.5 per cent Catholic to the average 14.4 per cent. Yet a bare 15.5 per cent of electors polled Yes and West Adelaide rejected federation. Furthermore, Labour's one Catholic parliamentarian, Hourigan, the Hindmarsh tanner and councillor, was a most dedicated opponent of the Bill.

The influence of the church would thus appear to have been very limited. In reality the Protestants seemed more concerned with their own affairs: the Wesleyans kept to their 'Young Peoples' Sunday', the various Methodists were preoccupied with union, and at the Synod the burning issue was not federation but the ethics of cremation. Despite unequivocal Catholic support, the colony's Little Rome voted No. Probably the major influence of religion in South Australia was indirect. Holder, the campaigner *par excellence*, whose role was acknowledged to have been decisive, was both Treasurer and Wesleyan lay preacher. As such he possessed a dual aura in matters economic. In his extensive tours of the northern 'wheatlands' he brought the Gospel of Federation at No Cost. He prophesied financial damnation for the depressed and sparsely populated colony should she fail to gain her Salvation by entering into the Kingdom of Australia. One paper rejoiced that 'his perorations were little sermons'.[93] The opposition lamented that 'Holder's statements are taken for the gospel truth because of his Christian profession'.[94]

CONCLUSIONS

Probably it was to be expected that in the depressed nineties economic appeals would dominate the South Australian campaign: economic considerations were evident even in the most peripheral issues. Baker, the political theorist, alluded to federalism in order to point to the *prosperity* of functioning federations: very little federal sentiment *per se* was apparent, and Baker declared that South Australians 'did not wish to be governed even concerning the matters which were to be handed over to the federation by a mob in Collingwood or Pyrmont'.[95]

Again, immigration and defence may well have been fundamental to the growth and sustenance of the federal movement but they assuredly did not win votes in the referendum. Immigration control was less important than saving revenue on the Northern Territory, and the Billites neglected to woo Labour though the prohibition of 'Asiatics and servile races' was on the party platform: nor did they seize upon the incident of the leper, who, moreover, was a resident of the city's Chinatown in West Adelaide. Perhaps the colony's much vaunted central position tended to make her more isolationist than others, like a mid-western State in America. But whatever the reason, discussion of defence scarcely rose above the piggy-bank level of the *Northern Territory Times*, the Anti-Billites (unlike their approach to free trade where they equivocated) attacked confidently, and the delegates, shrewd and able politicians, muffled the war drums. In reality the colony was more afraid of possible internal extravagance than of a potential external foe.

Further, even if the churches exerted a general influence, it would be difficult to determine which of their appeals proved persuasive. Although they related federation to Christian duty, the ties of blood, language and religion, peace on earth and the Divine Will, they were also concerned with more mundane aspects. The Methodist paper described fiscal barriers and preferential railway rates as 'a disgrace to our Christianity'. A Mount Gambier Presbyterian preached that border duties were calculated to promote 'peace and goodwill' and declared the Bill to be 'the outcome of the brightest brains of some of the best businessmen of Australia'.[96]

It has been argued too that the peculiar composition of the two groups of campaigners rendered their economic-centred appeals the most credible of all and that the response indeed produced an unmistakable correlation between economic interest and voting in the referendum. The support, opposition, and variations in the case studies were good illustrations of regional economic interests, for as Gordon said, 'the question of federation was largely considered from the standpoint of their pockets'.[97]

However, in one sense at least the colony was an economic entity, and the stress on the Barrier, the River trade, and the like was only in part directed to the places directly involved. Appeals of this nature had a wider application because of the enormous *revenues* the colony derived from the traffic: in 1898 the Barrier traffic brought in £394,784 and rail receipts, the largest single item, provided over one third of the colony's total revenue. Where no clear purely local threat was apparent, such appeals from the men of stature who had governed South Australia for many years must have carried great weight with the electors: the colony, Symon urged, must not become another bankrupt Newfoundland which stood out of the Canadian Dominion. Primary producers who sought government aid, and the taxpayers in general, who footed the bills, had a vested interest in the financial viability of the State.

This is not, of course, to exclude non-economic motives entirely: few but the religious bigot or doctrinaire Marxist would seek to impose a monocausal interpretation on history. None the less they were undoubtedly subordinate, and in South Australia federation was regarded as a business merger. The notice of the

Commonwealth League reads like a business prospectus. The delegates campaigned more like founders of the Australian Company than an Australian Commonwealth. In the final analysis acceptance or rejection of the Bill in 1898 seems to have depended less on White Nationhood or Christian Brotherhood than on the anticipated effects on the boot industry and the incidence of codlin moth. The love of federalism and class loyalties as such were less important than the price of potatoes and the prospects for wheat, flour and dairy produce. Truly, in the best traditions of Australia politics, these were bread and butter issues.

APPENDIX

1898 S.A. Referendum

City Electorates	Roll	Yes	No	Inf.	Total	% Voters to Roll	% Yes to Roll	% Yes to Formal Votes
East Adelaide	6,480	1,171	935	31	2,137	32·98	18·07	55·60
West Adelaide	5,013	777	818	17	1,612	32·16	15·50	48·71
North Adelaide	7,588	2,117	1,024	35	3,176	41·86	27·90	67·40
Port Adelaide	8,092	1,679	1,469	49	3,197	39·51	20·75	53·34
East Torrens	12,828	3,141	2,043	50	5,234	40·80	24·49	60·59
West Torrens	7,350	1,016	1,931	40	2,987	40·64	13·82	34·48
Sturt	9,986	2,641	1,443	38	4,122	41·28	26·45	64·67
Totals	57,337	12,542	9,663	260	22,465	39·2	21·9	56·5
Country								
Albert	3,663	1,556	407	21	1,984	54·16	42·48	79·27
Barossa	4,765	1,546	412	51	2,009	42·16	32·44	78·96
Burra	4,469	1,418	365	23	1,806	40·41	31·73	79·53
Encounter Bay	2,186	749	286	9	1,044	47·76	34·26	72·37
Flinders	3,959	699	330	22	1,051	26·55	17·66	67·93
Frome	6,300	1,597	482	36	2,115	33·57	25·35	76·82
Gladstone	5,869	1,461	686	39	2,186	37·25	24·89	68·05
Gumeracha	4,044	998	380	16	1,394	34·47	24·68	72·42
Light	4,767	1,633	337	32	2,002	42·00	34·26	82·89
Mount Barker	3,519	1,052	636	27	1,715	48·74	29·89	62·32
Newcastle	4,837	1,485	297	20	1,802	37·25	30·70	83·33
Noarlunga	2,668	864	249	10	1,123	42·09	32·38	77·63
Onkaparinga	3,786	917	596	13	1,526	40·31	24·22	60·61
Stanley	3,416	1,398	354	26	1,778	52·05	40·93	79·79
Victoria	5,149	1,863	572	41	2,476	48·09	36·18	76·51
Wallaroo	5,503	1,165	478	27	1,670	30·35	21·17	70·91
Wooroora	3,295	1,040	386	29	1,455	44·16	31·56	72·93
Yatala	3,060	723	246	10	979	31·99	23·63	74·61
Yorke Peninsula	3,021	935	150	—	1,085	35·92	30·95	86·18
Northern Terr.	774	159	8	4	171	22·09	20·54	95·21
Totals	79,050	23,258	7,657	456	31,331	39·7	29·4	75·2
Grand Totals	136,387	35,800	17,320	716	53,836	39·5	26·2	67·4

Source: Based on *South Australian Register,* 20 June 1898, p. 6.

6

ASPECTS OF CAMPAIGNS IN SOUTH-EASTERN NEW SOUTH WALES AT THE FEDERATION REFERENDA OF 1898 AND 1899

Patricia Hewett

This paper presents in part the results of an investigation stimulated by the Parker-Blainey discussion of regional economic and political interests in voting patterns at the federation referenda of 1898 and 1899. That discussion highlighted the complexity of pressures to which voters were subject and suggested the possible virtues of further study, at a 'grass-roots' level, of sample campaigns. Technical difficulties, such as the lack of data for booth by booth analyses and the impossibility of precisely identifying the active electorate, alone make firm correlations between the balance of interests and patterns of voting difficult—if not impossible—to achieve. But some approach to a realistic appreciation of the atmosphere in which the vote was taken may usefully be made by examining the tone of local campaigns in selected areas and the response to them, particularly as reflected in local newspapers.

For this purpose, a set of sample electorates in south-eastern New South Wales has been chosen. These electorates stretched along the south coast from Illawarra to the Victorian border, included the Victorian border electorates of Eden-Bombala and Monaro, and extended north-west as far as Boorowa. They have a special interest in that they may be divided into three distinct groups: (i) a block of six electorates to the south-west of Sydney (Boorowa, Yass, Queanbeyan, Braidwood, Goulburn, Argyle) which voted firmly against the Bill at both referenda; (ii) a block of three electorates on or close to the Victorian border (Bega, Eden-Bombala, Monaro) which voted strongly in favour both times; (iii) a block of five electorates along the south coast (Illawarra, Kiama, Shoalhaven, Bowral, Moruya) which swung from an unfavourable majority in 1898 to a favourable majority in 1899.

No newspaper reader in this region could have failed to recognize the prominence of the federal issue in the late 1890s for it was blazoned abroad in even the smallest and least politically-minded weeklies. In fact, so great was the spate of meetings, debates and newspaper reports in large country towns that many residents declared themselves utterly confused by the mass of contradictory arguments presented for their benefit. As one Bowral elector put it in 1898:

I'm willing to listen to almost anything now if it will only lighten the darkness a little. I have heard so much against each side, I've read so much argument for and against, that I have not the least notion which is right. One side is certainly wrong, but there is such an apparency of truth in both parties that I cannot detect the truth from the lies.[1]

In the following year, an equally puzzled journalist at Yass complained that:

As fast as some sensible friend of mine points out all the advantages of Federation under the amended William another reliable friend comes along and tells me the first friend was no end of a liar. And they both conclusively and definitely PROVE what they say.[2]

The cost of the proposed scheme of federation was a key question in all campaigns: local papers devoted more space to the discussion of the financial arrangements of the Bill than to any other federal matter, and presented electors with blatantly contradictory sets of financial propaganda. Anti-federal articles claimed that the operation of the 'Braddon blot' would increase taxation in New South Wales by at least 10s 6d per head while other colonies would find their burdens lightened by 14s 6d per head.[3] 'You and the people of New South Wales', ran a typical argument to the Braidwood electors in 1899, 'are really asked to vote that your colony shall be the Financial Milch Cow, not for your own colony, but to assist the other necessitous colonies who . . . CANNOT AFFORD TO FEDERATE WITHOUT YOUR MONEY.'[4] Such assertions were met from the federalist camp with flat

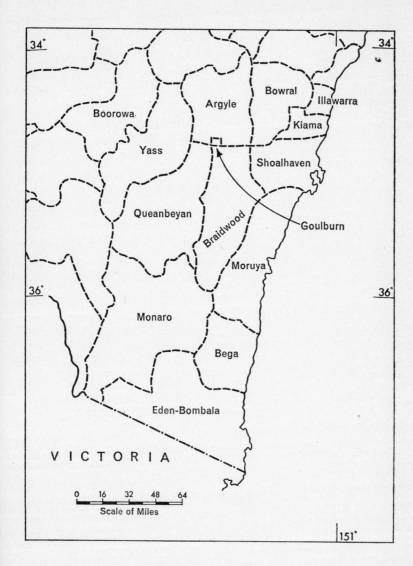

South-eastern N.S.W. electorates after the 1893 revision
(From a map compiled by A. W. Martin)

denials and the equally assured claims that federation would cost the taxpayer a mere 3s 6d (or thereabouts) extra per year.

Such obviously contradictory propaganda brought indignant protests—in letter and in verse—in local papers. The confusion and frustration reflected in such contributions are admirably summed up in the following lines from a poem entitled 'Federal Finance':

> Four loaves of bread and a bushel of wheat
> Divided by twopence and sixteen feet,
> Are equal to seventy pounds of steam,
> And that is the cost of the Federal scheme!
> On you add a sheep's head to a bucket of chaff,
> And you multiply both by a mile and a-half,
> And the square of the base will be equal to what
> We can learn of this awful financial rot![5]

Hopes for a new clarity were raised in 1898 by the appointment of a Federal Finance Committee, whose task it was to produce an official report on the cost of federation. An editorial of 13 May claimed:

As far as it is possible to gauge the position today, this colony has decided to await the report of the Federal finance trio who are at present engaged in an effort to extricate from the maze a true statement of what the finances of this colony will be under the Federal government. The report, and that financial pivot, will most likely turn the tide at the Federal ballot on the 3rd June, and until it sees the light of day thousands of votes will hang in the balance. The sooner it is forthcoming the better, and the more concise it is when it does appear the greater will be its value.[6]

But the Committee's report did not simplify matters. According to the anti-federalists it 'sounded the death-knell of the Bill, and placed it beyond the possibility of acceptance by the people of this colony',[7] while, according to the Billites, it was 'a triumph for the federal cause'.[8] The former claimed that it reported the federal scheme as inflicting on the people of New South Wales 22s 6d per head taxation for the support of the necessitous States,[9] and the latter that, according to its calculations, extra taxation would only amount to 3s 6d per person.[10]

Similar confusion was everywhere evident on the vital question of intercolonial free trade. The issue here was ostensibly straightforward enough: an agreement was advocated to allow trade from the border areas of New South Wales to flow freely to its natural outlets in Victoria, South Australia, or Queensland. But this issue was complicated by the cross-effects of others. It was blurred, for example, in the country electorates by jealousy and frequently expressed antagonism towards the 'Sydney tyranny'[11] which, in the words of the *Bega Free Press*, 'devours every town and village in the colony'.[12] According to the *Yass Courier*:

As for the bitter wail . . . that the interests of Sydney have been sacrificed by the Federal 'Convention' Delegates, it would not, even if there were stronger grounds for it, evoke sympathy in the *country districts* of New South Wales. Sydney has long forfeited any claim she may ever have had to the kindly regard of the provinces. Her 'rings' and 'cliques', commercial and financial, have long wielded an absolute predominance to the detriment of the 'country' interests. Any lowering of Sydney's position as archfactor in New South Wales politics will be hailed with rejoicing by country districts.[13]

Furthermore, it was generally recognized that the question of removing border duties was linked with that of modifying the system of differential railway rates which existed to foster Sydney's monopoly of New South Wales commerce. The anti-federal argument alleged that if New South Wales 'lost trade in the Riverina and on the northern borders, the first thing that would happen would be a retrenchment in the railway service'.[14] This, it was said, would undoubtedly be brought about by the Inter-State Railway Commission to be set up under the federal scheme, and would involve an increase in rates and a lowering of employees' wages. Pro-federalists attacked such claims with contradictory but equally firm statements. The Commission 'can neither increase our rates nor lower the wages of our employees', said one newspaper.[15] 'Federation . . . means lower rates and fares', said another,[16] while, according to a third, unless the present 'cut-throat competition which is carried out by differential rates is stopped, the next cut must be into the wages of our railway employees in New South Wales.'[17]

Parliamentary members were apparently of little use in guiding their electorates through the maze of confusing arguments. In May 1899, the *South Coast Herald* scornfully remarked: 'The political fence is lined thickly just now with long-faced undecided politicians. There they sit, like so many meditative crows, now looking east, now west, giving tentative hops along the rail, as though preparing to get down, but settling back again into the long-faced undecided mood.'[18]

Such caution seems to have borne little fruit, for the members representing at least five of the six consistently anti-federal electorates in south-eastern New South Wales supported the Bill in 1899, two of them having done so during the first referendum campaign. Likewise, two of the three strongly pro-federal border electorates were represented by Anti-Billite parliamentarians in 1898 (although both these men changed to support of the Constitution the following year).

Indeed, in some instances political influences served merely to add to the confusion. There was, for instance, no simple way of relating the conventional free trade-protection division to federation. There can be no doubt about the bewilderment caused by Premier George Reid's 'Yes-No' policy, summed up in his piously expressed hope that 'Heaven would forgive him for his sin in voting for the Convention Bill.'[19] That Reid, one of the chief engineers of the federal plan, should adopt such an attitude was pleasing neither to fervent Billites nor anti-federalists, though the latter joyfully hailed it as evidence of the Constitution's doubtful qualities. To the average elector it must have seemed incomprehensible:

The attitude taken up by Mr. Reid [ran a typical newspaper article] is so remarkably enigmatical, as to prove to both supporters and opponents a conundrum of the first order . . . No speech has yet been delivered by the enemies to Federation . . . in which the measure has been . . . so completely torn to 'rags and tatters' . . . By what process of logic Mr. Reid can after those speeches reconcile himself to give a vote in its favour is a mystery.[20]

Nor was Reid's the only confusing political influence. The Labor Party, officially opposed to the Federal Constitution, appears to have been far from unanimous in its opposition. Despite its official part in the anti-federal campaign, some of its members openly supported and addressed Billite meetings. The division of opinion in the party was sufficiently sharp to prompt the claim in one editorial that 'Whatever else the present Federal controversy succeeds in doing, it will ensure one of two things—

a split in the ranks of the New South Wales Labour Party, or its total extinction.'[21]

Confusion, then, would seem to have been an undoubted characteristic of the referenda campaigns as viewed by the electorate. Pro and anti-federal propagandists alike presented a maze of argument on practically every main provision of the Bill, thus producing a sufficiently broad range of conviction to accommodate every conceivable practical or idealistic interest in New South Wales. To find a rational way through conflicting sets of arguments was extremely difficult for the ordinary voter. Furthermore, as we have seen, political leadership sometimes proved an additional hindrance to the clear and objective presentation of a case to electors. Perhaps the previously quoted words of the Bowral elector of 1898 can now be seen to be scarcely surprising: 'I have heard so much against each side, I've read so much argument for and against, that I have not the least notion which is right . . . there is such an apparency of truth in both parties that I cannot detect the truth from the lies.'

It is reasonably certain however, that for many members of the electorate rational analysis of the federal scheme before them was overridden by a burning spirit of patriotism. Nationalistic sentiment inspired the composition of a spate of anthems, songs and prayers, including the following rousing and widely published chorus:

> Australians rise! Why longer wait
> While wrangling politicians prate
>   On themes that new dissensions breed?
> Arrest this paltry party strife
> That bars us from the larger life
>   And panders to provincial greed.
> Australians rise! no longer wait,
> Unfurl the flag and federate![22]

Sentiments of this kind may, of course, have reflected practical approval for the particular scheme of federation then under discussion; but, more obviously, they could be shared by many an ill-informed yet enthusiastic elector. Those electors who assisted in the singing of 'Hurrah, Hurrah for the Flag that Sets Us Free!' at the Captain's Flat torchlight procession on the eve of the second referendum,[23] presumably recorded Yes votes at the polls the next day; but whether they did so because convinced of the merits of the Constitution offered to them, or because they were willing to accept any plan which would ensure the establishment of the Australian nation, it is impossible to ascertain. At any rate, it can be said that patriotic sentiment added yet another subjective and inscrutable element to the referenda campaigns.

Ambiguity and confusion of the kinds so far outlined were general throughout the electorates under discussion. Their presence underlines the difficulty of finding a rational basis for explaining the vote recorded in any particular case. There were, however, variations in the presentation and content of campaigns between town and country and, more broadly, between the three blocks of electorates. These variations require examination, as possible factors in the differing voting 'tone' of constituencies.

The most obvious variations were in the intensity rather than the content of propaganda. While most main country towns seem to have been inundated with literature, debates and speeches by politicians of varying degrees of efficiency and fame, their outlying districts were often only cursorily submitted to such treatment. This situation prompted 'True Federalist' to write impatiently to the *Yass Courier* in 1899:

It is not the city of Yass which wants educating but the whole electorate with about half of which Yass is entirely out of touch . . . Cannot everybody see that there are the outlying parts who killed the bill here last year, and will probably do so again for all the alleged local federal league leaders seem to care or understand.[24]

A similar complaint, in milder vein, was expressed in a letter from the Queanbeyan branch of the New South Wales Federal Association to the central body of that organization in 1898: 'The people in the town of Queanbeyan are enthusiastically in favour of the Bill, but it would be desirable to awaken greater interest in the matter amongst the people in the outlying districts.'[25] In support of these charges came reports from the Warroo district, in Yass electorate, that 'very little interest seems to be taken with regard to Federal matters',[26] and from Sutton, in Queanbeyan electorate, that 'there seems to be very little interest taken in Federation in this locality'.[27]

Variation in the intensity of the campaigns can be seen on a broader scale between the three blocks of electorates. The border group of Bega, Monaro and Eden-Bombala suffered most severely from neglect in this unequal distribution of propaganda. Their physical and subsequently political remoteness from the capital city seems to have rendered them relatively free of 'high pressure' campaigning, and to have prevented such large-scale public enthusiasm as flourished to their north. In fact, a letter to the *Manaro Mercury,* just four weeks before polling day in 1898, bewailed the silence prevailing in the writer's electorate:

What about Federation? Are you 'leading lights' going to allow this monstrous question to take its chance without as much as making some move to arrange for a Federal Delegate, or someone versed in the subject to come and explain the 'Bill'. I doubt if there is a district in the colony where this subject has been treated with such great silence . . . Manaro, you are just about as slow as the snail, no wonder people ask you where you are, in what colony are you?[28]

In view of this situation it is scarcely surprising that at the first referendum Monaro showed the second smallest ratio of active to potential electors in the fourteen electorates of south-eastern New South Wales, with only 826 out of 2,213 qualified voters going to the polls.[29]

By contrast to the border electorates, the six consistently anti-federal electorates to the north were subject to a high degree of propaganda. Of course, the prevalence of such propaganda varied from town to town and from settlement to settlement, but at least in the main townships (and possibly also, broadly speaking, in the smaller rural settlements), of the anti-federal region, its volume appears to have been greater, and the manner of its presentation more forceful, complicated and bewildering, than in places of corresponding importance in the border district. In 1898 the city of Goulburn, for example, was subjected to speeches from Edmund Barton, W. J. Lyne, W. P. Cullen, Sir Arthur Renwick, Daniel O'Connor, J. C. Watson, W. J. Ferguson, John Haynes, E. D. Millen, J. Ashton, G. H. Reid, W. M. Hughes, W. P. Crick, E. W. O'Sullivan and at least five other enthusiasts—a selection of gentlemen sufficiently varied to ensure the invocation of practically every type of pro- and anti-Billite argument in use in New South Wales, and far wider than any to be found in a single district of the three pro-federal electorates.

In fact, so intense were the campaigns in the anti-federal electorates, that the defeat of the Bill in 1898 was accounted for by a Braidwood citizen in terms of the surfeit of anti-federal rumours which had beset his fellow voters:

> Anti-Billites certainly were very industrious in disseminating the 'bogy' scares broadcast, which owing to the imperfect knowledge which unfortunately existed on the subject had an alarming effect upon a certain class, particularly the wild and utterly unreliable statements made respecting the cost of federation, which induced a large number to vote against the bill.[30]

In the following year a letter to the *Burrowa Times* from 'Pat of Mullingar' made explicit the way in which the forceful contradictory nature of the 1899 campaign was effecting an attitude of bewilderment and distrust towards the Bill in Burrowa electorate:

> What I seek [he wrote] is enlightenment on many of the debateable points; and there are only too many in the bush who are in a similar plight, looking for guidance, but failing to discover it in the conflict of opinion that now prevails among those who profess to thoroughly understand the merits of the situation—financially and otherwise . . . In the face of the inconsistencies of the character mentioned, the general public view the question with a certain amount of natural suspicion, and have been induced to canvass the motives of its most fervid advocates.[31]

If we partly attribute the small vote in the border electorate of Monaro to a comparative lack of propaganda in that region, it seems equally reasonable to see the forceful nature of the campaigns in the anti-federal electorates as an important factor contributing to the majority No votes. The cautious, distrustful attitude towards the Bill expressed by 'Pat of Mullingar' seems at once the natural outcome of the confusion of the campaigns, and the natural cause of much anti-federal voting.

This indirect anti-federal influence was apparently more significant in the six consistently No voting electorates than elsewhere in south-eastern New South Wales. However, it was also obviously active in the five south coast electorates which swung to a barely favourable majority in 1899. Probably it helped produce the high percentage of anti-federal votes recorded in this region. In 1898 a Kiama newspaper rather facetiously expressed its concern at the confusing situation by quoting the following paragraph from the *Methodist*:

It is a fortunate thing that the polling day for the voting on the Federal Convention Bill is rapidly drawing near. So many meetings have been held, so many contradictions have been heard, so many different calculations have been made, that people are getting bewildered. Even the 'Daily Telegraph', which usually is pretty clear in the expression of its views, has got hopelessly mixed. In a recent article the writer, after quoting all sort of figures, arrives at the following conclusion:—'Towards the sum we may expect from post and telegraph set clpnd down L gv glirnsf RRRDL Telegraphs CC.' That's just about the spot most people will land after reading the arguments and endeavouring to follow the calculations of the writers and speakers on Federation.[32]

The *Ulladulla and Milton Times,* published in the south coast electorate of Moruya, provided several excellent examples of anti-federalist feeling caused by confusion in 1899. To one man 'Federation meant that he and his people would be deported to Victoria. He was comfortable enough at the Camp and had no desire to be sent from the land of his forebears. That his vote went against the Bill was only to be expected'. One Ulladulla resident 'is alleged to have declared that Federation meant that a duty of 4d. would be imposed on a 2d. stamp'. Another elector summed up the situation thus: 'I'm aginst the Bill, and I'll tell ye why. If we get Federation the price of beef 'ud go up 2d. a lb., and how 'ud a pore worukin man manage to git mate thin?'[33]

Although variations in the intensity of propaganda throw some light on the pattern of voting in south-eastern New South Wales, they clearly cannot constitute anything approaching a comprehensive explanation of this pattern. Local interests connected with the federal issue must also be taken into account.

It should be said that the operation of such interests is not easy to identify, since a significant feature both of press comment on federation and of the campaigns of visiting and local speakers was the tendency to concentrate on 'national' rather than local interests, as if, by common consent, argument along narrow parochial lines was considered unworthy of the greatness of the question under discussion. Thus, for example, there were hints that many people in the city of Goulburn and its rural environs (embracing the Goulburn, and parts of the Argyle, Queanbeyan and Braidwood electorates) were concerned at the implications of federation for local trade. Would traffic along the southern line, and Goulburn's position as an inland centre for the marketing of rural products, be adversely affected by the introduction of intercolonial free trade and the likely drawing away of Riverina trade to Victoria? These were questions of considerable importance to local railwaymen and traders. The *Goulburn Evening Penny Post* never discussed federal prospects in such crude terms, but an occasional blunt letter to the editor did, and in 1898 the Goulburn Federal League came out plainly with the accusation that local anti-federalists were moved by fears of railway and trade losses.[34]

Given the tendency of the Goulburn press to play down specific fears of this kind, it is perhaps reasonable to conclude that in this area narrowly local matters may not have been more important in moving voters than the broader, highlighted arguments which concerned questions like the effect of federation on the colony's tax burden. There are many indications that the same may have been true elsewhere.

In the electorate of Bowral, for example, the campaigns revealed strong rivalry between the township of Moss Vale and the settlements of Bowral and Mittagong. A week after the first referendum had been held, the *Robertson Advocate* had this to say about local rivalry:

Moss Vale pushed and urged itself into sentiment and song and hoarseness over its advocacy of the Federal Bill, therefore Bowral laid low and voted against it for all its was worth. Each town today pats itself on the back and claims the victory. The Moss Vale branch of the Federal League will keep its warpaint on and sharpen up its battle cry preparatory to renewed efforts and more victory; therefore Bowral will lie lower with its other eye open and alert to fresh honours and glory.[35]

This impression of rivalry is supported by a number of other hints in local newspapers. Furthermore, the polling returns for 1898 show that Moss Vale voters did indeed support the Constitution, with 112 Yes to 94 No votes, while the other two towns cast firm anti-federal votes—the Bowral vote being 85 in favour and 193 against the Bill, and the Mittagong returns 55 in favour and 104 against.[36]

At an 1899 meeting of the Geebung Club in Berrima a similar return was foretold for the second referendum. Mr O'Tell said Moss Vale was very strong on federation, was going to vote Yes straight out on 20th; that alone, he considered, would be sufficient justification for Bowral and Mittagong voting No.[37] Yet his prediction was not fulfilled, for at the second referendum all three townships returned pro-federal majorities, with Bowral voting 159 to 126 in favour, Mittagong 116 to 101, and Moss Vale 182 to 91.[38] Provincial jealousies then, though perhaps exerting some influence on voting returns, were clearly not the predominant issue for the residents of Bowral electorate. Newspapers make it clear that the voters of all three townships shared the manifold influences contained in the general propaganda of the campaigns, while angry and worried letters to the press revealed electors' full participation in the subsequent caution and bewilderment. In Moss Vale, furthermore, the local Federal Association indulged to an unusual degree in the promotion of nationalistic sentiment, through monster demonstrations. According to the *Bowral Free Press*, 'had it not been for the vigorous canvassing, speechifying, flag waving, vocal efforts and free drives, the polling at the local booth would certainly have been reversed'.[39]

Similarly, the change in the coastal voting block from opposition to the Bill in 1898 to its support in 1899 is more easily seen in terms of the Australia-wide trend towards a rise in Billite support than in terms of any particular local interest. According to the press of south-eastern New South Wales, this upward trend was largely due to increased nationalistic sentiment, greater knowledge of—and hence interest in—the Bill, fairer voting arrangements, and a growing feeling that federation was inevitable. As four of the five south coast electorates (Bowral being the exception) required but a small adjustment in the ratio of pro- to anti-federal votes to effect a swing to a Billite majority, the change does not appear to be of great local significance.[40]

Newspaper evidence suggests, however, that in the three pro-federal border electorates one matter of potential 'local' interest was more influential than in the south coast or anti-federal blocks. The papers of the border electorates stressed to an unusual degree the importance of the issue of intercolonial free trade. The *Manaro Mercury,* in particular, became a fierce advocate of the Bill, and in a way unusual for a country newspaper harped on economic benefits (often implicitly local) that would follow from its acceptance. The following editorial of April 1899 may be taken as giving characteristic expression to these views:

[Sydney capitalists and anti-federalists] would retain the monopoly of commerce which the policy of centralisation has given to the capital since its birth, and cast aside the interests of all other colonists who have gone into the interior and opened up vast tracts of country which a few decades since were unknown. To the selfish and insignificantly small minority the question of the advantages of federation does not appeal in the slightest degree. They would, if it lay in their power, treat the producers in the country as mere machines for raising marketable commodities for the enrichment of the city traders . . . If one portion of the seaboard is more accessible, for the purposes of trade, than Sydney, and is necessary to the development of a portion of the colony, facilities for the dispatch of products from that part should be secured to the producers, who should not be heavily taxed by being compelled to trade with Sydney alone, and in many instances send their goods over hundreds of miles of railway line. It is to the interests of the whole of the colonists of the group that the natural channels of trade should be opened out and that the present handicaps to profitable production should be swept away.[41]

The discontent with the trading arrangements of New South Wales reflected here, and the clearly expressed desire for commercial decentralization, were not found merely in Monaro newspapers. 'Centralization is the be-all and end-all of Sydney', grumbled the *Bega Free Press,* 'every pound of tea, and every necessity of life and business must be drawn from Sydney to the disadvantage of country business'.[42] From Eden electorate came the following statement:

Under federation these oppressive duties will be swept away, and the markets of all the colonies will be thrown open to our pastoralists, our agriculturalists, our fruit growers, our miners, our dairymen and manufacturers. The establishment of manufactories means the employment of more workers, and greater demand for coal, the development of the iron industry and the cloth and woollen trades in our midst.[43]

In these eastern border electorates, generalized anti-Sydney feeling merged with a wider sense of the necessary interdependence, for mutual prosperity, of the colonial economies. If local propagandists could offer few instances of local trade severely hampered by 'border barbarities', indignation at the difficulties which beset neighbouring electorates along the Murray to the westward was still vicariously shared. When New South Wales rang with the accusation that those on the Victorian border were supporting the Federal Bill for purely selfish commercial motives, the *Manaro Mercury* saw no reason to apologize:

The border vote of 3rd June [1898] was the strongest possible effort to free that portion of New South Wales from the outrageous handicaps which had been placed upon it by the system of centralization, and it showed that those who fought against the border duties were content to be under the rule of Victoria if necessary rather than continue existence in New South Wales governed by existing conditions.[44]

In 1899 the amended Federal Constitution raised a fresh issue, immediately recognizable as of distinct local interest to all three blocks of electorates in south-eastern New South Wales. The provision under the amended Bill whereby the federal capital city was to be established at least 100 miles from Sydney, but in the bounds of the mother colony, immediately roused the aspirations of many a district and township to be selected for the honoured site.

Perhaps optimism was highest in the border electorates. Monaro electors were strongly urged 'to record an unanimous vote in favour, as there is to them the prospect of the Federal Capital being within their territory',[45] while in Eden-Bombala active steps were taken to secure the coveted city. A Federal Capital League was formed, and a manifesto 'setting out the claims of Southern Monaro to the Federal City'[46] was published and issued to residents of Bega and surrounding districts. The township of Bombala, in fact, believed that it itself possessed sufficient qualifications and natural advantages to prove the ideal site for the national centre, and it quoted and heartily endorsed the following estimate of its suitability:

[Bombala] is near the coast, which offers a splendid harbour for large shipping, is midway between Sydney and Melbourne, and practically halfway between Adelaide and Brisbane. Further, the necessary territory is chiefly Crown land, and the cost of territorial acquisition will be consequently trifling.[47]

The anti-federal electorates also laid claims for the national capital site, and the 1899 campaign was marked particularly by much discussion on the likelihood of the selection of the district of Yass. As early as February a meeting was held to promote this possibility, and the following resolution was passed: 'That in the opinion of this meeting the claim of Yass district to be chosen as the site for the contemplated Federal territory is manifestly evident by reason of its many natural advantages'.[48] Yass, meanwhile, accused Goulburn of 'straining every muscle and nerve to secure the capital',[49] a claim which probably helps explain the fall in the size of the anti-federal majority in that city from 298 in 1898 to 138 in 1899. It is interesting to note that the township of Towrang, close to Goulburn and also suggested as a possible site for the federal capital, was one of the three out of twenty-one polling places in Argyle electorate to vote in favour of the Bill in 1899. It returned 21 to 16 anti-federal votes.[50]

Subsequent to the poll of 1899, the anti-federal *Goulburn Evening Penny Post* reported proudly that:

The six clustering constituencies with Goulburn as the commercial centre stood unshaken. Goulburn, Argyle, Queanbeyan, Braidwood, Burrowa and Yass withstood the temptation of the capital bribe which the Premier, with the loose principles of a Leviathan hucksterer, dangled before the eyes of residents all along the Southern line, and kept their trust unsullied.[51]

In the eligible electorates of the south coast, the issue does not appear to have been so great, though one newspaper claimed that 'Shoalhaven means to make a claim for the site of the federal city.'[52] A small attendance was reported at a 'Federal Capital site' meeting held at Nowra in Shoalhaven electorate, at which the principal movers supported 'the claims of the country between Jervis Bay and Goulburn . . . as a most suitable site for the federal city'.[53] Perhaps then, the capital issue resulted in a few pro-federal votes on the south coast also.

The impossibility of precisely estimating the influence of this or any other particular issue in any part of south-eastern New South Wales will, however, be recognized. As has been demonstrated, the campaigns in every electorate were of such a complex nature that it is not feasible to separate any one issue from the mass of propaganda and weigh up its importance separately. The federal capital, and all other local interests were only elements interconnected with a host of others which together made up the campaigns.

In general, our discussion of the campaigns in south-eastern New South Wales has produced negative results: clear explanations of why the respective groups of electorates voted as they did have not emerged. As suggested earlier, lack of useful statistical data and the technical impossibility of identifying the active electorate must on one level vitiate any effort to correlate interests and voting figures. But beyond that it is clear from our examination of campaign content that clear-cut local interests usually operated in narrow spheres, and were largely counteracted by the attention local speakers and newspapers gave to wider, 'national' questions. When surveying the pattern of campaigning from electorate to electorate, one cannot satisfactorily estimate the real weight of particular issues affecting the voting outcome.

But one major negative observation emerges, and though simple, it is a salutary point for the historian to note. There is much evidence to suggest that one crucial effect of the *variety* which marked campaigning was to produce in many electors' minds an overwhelming sense of confusion. What is more, the confusion appears to have been greatest where the intensity of campaigning was greatest, viz. in the block of steadily anti-federal electorates. How far, one is tempted to ask, was this negative vote largely a cautious, even despairing, reaction to lack of understanding? At all events, the historian may take comfort from the irrationality of voters' reactions to the questions that confronted them, reflecting that, if electors could 'not detect the truth from the lies', then his chances of plumbing their minds for clear evidence of motivation are not very great. He might philosophically reflect, with the *Bega Free Press*'s versifier, on the absurdity of the things men said and believed about federation:

> The cost of the scheme you can easily see,
> For three sevens are seventy three,

Allowing a margin for possibly more,
Then three times nine are a hundred and four!
Subtracting, say, six from seventy four,
We get ten shillings a head or more;
Then add three bushels and nineteen quarts,
And what becomes of the Freetrade ports?
Suppose you multiply three half-crowns
By a ton, three-quarters, and thirteen poun's,
And then you add two thousand of bricks,
And divide the balance by three feet-six?
You take the penny postage away
And it then becomes as clear as day
That the weight of a dead mosquito's tail
Is as long as the price of a two inch nail![54]

Federal Referenda Results in South-Eastern New South Wales 1898 and 1899

Electorates		Electors on roll	Total ballots	Informal votes	Yes votes	No votes	Majority For	Majority Against
Opposed to Bill each time								
Boorowa	1898	2,088	880	9	412	459		47
	1899	2,153	1,403	13	520	870		350
Yass	1898	1,980	965	—	413	532		139
	1899	2,060	1,297	8	599	690		91
Argyle	1898	2,118	1,182	10	384	788		404
	1899	2,197	1,289	12	483	794		311
Goulburn	1898	2,166	1,173	5	435	733		298
	1899	2,199	1,616	12	733	871		138
Braidwood	1898	2,160	768	11	268	489		221
	1899	2,210	1,093	10	489	594		105
Queanbeyan	1898	1,786	990	3	480	507		27
	1899	1,924	1,404	11	623	770		147
In favour of Bill each time								
Monaro	1898	2,213	822	4	613	205	408	
	1899	2,269	1,084	8	842	234	608	
Bega	1898	2,135	1,056	6	735	315	420	
	1899	2,191	1,292	7	1,021	264	757	
Eden-Bombala	1898	1,970	1,080	4	843	233	610	
	1899	2,131	1,350	8	1,157	185	972	
Opposed to Bill 1898 and in favour 1899								
Bowral	1898	1,841	936	5	339	592		253
	1899	1,915	1,262	3	655	604	51	
Illawarra	1898	2,072	1,037	9	481	547		66
	1899	2,094	1,492	7	777	708	69	
Kiama	1898	2,041	927	12	451	464		13
	1899	2,052	1,172	10	595	567	28	
Shoalhaven	1898	2,092	1,012	9	494	509		15
	1899	2,230	1,307	13	673	621	52	
Moruya	1898	2,022	945	2	469	474		5
	1899	2,144	1,317	20	773	524	249	

ABBREVIATIONS

A.N.L.	National Library, Canberra
CO	Colonial Office, London
H.S.	*Historical Studies, Australia and New Zealand*
La T.L.	La Trobe Library, Melbourne
M.L.	Mitchell Library, Sydney
Parl. Deb.	*Parliamentary Debates*
P.P.	*Parliamentary Papers*
P.R.O.	Public Record Office, London
S.M.H.	*Sydney Morning Herald*
V. & P.	*Votes and Proceedings*

REFERENCES

Preface

1 Alfred Deakin, *The Federal Story* (Melbourne, 1963), p. 3.
2 C. M. H. Clark, *Select Documents in Australian History, 1851-1900* (Sydney, 1955), p. 444.
3 G. Blainey, 'The Role of Economic Interests in Australian Federation', in J. J. Eastwood and F. B. Smith (eds), *Historical Studies, Selected Articles* (Melbourne, 1964), p. 193.
4 J. Quick and R. R. Garran, *The Annotated Constitution of the Australian Commonwealth* (Sydney, 1901).
5 L. F. Crisp, *Australian National Government* (Melbourne, 1965), p. 39.
6 Deakin, op. cit., p. 173.
7 B. R. Wise, *The Making of the Australian Commonwealth 1889-1900* (London, 1913).
8 Melbourne, 1965.   9 J. Reynolds, *Edmund Barton* (Sydney, 1948).
10 L. F. Fitzhardinge, *William Morris Hughes, A Political Biography* (Sydney, 1964), vol. 1.
11 B. E. Mansfield, *Australian Democrat: the Career of Edward William O'Sullivan, 1846-1910* (Sydney, 1965).
12 G. O'Collins, *Patrick McMahon Glynn* (Melbourne, 1965).
13 W. G. McMinn, 'George Reid and Federation: the Origin of the "Yes-No Policy" ', *H.S.*, vol. 10, no. 38, 1962; L. E. Fredman, 'Yes-No Reid: a Case for the Prosecution', *Journal of the Royal Australian Historical Society*, vol. 50, July 1964.
14 W. G. McMinn, 'Sir Henry Parkes as a Federalist', *H.S.*, vol. 12, no. 47, 1966.
15 R. L. Reid, 'South Australian Politicians and the Proposals for Federation', in E. L. French (ed.), *Melbourne Studies in Education, 1960-1961* (Melbourne, 1962).
16 J. Bastin, 'Federation and Western Australia: A Contribution to the Parker-Blainey Discussion', *H.S.*, vol. 5, no. 17, 1951.
17 The relevant articles are conveniently collected in J. J. Eastwood and F. B. Smith (eds), op. cit.
18 L. F. Crisp, *The Parliamentary Government of the Commonwealth of Australia* (London, 1949), ch. 1 ('The Fathers and their Constitution').
19 Eastwood and Smith (eds), op. cit., p. 192.
20 'The Role of Economic Interests in Australian Federation', ibid., pp. 179-94.
21 See esp. N. G. Butlin, *Investment in Australian Economic Development, 1861-1900* (Cambridge, 1964).
22 H. L. Hall, *Victoria's Part in the Australian Federation Movement, 1849-1900* (London, 1931); J. M. Ward, *Earl Grey and the Australian Colonies 1846-1857* (Melbourne, 1958).
23 As demonstrated by the first two volumes in this series: Geoffrey Sawer, *Australian Federalism in the Courts* (Melbourne, 1967); Alfred Deakin (ed. J. A. La Nauze), *Federated Australia: Selections from letters to the Morning Post 1900-1910* (Melbourne, 1968).

1 Victoria's Campaign for Federation

[1] *Argus*, 15, 16, 18 June 1883; *Age*, *S.M.H.*, 15 June; *Border Post*, 18 June.
[2] 21 Apr. 1883. supp. 1.
[3] D. C. Gordon, *The Australian Frontier in New Guinea 1870-1885* (New York, 1951), pp. 100-13; J. D. Legge, *Australian Colonial Policy* (Sydney, 1956), ch. 2.
[4] 'Annexation of Islands in the Pacific Ocean', *V. & P.* (Vic.), 1883 (2nd session), vol. 2, no. 23; 'Australasian Convention, 1883. Report of the Proceedings', ibid., 1884, vol. 2, no. 25, p. 1007.
[5] 'Annexation of Islands in the Pacific Ocean', pp. 1059-60.
[6] CO 881/6, no. 95; W. P. Morrell, *Britain in the Pacific Islands* (Oxford, 1960), pp. 198-200.
[7] Derby to Australian Governors, 11 July 1883, Sec. of State for Colonies Outward Despatches (Vic. Archives); Gordon. op. cit., ch. 7; Paul Knaplund, 'Sir Arthur Gordon on the New Guinea Question, 1883', *H.S.*, vol. 7, no. 27, 1956.
[8] *Argus*, 19 July 1883, p. 7.
[9] *Parl. Deb.* (Vic.), vol. 43, p. 137; *Argus*, 16 July 1883, p. 9 and 17 July, p. 5 for comment on parliamentary and popular opinion.
[10] Agents-General to CO, 21 July 1883, CO 881/6, no. 96.
[11] CO 881/6, no. 96; *Argus*, 17 July 1883 (Higinbotham); *Parl. Deb.* (Vic.), vol. 45, p. 361 (Shiels).
[12] 'Annexation, Federation and Foreign Convicts. Correspondence', *V. & P.* (Vic.), 1884, vol. 3, no. 38, p. 22.
[13] *Parl. Deb.* (Vic.), vol. 43, pp. 320-1; 'Annexation of Islands in the Pacific Ocean', pp. 1065-7.
[14] 30 July 1883, editorial.
[15] 'Annexation or Protectorate of Islands . . . Resolutions', *V. & P.* (Vic.), 1883, vol. 3, no. 47; 'Annexation . . . Resolutions', ibid,. 1884, vol. 2, no. 23; CO 881/6, no. 95.
[16] CO 881/6, no. 95; 'Australasian Convention, 1883. Report of the Proceedings' (Derby's Despatch), *V. & P.* (Vic.), 1884, vol. 2, no. 25, pp. 1021-2; Gordon, op. cit., ch. 9.
[17] *Age*, 12 Nov. 1883, p. 4; note the serious debate on federation in Sept. 1882, *Parl. Deb.* (Vic.), vol. 40, pp. 1646-71 and vol. 41, pp. 2039-40, 2380-2.
[18] *Parl. Deb.* (Vic.), vol. 45, p. 201; *Argus*, 11 May 1883.
[19] 'Australasian Convention, 1883. Report of the Proceedings', *V. & P.* (Vic.), 1884, vol. 2, no. 25, pp. 1047-9.
[20] Ibid., p. 1050.   [21] CO 881/6, no. 95.
[22] 'Australasian Convention on Annexation and Federation. Further Correspondence', *V. & P.* (Vic.), 1883, vol. 3, no. 42, pp. 1031-3.
[23] *Argus*, 10 Dec. 1883, p. 5.
[24] J. Quick and R. R. Garran, *The Annotated Constitution of the Australian Commonwealth* (Sydney, 1901), pp. 111-12.
[25] 'Australasian Convention, 1883. Report of the Proceedings', *V. & P.* (Vic.), 1884, vol. 2, no. 25, pp. 1021-2; *Argus*, 30 Nov.-10 Dec. 1883; Alfred Deakin, *The Federal Story* (Melbourne, 1963), pp. 11-16.
[26] Sir William Des Voeux, *My Colonial Service* (London, 1903) vol. 2, p. 113.
[27] CO 309/129/9.   [28] *The Federal Story*, p. 15.
[29] *Argus*, 11 Dec. 1883, p. 8.   [30] Ibid., p. 4.
[31] *Parl. Deb.* (N.S.W.), 11 Dec. 1883, pp. 919-28; *S.M.H.*, 10 Dec. 1883.
[32] *The Federal Story*, pp. 16-17.
[33] *Prosper the Commonwealth* (Sydney, 1958), p. 88.
[34] *Australia and New Zealand* (London, 1873) p. 387.
[35] *My Reminiscences* (London, 1917), p. 52.

36 *Argus*, 13 Nov. 1883, p. 5.
37 *Age*, 14 Mar. 1883, editorial; 16 June 1883, editorial; *Argus*, 7 July 1883, editorial.
38 e.g., *Leader*, 13 June 1885; CO 448/1B/173; E. S. Parkes to Selby, 20 Nov. 1884, Bank of Australasia records (London).
39 Hugh R. Reid, *A Customs Union for Australasia* . . . (Melbourne, 1883), p. 3; cf. *Parl. Deb.* (Vic.), vol. 45, p. 363 (Shiels).
40 *Argus*, 1 May 1885, p. 3.
41 Dr J. M. Tregenza drew my attention to the notebook in the Pearson Papers (La T. L.) which lists Pearson's editorial contributions.
42 *Argus*, 12 Jan. 1883, editorial; 17 June 1886, p. 5.
43 H. Mayer, *The Press in Australia* (Melbourne, 1964), p. 19.
44 N. G. Butlin, *Investment in Australian Economic Development 1861-1900* (Cambridge, 1964), pp. 364-9.
45 Joy E. Parnaby, 'The Economic and Political Development of Victoria, 1877-1881', unpublished Ph.D. thesis, University of Melbourne, 1951, ch. 6; C. D. Allin, *A History of the Tariff Relations of the Australian Colonies* (Minneapolis, 1918), pp. 165-71; Garran, op. cit., pp. 46-9; *Parl. Deb.* (Vic.), vol. 49, p. 1538.
46 *Argus*, 10 Jan. 1884, p. 6.
47 Service in *Age*, 9 Jan. 1885, p. 6; *Argus*, 24 Apr. 1884, p. 9; 2 May 1887, p. 7.
48 *Age*, 12 Nov. 1883, editorial.
49 Derby to Gladstone, 7 Dec. 1883 and Gladstone to Derby, 8 Dec. 1883, Gladstone Papers (British Museum); Gordon, op. cit., pp. 195-8.
50 CO 881/6, no. 95; CO 309/126/193; CO 309/128/206-7.
51 CO 309/127/37; CO 309/128/290; 'Annexation, Federation, and French Convicts', *V. & P.* (Vic.), 1884, vol. 3, no. 38, pp. 113-26.
52 *Parl. Deb.* (Vic.), vol. 45, pp. 196-644 *passim*; *Argus*, 21 June 1884, p. 5.
53 'High Commissionership of the Western Pacific', *V. & P.* (Vic.), 1884, vol. 3, no. 44; 'Protectorate of New Guinea. Correspondence', ibid., vol. 4, no. 60; *Age*, 20 June 1884, editorial.
54 Gladstone Papers, vol. 46 (Childers's letters), vol. 560 (Cabinet Papers); CO 881/6, no. 103; Marjorie C. Jacobs, 'Bismarck and the Annexation of New Guinea', *H.S.*, vol. 5, no. 17, 1951.
55 Vic. Premier's Telegram Book (Tel. Book) (Vic. Archives, State Library of Victoria), 8, 19, 26 Aug. 1884.
56 W. B. Dalley, *Speeches on the Proposed Federal Council for Australasia* (Sydney, 1884), p. 37.
57 Tel. Book, Sept.-Oct. 1884; Dalley to Griffith, 16 Oct. 1884, Griffith Papers (Dixson Library, Sydney); *Argus*, 14 Jan. 1886, p. 6; Gordon, op. cit., pp. 226-30.
58 Tel. Book, 5 Nov. 1884; *Parl. Deb.* (Vic.), vol. 47, pp. 2300-1.
59 *Argus*, 23 Sept. 1884, p. 6.
60 Tel. Book, 1 Oct. 1884; Loch to Sec. of State (Confidential), 9 Oct. 1884, Vic. Governors' Despatches; *Parl. Deb.* (Vic.), vol. 47, p. 2114.
61 Dalley, op. cit., p. 50.
62 Tel. Book; also *Argus*, 20 Dec. 1884, pp. 8-9; 7 Jan. 1885, p. 6; 8 Jan. 1885, p. 6.
63 *Argus*, 14 Jan. 1885, p. 6.
64 To C. Crisp, 29 Dec. 1884, Crisp Correspondence (A.N.L.).
65 CO 309/128/365; CO 309/129/320, 321, 326; Tel. Book, 5 Feb. 1885.
66 *Parl. Deb.* (Vic.), vol. 48, p. 214; vol. 50, pp. 2135-6.
67 *Oceana or England and her Colonies* (London, 1886), pp. 98-9.
68 Gray correspondence (La. T. L.), 8 Mar. 1885.
69 CO 309/129/332, 337; *Argus*, 12-19 Feb. 1885; Tel. Book, 13 Feb. 1885.
70 *Parl. Deb.* (Vic.), vol. 68, p. 2496.
71 *Argus*, 27 Feb. 1885, p. 6; 25 Feb., p. 6.

72 Ibid., 19 Feb. 1885, editorial; 16 Apr. 1885, p. 9; Dalley to Lord Loftus, 23 Feb. 1885, Letters to Lord Loftus (M.L.).

73 Tel. Book.

74 *Argus*, 12 Mar. 1885, p. 4; 17 Mar. 1885, p. 5.

75 Tel. Book, 17, 20 July 1885; *Age*, 17 July 1885, p. 5; 21 July 1885, p. 5; *Argus*, 8 Aug. 1885, p. 9; Quick and Garran, op. cit., p. 114; C. W. Dilke, *Problems of Greater Britain* (London, 1890), pp. 264-6.

76 *Bulletin*, Sydney, 29 Aug. 1885, p. 3 (and following quotation also).

77 *Parl. Deb.* (Vic.), vol. 49, pp. 1513-44; vol. 50, pp. 1587-612.

78 Tel. Book, 18, 20 Nov. 1885; Governors' Papers (Vic. Archives), Bundle 16 (Federal Council).

79 *Parl. Deb.* (Vic.), vol. 48, pp. 41, 212-14.

80 Derby to Loch, 18 May 1885, Vic. Governor's Inward Despatches (Vic. Archives).

81 CO 881/6/112A; 'The New Hebrides. Correspondence', *V. & P.* (Vic.), 1886, vol. 2, no. 35; Judith B. McCullough, 'The Australian Reaction to the New Hebrides Crisis of 1886: a Study in Australian Nationalism', unpublished M.A. thesis, University of Melbourne, 1956, ch. 2: in the next few pages I owe much to her work.

82 *Argus*, 20 Apr. 1886, p. 7; *Age*, 24 Mar. 1886, editorial.

83 Tel. Book, 27 Mar. 1886.

84 'The New Hebrides. Correspondence', p. 1319.

85 CO 309/130/683.   86 CO 309/130/707.

87 'The New Hebrides. Correspondence', p. 1322.

88 8, 15 May 1886.

89 CO 881/6/112; CO 309/130/690.

90 A. Ross, *New Zealand Aspirations in the Pacific in the Nineteenth Century* (Oxford, 1964), pp. 218-29.

91 McCullough, op. cit., ch. 3.

92 W. P. Morrell, op. cit., pp. 200-4; CO 881/7/118; Tel. Book, June-July 1886; McCullough, op. cit., chs 4-5.

93 Morrell, op. cit., pp. 200-4; J. M. Ward, *British Policy in the South Pacific, 1786-1893* (Sydney, 1948), pp. 300-2; CO 881/7/118.

94 10 Aug. 1886, 25 Feb. 1887, Berry Papers (La T. L.); Tel. Book.

95 Cf. Deakin, op. cit., pp. 24-5.

96 Deakin to C. H. Pearson, 26 Feb. 1887, Pearson Papers; Berry to Gillies, 18 Mar. 1887, letter-book, Berry Papers.

97 Tel. Book, 24, 28 Mar. 1887.

98 *Proceedings of the Colonial Conference, 1887* (C.5091), pp. 24-5.

99 *Argus*, 28 Apr. 1887, p. 5; 9 June 1887, p. 9.

1 *Parl. Deb.* (Vic.), vol. 68, p. 2493.

2 Ibid., vol. 61, p. 1642; *Imperial Federation*, London, May 1888, p. 96; *Argus*, 10 Feb. 1888, p. 4; 15 May 1888, p. 9; *Proc. Royal Colonial Institute*, 1887-8, p. 343.

3 Berry to Gillies, 25 Oct. 1887, letter-book, Berry Papers; *Parl. Deb.* (Vic.), vol. 54, pp. 262-70.

It will be observed that I have not placed great reliance on Deakin's account in *The Federal Story* (pp. 23-4) which is misleading in several particulars, especially in neglecting the co-operation by the Australian colonies including N.S.W. on the New Hebrides question. J. A. La Nauze's admirable account of the Conference (*Alfred Deakin*, Melbourne, 1965, vol. 1, pp. 95-104) needs to be modified by Service's evidence (see preceding note). Despite Service's statement, English observers did consider Deakin's speech to be the strongest.

4 CO 309/131/659; Gillies to Berry, 6 Sept. 1887, Berry Papers; CO 309/131/282, 290, 297, 317.

5 25 Oct. 1887, letter-book, Berry Papers.

6 Deakin, *Parl. Deb.* (Vic.), vol. 54, p. 272.

7 Richard A. Preston, *Canada and 'Imperial Defense'* (Durham, N.C., 1967), pp. 98-102; CO 881/7, no. 115; CO 309/129/184; Vic. Governors' Papers, Bundle 16 (Naval Defences); H. Mortimer-Franklyn, *The Unit of Imperial Federation* (London, 1887), ch. 6.

8 *Parl. Deb.* (Vic.), vol. 56, pp. 2186-202, 2254-62.

9 Henry Parkes, *Fifty Years in the Making of Australian History* (London, 1892), pp. 497-8.

10 Preston, op. cit., p. 119.

11 *Parl. Deb.* (Vic.), vol. 48, pp. 82, 85.

12 W. P. Reeves, *State Experiments in Australia and New Zealand* (London, 1902), vol. 1, p. 149.

13 *Argus,* 14 May 1887, p. 13; 10 Apr. 1888, p. 8.

14 *Parl. Deb.* (Vic.), vol. 45, p. 202; *Argus,* 24 Apr. 1884, p. 9.

15 *Imperial Federation,* May 1887, pp. 106-7.

16 *Proc. Royal Colonial Institute,* 1886-7, p. 39.

17 *Parl. Deb.* (Vic.), vol. 48, p. 107.   18 *Argus,* 26 Nov. 1887, p. 7.

19 Morrell, op. cit., pp. 261-2; Jacobs, op. cit.

20 E. E. Morris, *A Memoir of George Higinbotham* (London, 1895), pp. 205-6.

21 Barbara R. Atkins, 'The Problem of the Representation of Australia in England', unpublished M.A. thesis, University of Melbourne, 1959, pp. 238-49.

22 *Imperial Federation,* May 1887, supp. p. 106; *Argus,* 7 Feb. 1888, p. 8.

23 25 Feb. 1887, Berry Papers.

24 *Argus,* 10 Mar. 1887, p. 7; 16 July 1887, p. 9; *Bulletin,* 21 May 1888, p. 5.

25 *Parl. Deb.* (N.S.W.), 1887-8, pp. 1476-522.

26 *S.M.H.* and *Daily Telegraph,* 23-5 Nov. 1887; *Bulletin,* 2 Dec. 1887, p. 5.

27 *Australasian,* 3 Dec. 1887, p. 1081; *Parl. Deb.* (Vic.), vol. 56, p. 2211; Tel. Book, 25, 29 Nov. 1887; CO 309/131/399, 438.

28 *Argus,* 7 Dec. 1887, p. 5.

29 *Argus,* 14 Dec. 1887, p. 7; *Parl. Deb.* (Vic.), vol. 57, p. 731; Parkes to Gillies, 29 Dec. 1887, Vic. Premiers' Corresp. (Vic. Archives).

30 'Inspection of Colonial Forces by an Imperial General Officer. Correspondence', *V. & P.* (Vic.), 1889, vol. 3, no. 57.

31 Parkes to Gillies, 3 Apr., 4 May, 13 Sept. 1888. Vic. Premiers' Corresp.; Gillies to Parkes, 13 Apr., 26 Apr., 29 June 1888, ibid.; Alan Gross, 'Maribyrnong', *Victorian Historical Magazine,* no. 86, 1947, p. 60; *Parl. Deb.* (Vic.), vol. 59, pp. 2345-7, vol. 62, p. 2001.

32 CO 881/8, no. 129 and CO 881/9, no. 130 contain almost all the relevant despatches; Vic. Premiers' Corresp. and Tel. Books; *Argus,* 12-14 June 1888; Myra Willard, *History of the White Australia Policy to 1920* (Melbourne, 1923), ch. 4.

33 e.g., *Argus,* 2 Feb. 1887, p. 4.

34 W. F. Walker, *Parl. Deb.* (Vic.), vol. 40, p. 1658.

35 *Report of the Delegates representing the Victorian Chamber of Manufactures at the Intercolonial Free-Trade Conference . . . 1887* (Melbourne, 1887); Reid, op. cit.; H. R. Hogg, *Intercolonial Free Trade in Australia* (Melbourne, 1883); *Argus,* 26 Sept. 1883, p. 9.

36 Berry, *Parl. Deb.* (Vic.), vol. 50, p. 1778.

37 The answer has not been found in the official correspondence.

38 'Victoria and Tasmania. Treaty for Intercolonial Free Trade', *V. & P.* (Vic.), 1885, vol. 4, no. 85; *Parl. Deb.* (Vic.), vol. 50, pp. 1775-87; vol. 54, p. 680 (Deakin); *Argus,* 29 Jan. 1885, p. 5; 5 Mar., p. 7; 14 Mar., p. 8; 14 Nov., editorial; 29 Jan. 1886, p. 7; *Age,* 13 July 1885, p. 6; *Australasian Commercial Congress, 1888. Report* (Melbourne, 1889) for Service and Douglas; F. T. Derham letter-books, 1885-6 (University of Melbourne Archives); Gillies to Griffith, 21 Aug., 13 Oct. 1886, Griffith Papers (Dixson Library).

39 *Report of the Proceedings at the Intercolonial Free Trade Conference of Delegates from the Chambers of Manufactures* (Melbourne, 1887).
40 *Argus*, 7 June 1888, p. 5; 8 June, p. 6.
41 *Australasian Commercial Congress, 1888. Report* (Melbourne, 1889).
42 *Argus*, 3 Nov. 1887, p. 7; 26 Aug. 1888, p. 5. For minority farmers wanting intercolonial free trade, ibid., 25 May 1888, p. 7; 14 Nov., p. 13; *Parl. Deb.* (Vic.), vol. 58, p. 986.
43 *Age*, 8 Jan. 1889, p. 6.
44 *Argus*, 20 June 1888, p. 8; 26 June, p. 5; 3 July, p. 5.
45 *Parl. Deb.* (Vic.), vol. 57, pp. 668-71; *Argus*, 27 Aug. 1888, p. 7.
46 *Argus*, 22 Aug. 1888, p. 7.   47 Ibid., 21 Sept. 1889, p. 5.
48 *Parl. Deb.* (Vic.), vol. 60, pp. 923-1004; vol. 61, pp. 1005-146.
49 22 Aug. 1889, p. 7; 23 Sept., editorial.
50 Melbourne Chamber of Commerce Minute-book, 16 July 1889 (La T. L.).
51 e.g., *Age*, 20 Aug. 1888, editorial; *Parl. Deb.* (Vic.), vol. 45, p. 333; vol. 50, p. 1600.
52 *Age*, 14 Sept. 1888, editorial.   53 Ibid., 12 July 1888, editorial.
54 Ibid., 3 May 1889, editorial.   55 Ibid., 21 Aug. 1888, editorial.
56 Ibid., 20 Apr. 1888, editorial.   57 *Leader*, 18 Feb. 1888.
58 *Australasian Commercial Congress*, p. 24.
59 *Argus*, 12 Nov. 1888, p. 4; cf. Service, ibid., 15 May 1888, p. 9.
60 La Nauze, op. cit., vol. 1, p. 116.
61 3 May 1889, editorial.
62 *Federal Council of Australasia. Official Record of Debates* (Hobart, 1889), p. 79.
63 *The Federal Story*, p. 18.
64 *Sir H. Parkes' Federation Scheme: Extracts from Lord Carrington's Diary* (M.L.).
65 Parkes Papers, A 1044 (M.L.), cited by A. W. Martin, *Henry Parkes* (Melbourne, 1964), p. 23.
66 Vic. Premiers' Secret Files, 89/5 (Vic. Archives).
67 Ibid.
68 Dilke Papers (British Museum).
69 *Parl. Deb.* (Vic.), vol. 51, p. 474; vol. 55, p. 1046; vol. 59, p. 2327.
70 *Argus*, 4 July 1889, editorial; 9 and 19 Sept., editorial; *Age*, 6 Sept., p. 5; 7 Sept., p. 8.
71 Parkes, op. cit., pp. 585-603; La Nauze, op. cit., vol. 1, pp. 115-18; D. McR. McCallum, 'Sir Henry Parkes and Federation', *Journal of the Royal Australian Historical Society*, vol. 34, pt. 1, 1948; W. G. McMinn, 'Sir Henry Parkes as a Federalist', *H.S.*, vol. 12, no. 47, 1966.
72 'Reflections upon a Wandering Life in Australasia', *Atlantic Monthly*, vol. 63, 1889, p. 816.
73 e.g., *Parl. Deb.* (Vic.), vol. 47, p. 1712.
74 26 Mar. 1887, p. 5.   75 Op. cit., p. 25.
76 I am grateful to Marian Aveling and to Professors J. A. La Nauze, A. W. Martin and N. B. Nairn for their most helpful comments on this essay.

2 *'Absolutely Free'*

1 R. R. Garran, *Prosper the Commonwealth* (Sydney, 1958), pp. 184, 415.
2 *Official Record of the Debates of the Australasian Federal Convention. Third Session. Melbourne, 1898* (Melbourne, 1898), vol. 2, p. 2367. Cited henceforth as '*Debates* (Melbourne, 1898)'.
3 76 C.L.R. at p. 381. It is proper to say that two respected legal scholars think I am mistaken in suggesting that the italicized words were meant to imply a sequence of events in time. While I cannot see that 'added' can have any other meaning in this context, and while (as a matter of history) the original version of S. 92 was framed *before* S. 51 (i), I must accept

their views; but I have let my comment stand to illustrate the puzzles of an historian confronted with what certainly appears to be (as I have said above) 'a kind of history'.

4 Henry Parkes, *Fifty Years in the Making of Australian History* (London, 1892), p. 604.

5 A printed document, over the (printed) signature 'Sir Samuel Griffith', with notes in Griffith's hand, inserted in the bound volume 'Successive Stages of the Constitution of the Commonwealth of Australia', Griffith Papers, MS. Add. 501 (Dixson Library, Sydney).

6 Clark's Draft Bill is reprinted as an appendix to John Reynolds, 'A. I. Clark's American Sympathies and his Influence on Australian Federation', *Australian Law Journal*, vol. 32 (1958), pp. 62-75. Parkes acknowledged its receipt on 18 February 1891 (loc. cit., p. 65). There is a copy (Document 5) in the volume 'Successive Stages' referred to in note 5.

7 Clark's Draft Bill, Clauses 78, 79, 55. Of course the Federal legislature itself could enact, or consent to, an impairment of internal freedom of trade under these provisions, but Clark was well aware that Congress had not so acted in over a century, and that in various judgments the Supreme Court had taken notice of this fact. If he knew of the recent Wilson Act (August 1890) he would have realized that it impaired interstate free trade only in a very special case, the import and sale of liquor.

8 Copy in 'Successive Stages', Document 6. It was printed in Adelaide and dated '26/2/91'.

9 Kingston's Draft Bill, parts XII (iv) and XIII.

10 Alfred Deakin, *The Federal Story* (Melbourne, 1963), p. 47.

11 *S.M.H.*, 3 Mar. 1891.

12 *Official Report of the National Australasian Convention Debates. Adelaide March 22 to May 5* (Adelaide, 1897), p. 242. Henceforth cited as '*Debates* (Adelaide, 1897)'.

13 A document marked 'Confidential' included in 'Successive Stages' prints Parkes's original pre-Convention Resolutions, as reproduced in *Fifty Years*. It has corrections in Parkes's handwriting, and notes in Griffith's.

14 A. Inglis Clark to S. W. Griffith, 3 Mar. 1891, Griffith Papers, MS. Add. 450 (Dixson Library).

15 Enclosure in Clark to Griffith, 3 Mar. 1891. Note that in the bound volume of correspondence this document precedes the letter. It is not in Clark's hand, but he generally preferred to use an amanuensis (see Clark to Edmund Barton, 19 June 1889, Barton Papers, MS. 51/62 (A.N.L.), and in any case was having several copies made.

16 Document 1 in 'Successive Stages' and in the *Official Report of the National Australasian Convention Debates* (Sydney, 1891), p. 23.

17 'Successive Stages', p. [5].

18 Clark to Griffith, as cited in note 15.

19 Art. 1, S. 10 (ii).

20 *Proceedings and Debates of the Australasian Federation Conference* (Melbourne, 1890), p. 46. He was referring in detail to the case of *Guy* v. *Baltimore* (1879) 100 U.S. 434 (though he did not name it, and I am grateful to Professor G. Sawer for identifying it for me). He said (p. 45) that he had met with it since he came to Melbourne.

21 'Report of Committee for Trade and Plantations of Privy Council on proposed Australian Constitution, 1 May 1849', in A. Berriedale Keith (ed.), *Selected Speeches and Documents on British Colonial Policy* (London, 1918), vol. 1, p. 209.

22 J. M. Ward, *Earl Grey and the Australian Colonies 1846-1857* (Melbourne, 1958), p. 94.

23 *Debates* (Melbourne, 1890), p. 34.

24 See J. M. Ward, op. cit., pp. 458-64.

25 *Debates* (Melbourne, 1890), pp. 103-4.

26 J. Quick and R. R. Garran, *The Annotated Constitution of the Australian Commonwealth* (Sydney, 1901), pp. 84, 86. The sentence is quoted from a despatch by Denison, Governor of Tasmania, 28 Dec. 1849.

27 *Debates* (Melbourne, 1890), p. 56. My italics.

28 *Debates* (Sydney, 1891), pp. 24-5.

29 Ibid., p. 30.   30 Ibid., p. 50.

31 Ibid., p. 89.   32 Ibid., p. 528.

33 Ibid., p. 802.

34 As is shown in a paper by Mr Justice Neasey, of the Supreme Court of Tasmania, which I hope will be published.

35 Copy in 'Successive Stages'.

36 Copy in 'Successive Stages', Document 7.

37 'Successive Stages', Documents 9 and 10.

38 Ibid., Document 11.

39 For this and the Draft Bill ordered by the Convention on 31 March to be printed, 'Successive Stages', Documents 13 and 14 and, for the latter, also *Official Record of the Proceedings and Debates of the National Australasian Convention*, printed in the Parliamentary Papers of N.S.W., Victoria and Queensland for the session of 1891, and also separately.

40 Samuel Walker Griffith, *Some Conditions of Australian Federation* (Brisbane, 1896).

41 Samuel Walker Griffith, *Notes on Australian Federation: Its Nature and probable Effects* (Brisbane, 1896)—dated July at end of text.

42 Op. cit., p. 29.   43 Op. cit., pp. 30, 31.

44 By Augustus Mongredien (London, 1881), p. 175.

45 This, and not the complete absence of tariffs, was what Parkes (*Fifty Years*, p. 268) meant by 'pure' free trade, in a passage referred to by Professor G. Sawer, *Australian Federalism in the Courts* (Melbourne, 1967), p. 175.

46 *Debates* (Adelaide, 1897), p. 16.   47 Ibid., p. 17.

48 Ibid., p. 273.   49 Ibid., p. 300.

50 The Report is Paper no. 1, in the appendix to *Proceedings of the Australasian Federal Convention* (Adelaide, 1897).

51 W. McMillan to Barton, 10 Apr. 1897 (originally dated 9 Apr.), Barton Papers, MS. 51/1194 (A.N.L.).

52 'Draft of a Bill prepared by E. Barton, Esq., Q.C.; Hon. Sir John Downer, K.C.M.G., Q.C., M.P.; Hon. Mr O'Connor, M.L.C., Q.C.'. Barton Papers, MS. 51/1194 (A.N.L.). The Bill is dated 12/4/97.

53 *Debates* (Adelaide, 1897), p 830. The substance of Deakin's amendment ultimately became S. 113 of the present Constitution.

54 Ibid., p. 875.   55 Ibid., p. 876.

56 Ibid., p. 1141.   57 Ibid.

58 Ibid., p. 1144.

59 See the documents in CO 13/152 (P.R.O.). The Colonial Office's secret offensive, between the first and second sessions of the Convention was first discussed in detail by Dr B. K. de Garis in an Oxford D.Phil. thesis. See his contribution to this volume.

60 The debates were long drawn out and, in N.S.W., particularly unsystematic. See the various colonial *Parliamentary Debates* for June to Aug. 1897. There is a tabular statement of amendments suggested by the legislatures in *Proceedings of the Australasian Federal Convention held at . . . Sydney* (Sydney, 1898), pp. 81-153.

61 *Debates* (Adelaide, 1897), p. 1142.

62 *Parl. Deb.* (W.A.), vol. 10 (new series), pp. 296-7 (25 Aug. 1897).

63 *Notes on the Draft Federal Constitution framed by the Adelaide Convention of 1897. A Paper presented to the Government of Queensland by the Honourable Sir Samuel Walker Griffith, G.C.M.G., Chief Justice of that Colony.* Queensland, *Journals of the Legislative Council*, vol. 47, part 1, 1897 [June, 1897].

64 Ibid., p. 12. Griffith's italics.
65 Ibid., p. 1.   66 Deakin, op. cit., pp. 81-3.
67 *Official Record of the Debates of the Australasian Federal Convention. Second Session. Sydney 1897* (Sydney, 1897), p. 1038.
68 Ibid. (Sydney, 1897), p. 1041.
69 Ibid., p. 1053.
70 Ibid., p. 1058.   71 Ibid., p. 1064.
72 *Debates* (Melbourne, 1898), vol. 1, pp. 649-51.
73 These documents are printed in the Melbourne *Proceedings* (Melbourne, 1898), pp. 241-8.
74 *Debates* (Melbourne, 1898), vol. 1, p. 1015.
75 Ibid., p. 1018.
76 See F. R. Beasley, *Annual Law Review* (University of W.A. Law School), vol. 1 (1948-50), pp. 273-80. The above paragraph was inserted after reading his article. I had noticed the references to Clause 89 in the railway rate debate (*Debates*, Melbourne, 1898, vols 1 and 2, pp. 1250-512) but had not intended to give them in an already long article; I had not realized their importance as illustrating conceptions of the meaning of the Clause. After reading Professor Beasley's articles, however, I would draw attention to Downer's opinion that 'if trade and commerce between the states is to be absolutely free, then neither Commonwealth nor state should be able to make any law interfering with it', and to the interchange between Isaacs ('Clause 89 also prohibits the Commonwealth') and Barton ('It prohibits the Commonwealth too, perhaps'). (*Debates,* Melbourne, 1898, vol. 2, pp. 1335-7.).
77 *Debates* (Melbourne, 1898), vol. 2, p. 2365.
78 Ibid., p. 2367.   79 R. R. Garran, op. cit., p. 123.
80 *Debates* (Melbourne, 1898), vol. 2, pp. 2369-71.
81 Ibid., pp. 2373-4. He did not suggest any amendment; but was his promised re-consideration responsible for the insertion of the word 'commerce'?

3   *Colonial Office and the Constitution Bill*

1 For a copy of the Draft Bill as it stood at the end of the Adelaide session see the *Official Report of the National Australasian Convention Debates. Adelaide March 22 to May 5, 1897* (Adelaide, 1897), pp. 1220-43.
2 See B. K. de Garis, 'British Influence on the Federation of the Australian Colonies, 1880-1901', unpublished D.Phil. thesis, University of Oxford, 1965. For Grey's federal activity see J. M. Ward, *Earl Grey and the Australian Colonies 1846-1857* (Melbourne, 1958) and for Carnarvon and South Africa, C. F. Goodfellow, *Great Britain and South African Confederation, 1870-1881* (Cape Town, 1966).
3 The phrase is Bramston's, see CO 201/610, p. 281. For further discussion of the Constitution see the minutes on Jersey to Knutsford, 20 Apr. 1891, CO 201/612, p. 37.
4 Minute of 17 July on Hopetoun to Knutsford, 17 July 1891 (telegram), CO 309/136, p. 229.
5 e.g., Deakin to Loch, 6 May 1897, Chamberlain Papers, 9/1 (Birmingham University Library).
6 Loch to Chamberlain, 15 June 1897; Hopetoun to Chamberlain, 13 June 1897. Chamberlain Papers, 9/1.
7 Smith to Chamberlain, 30 July 1896, CO 18/221, pp. 269-77.
8 Smith to Chamberlain, 7 May 1897, CO 18/223, pp. 129-55.
9 Minute, 9 June 1897, on ibid.
10 Minute, 26 June 1897, CO 13/152, p. 171.
11 Minute, 29 June 1897, ibid.
12 Ibid.   13 Ibid.
14 Memorandum A, 'Australian Federal Constitution, Suggested Amendments';

Memorandum B, 'Australian Federal Constitution, Notes on Suggested Amendments'; Memorandum C, 'Australian Federal Constitution, Criticisms on the Bill', CO 13/152, pp. 208 ff.

15 Chamberlain to Reid (Confidential), July 1897 (copy), CO 13/152, pp. 206-7.

16 Kintore to Meade, 24 July 1893, CO 13/148, p. 150.

17 'Report of a Conference between Rt. Hon. J. Chamberlain, M.P. (Her Majesty's Secretary of State for the Colonies) and the Premiers of the Self Governing Colonies of the Empire at the Colonial Office, Downing St., London SW, June and July 1897', Misc. Confidential Print no. 111, CO 885/6, p. 4.

18 Ibid., p. 118.   19 Ibid.

20 Ibid., p. 2.   21 Ibid., pp. 99 ff.

22 The following summary and analysis of the seventeen amendments desired by the imperial government is based on Memoranda A and B, CO 13/152, pp. 208 ff.

23 Memorandum C, CO 13/152, pp. 208 ff.

24 The amendments suggested by each colony are conveniently set out in a parallel table in *Proceedings of the Australasian Federal Convention held at Parliament House Sydney, September 2nd to September 24th, 1897* (Sydney, 1897), pp. 81-153.

25 J. Quick and R. R. Garran, *The Annotated Constitution of the Australian Commonwealth* (Sydney, 1901), p. 229.

26 Dickson to Griffith, 21 Feb. 1900, Griffith Papers, Add. 452 (Dixson Library, Sydney).

27 Barton to Deakin, 20 Jan. 1900, Deakin Papers, MS. 1540/432 (A.N.L.).

28 These comprise marginal notes on Memoranda A and B and nineteen pages of notes on Memorandum C. Barton Papers, MS. 51/1196 (A.N.L.). In addition to the light they throw on the incident under discussion, these notes give valuable insight into the work of the Drafting Committee and their understanding of the meaning of many clauses in the Constitution.

29 Note on Memorandum B, regarding Clause 58, Barton Papers, MS. 51/1196.

30 Note on Memorandum B, regarding Clause 70, ibid.

31 *Official Record of the Debates of the Australasian Federal Convention. Second Session. Sydney 1897* (Sydney, 1897), p. 239.

32 Ibid., p. 240.   33 Ibid., p. 782.

34 Ibid., pp. 806-7.   35 Ibid., pp. 240-2, 251-2.

36 Ibid., p. 242. Downer was a member of the Drafting Committee. It seems unlikely that he would have made this remark if he had seen the Colonial Office memoranda at this stage; however this debate occurred soon after the resumption of the Convention and the most likely explanation is that Reid did not pass the memoranda on to the Committee until he had made some use of them himself.

37 Ibid., pp. 241-2.   38 Ibid., p. 253.

39 Ibid., p. 256.   40 Ibid., pp. 778-9.

41 *Official Record of the Debates of the Australasian Federal Convention. Third Session. Melbourne, 1898* (Melbourne, 1898), pp. 1611-16.

42 Ibid., pp. 336-7.

43 For a copy of the Bill as it stood at the end of the Melbourne Convention, see ibid., pp. 2523-44.

44 *Debates* (Sydney, 1897), p. 228.

45 For a brief account of the campaign and result in all colonies see Quick and Garran, op. cit., pp. 206-12.

46 *S.M.H.*, 28 Mar. 1898.

47 Madden to Chamberlain, 24 May 1898 (telegram), CO 309/147, p. 185.

48 Minutes of 25 May 1898, on ibid.

49 Minute: 3 Nov. 1897, CO 418/4, p. 319.

50 Minute: 31 May 1899, CO 13/153, p. 22.
51 'Notes on the Commonwealth of Australia Constitution Bill', Confidential Print, Australian no. 169, CO 418/6, pp. 409 ff.
52 Sir C. I. Ilbert's Memorandum on the Commonwealth Bill, 17 Nov. 1899; The Law Officers' Memorandum on the Commonwealth Bill, 21 Dec. 1899, CO 418/6, pp. 86-90, 101-15.
53 Minutes on Griffith to Chamberlain, 19 Oct. 1899, and on Griffith to Chamberlain, 14 Dec. 1899 (telegram), CO 234/69, pp. 83, 247.
54 Chamberlain to Beauchamp, 22 Dec. 1899 (telegram). Cd. 124, p. 26. *British Parliamentary Papers,* 1900, vol. 55.
55 This may be inferred from Deakin to Dilke, 14 Sept. 1899, Dilke Papers, Add. MSS 43877, f. 132 (British Museum).
56 Ibid.
57 Symon to Selborne, 17 Jan. 1900, CO 13/155, p. 399.
58 *Hansard's Parliamentary Debates,* 4th series, vol. 83, pp. 64-5.
59 Ibid., p. 404.   60 Ibid., pp. 77-8.

4   A.N.A. and Federation in South Australia

1 Brian Fitzpatrick, *The Australian Natives' Association 1871-1961* (Melbourne, 1961), p. 19.
2 James Hume-Cook, *The Australian Natives' Association* (Melbourne, 1931).
3 *Observer,* 6 Jan. 1890.
4 Ibid., 28 Jan. 1899.   5 Ibid., 9 Feb. 1901.
6 The Australian Natives' Association, S.A. Branch, *Valuable Facts* (Adelaide, 1907).
7 The following information is drawn from J. Hollinsworth [Pettman], 'The Australian Natives' Association in South Australia: The study of Nativist Nationalism 1887-1902', unpublished B.A. thesis, University of Adelaide, 1965, ch. 2.
8 See, for example, W. J. Sowden, *An Australian Native's Standpoint* (London, 1912).
9 Sowden in *Observer,* 5 Oct. 1901.
10 A.N.A. Board of Directors Minutes, 12 Nov. 1888.
11 Ibid.   12 Ibid., 21 Nov. 1889.
13 *Observer,* 23 Nov. 1889.   14 Hume-Cook, op. cit., p. 11.
15 Fitzpatrick, op. cit., p. 30.   16 *Observer,* 21 July 1900.
17 *South Australian Chronicle,* 25 Jan. 1890.
18 *Observer,* 25 Jan. 1890.
19 '1849' in *Chronicle,* 1 Feb. 1890.
20 'Volapuk', ibid.   21 Sowden, op. cit., p. 58.
22 *Observer,* 28 Jan. 1899.
23 Board Minutes, 30 June 1890.
24 Adelaide A.N.A. Committee Minutes, 6 Nov. 1893.
25 Adelaide A.N.A. General Minutes, 2 July 1894.
26 Adelaide A.N.A. Committee Minutes, 19 Nov. 1894.
27 Adelaide A.N.A. General Minutes, 3 Dec. 1894.
28 Australasian Federation League of South Australia, Provisional Committee Minutes, 25 Jan. 1895.
29 Ibid., 18 Jan. 1895.
30 *Rules* of the Australasian Federation League of South Australia (Adelaide, 1895).
31 S.A. Archives Research Note 364, G. N. Pitt, 1945.
32 Ibid.
33 R. S. Parker, 'Australian Federation: the Influence of Economic Interests and Political Pressures', in J. J. Eastwood and F. B. Smith (eds), *Historical Studies, Selected Articles* (Melbourne, 1964), p. 178.
34 Ibid.

5 The 1898 South Australian Referendum

1 J. J. Eastwood and F. B. Smith (eds), *Historical Studies, Selected Articles* (Melbourne, 1964), pp. 152-98.
2 *South Australian Register*, Adelaide, 26 Mar. 1898.
3 Ibid., 21 Mar. 1898.
4 *South Eastern Star*, Mount Gambier, 20 May 1898.
5 *Plain Dealer*, Kadina, 23 Apr. 1898.
6 *Orroroo Enterprise and Great Northern Advertiser*, 3 June 1898.
7 *Register*, 29 Apr. 1898.   8 Ibid., 4 Apr. 1898.
9 *Port Augusta Dispatch*, 6 May 1898.
10 *Port Pirie Advocate and Areas News*, 27 May 1898.
11 *Naracoorte Herald*, 31 May 1898.
12 *Mount Barker Courier, Onkaparinga and Gumeracha Advertiser*, 3 July 1898.
13 Tom Price M.P., *Register*, 7 May 1898.
14 Price, *Orroroo Enterprise*, 27 May, 1898.
15 *South Australian Advertiser*, 26 Mar. 1898.
16 *Kapunda Herald and Northern Intelligencer*, 20 May 1898.
17 *Laura Standard and Crystal Brook Courier*, 3 June 1898.
18 *Register*, 4 May 1898.
19 W. O. Archibald M.P., *Weekly Herald*, Adelaide, 30 Apr. 1898.
20 H. Adams, M.L.C., *People's Weekly*, Moonta, 21 May 1898.
21 Archibald, *Bunyip*, Gawler, 27 May 1898.
22 W. Russell, M.L.C., *Kadina & Wallaroo Times*, 21 May 1898.
23 E. G. Batchelor, M.P., *Southern Cross*, Adelaide, 6 May 1898.
24 *Northern Territory Times and Gazette*, 6 May 1898.
25 *Southern Cross*, 1 Apr. 1898.
26 J. Hutchinson M.P., *Register*, 19 Apr. 1898.
27 F. W. Coneybeer M.P., *Weekly Herald*, 21 May 1898.
28 *Mount Barker Courier*, 25 Mar. 1898.
29 *Laura Standard*, 12 May 1898.
30 *Register*, 23 May 1898.   31 Ibid., 3 June 1898.
32 *People's Weekly*, 4 June 1898.
33 The 'leper' was quarantined on Torrens Island where it was later discovered he suffered only from the action of a 'Chinese plaster' on his leg.
34 *South Eastern Star*, 20 May 1898.
35 Alfred Deakin, *The Federal Story* (Melbourne, 1963), p. 74.
36 Archdeacon Young, *South Eastern Star*, 24 May 1898.
37 *Census 1901*, part 7, table 9, pp. 549-51.
38 Quoted by Holder from *1891 Royal Commission on Intercolonial Free Trade*, p.v.
39 *S.A. Directory for 1899*, p. 870; *S.A. Post Office Directory*, 1899-1900, p. 890.
40 *S.A. Directory for 1899*, pp. 873, 874.
41 Ibid., p. 912; *S.A.P.O. Directory*, p. 960.
42 *Advertiser*, 6 May 1898.   43 Ibid., 3 May 1898.
44 *Register*, 27 Apr. 1898.   45 *Advertiser*, 25 May 1898.
46 *Weekly Herald*, 23 Apr. 1898.
47 *Statistical Register for 1898*, part 4, no. 1, p. 37.
48 Ibid., no. 2, pp. 56, 60, 79.
49 Ibid., p. 51.   50 *Register*, 14 Mar. 1898.
51 S.A. was the only colony where women had the vote.
52 *Advertiser*, 22 Mar. 1898.   53 Ibid., 10 May 1898.
54 *Register*, 30 Apr. 1898.   55 *People's Weekly*, 21 May 1898.
56 *Southern Yorke's Peninsula Pioneer*, Yorketown, 27 May 1898.
57 Ibid., 3 June 1898.   58 *Plain Dealer*, 28 May 1898.
59 *Register*, 1 May 1896.   60 *Advertiser*, 27 Apr. 1898.

61 *Register*, 18 Apr. 1896.
62 *Advertiser Supplement*, 14 May 1896.
63 *Register*, 21 May 1898.   64 Ibid., 30 May 1898.
65 *Statistical Register for 1897*, part 3, no. 17, pp. 30-3.
66 Said by local growers in support of import restrictions, *Register*, 4 Mar. 1898.
67 *Border Watch*, Mount Gambier, 23 Apr. 1898.
68 *Mount Barker Courier*, 15 Apr. 1898.
69 Eastwood and Smith, op. cit., p. 183.
70 Cockburn, then Chief Secretary, later Minister of Agriculture, *Parl. Deb.* (S.A.), 26 July 1890, p. 271.
71 *Register*, 15 Apr. 1898.
72 *Port Augusta Dispatch*, 6 May 1898.
73 Archibald, *Weekly Herald*, 30 Apr. 1898.
74 *Statistical Register for 1898*, part 4, table 2, pp. 44-93; table 11, p. 99.
75 *Register*, 2 June 1898.
76 *Port Augusta Dispatch*, 20 May 1898.
77 *South Eastern Star*, 31 May 1898.
78 *Naracoorte Herald*, 6 May 1898.
79 Report of the S.A. Railways Commissioner, *P.P.* (S.A.), 1898-9, vol. 2, no. 47.
80 *1891 Royal Commission on Intercolonial Free Trade*, p. 146.
81 Ibid., p. 133.   82 Ibid.
83 Eastwood and Smith, op. cit., p. 181.
84 Ian Mudie, well-known S.A. poet and historian of the Murray.
85 Report of the Inter-State Royal Commission on the Murray, *P.P.* (S.A.), 1903, vol. 2, no. 22, p. 199.
86 Ibid.
87 *Statistical Register for 1898*, no. 29. Items as low as £1 in value are recorded.
88 The River Murray Trade, 1890-1-2, Paper 38, *P.P.* (S.A.), 1893, vol. 2.
89 *Census of 1881*, table 7, pp. 260, 263, 269, 273.
90 Eastwood and Smith, op. cit., p. 191.
91 *Northern Territory Times*, 3 June 1898.
92 *Australian Christian World*, Adelaide, 17 June 1898, p. 1.
93 *Port Pirie Advocate and Areas News*, 10 June 1898.
94 *Weekly Herald*, 4 July 1898.   95 *Register*, 19 Apr. 1898.
96 *South Eastern Star*, 24 May 1898.
97 *Naracoorte Herald*, 28 May 1898.

6   *Referenda Campaigns in S.E. New South Wales*

1 *Bowral Free Press*, 1 June 1898.
2 *Yass Evening Tribune*, 15 June 1899.
3 *Goulburn Evening Penny Post*, 10 June 1899.
4 *Braidwood and Araluen Express*, 16 June 1899.
5 *Bega Free Press*, 12 May 1898.
6 *Robertson Advocate*, 13 May 1898.
7 *Bega Standard*, 24 May 1898.
8 *Kiama Independent*, 24 May 1898.
9 *Bega Standard*, 24 May 1898.   10 *Bega Free Press*, 2 June 1898.
11 *Kiama Reporter*, 6 May 1899.   12 *Bega Free Press*, 4 May 1899.
13 *Yass Courier*, 15 Apr. 1898.
14 *Goulburn Evening Penny Post*, 6 May 1899.
15 *Scrutineer*, 7 June 1899.
16 *Queanbeyan Observer*, 27 May 1898.
17 *Yass Courier*, 3 June 1898.
18 *South Coast Herald and Illawarra Guardian*, 5 May 1899.

[19] *Braidwood Dispatch*, 15 June 1898.
[20] *Kiama Independent*, 21 May 1898.
[21] *Manaro Mercury*, 29 May 1898.
[22] *Bega Free Press*, 12 May 1898.
[23] *Queanbeyan Age*, 28 June 1899.   [24] *Yass Courier*, 2 June 1899.
[25] *Queanbeyan Observer*, 10 May 1899.
[26] *Yass Courier*, 5 May 1899.
[27] *Queanbeyan Observer*, 13 June 1899.
[28] *Manaro Mercury*, 6 May 1898.   [29] See appendix.
[30] *Braidwood Dispatch*, 8 June 1898.
[31] *Burrowa Times and Binalong, Frogmore, Reid's Flat and Rye Park Advertiser*, 13 May 1899.
[32] *Kiama Independent*, 14 May 1898.
[33] *Ulladulla and Milton Times*, 24 June 1899.
[34] *Goulburn Evening Penny Post*, 7 May 1898.
[35] *Robertson Advocate*, 10 June 1898.   [36] Ibid., 7 June 1898.
[37] *Scrutineer and Berrima District Press*, 10 June 1899.
[38] *Bowral Free Press*, 24 June 1898.
[39] Ibid., 11 June 1898.   [40] See appendix.
[41] *Manaro Mercury*, 21 Apr. 1899.
[42] *Bega Free Press*, 4 May 1899.
[43] *Eden Free Press*, 7 June 1899.
[44] *Manaro Mercury*, 13 June 1898.   [45] Ibid., 12 June 1898.
[46] *Bega Standard*, 11 Apr. 1899.
[47] *Bombala Herald and Delegate, Cooma, Eden and Coast Districts General Advertiser*, 7 Apr. 1899.
[48] *Yass Courier*, 17 Feb. 1899.   [49] Ibid., 21 Mar. 1899.
[50] In 1898 Towrang returned 13 pro and 15 anti-federal votes.
[51] *Goulburn Evening Penny Post*, 22 June 1899.
[52] *Leader*, 3 Mar. 1899.
[53] *Shoalhaven News and South Coast District Advertiser*, 11 Mar. 1899.
[54] *Bega Free Press*, 12 May 1898.

INDEX